UNIVERSITY OF NORTH CAROLINA
STUDIES IN THE ROMANCE LANGUAGES AND LITERATURES
Number 59

HISPANIC STUDIES IN HONOR OF
NICHOLSON B. ADAMS

HISPANIC STUDIES IN HONOR OF
NICHOLSON B. ADAMS

EDITED BY

JOHN ESTEN KELLER   AND   KARL-LUDWIG SELIG

CHAPEL HILL

THE UNIVERSITY OF NORTH CAROLINA PRESS

DEPÓSITO LEGAL: V. 1.087-1966

ARTES GRÁFICAS SOLER, S. A. — VALENCIA. — 1966

TABLE OF CONTENTS

	Page
BIOGRAPHY AND PUBLICATIONS	9
ORIGEN Y SEMÁNTICA DE LA PALABRA "CHÉVERE" by José Juan Arrom	17
EL IMPACTO DEL CULTERANISMO EN EL TEATRO DE LA EDAD DE ORO by James A. Castañeda	25
RELECCIÓN DE LOS PRIMEROS PÁRRAFOS DE *NIEBLA* DE UNAMUNO by F. S. Escribano	37
MELANCHOLY AND DEATH IN CERVANTES by Otis H. Green	49
ATTACKS ON LOPE AND HIS THEATRE IN 1617-1621 by Ruth Lee Kennedy	57
RELIGIOUS HISPANISMS IN AMERICAN INDIAN LANGUAGES by Lawrence B. Kiddle	77
CRACKS IN THE STRUCTURE OF CALDERÓN'S *ALCALDE DE ZALAMEA* by Sturgis E. Leavitt	93
AN UNNOTICED COMPLEMENT TO "CONCOLORCORVO" by John Kenneth Leslie	97
THE SPANISH SOURCES OF PAUL SCARRON'S *JODELET DUELLISTE* by Raymond R. MacCurdy	107
LOPE DE VEGA'S *ARTE NUEVO DE HACER COMEDIAS*: POST-CENTENARY REFLECTIONS by J. H. Parker	113

	Page
CERVANTES AND THE *AMADÍS* by Edwin B. Place	131
SOME BAROQUE REFLECTIONS ON THE GREEK ANTHOLOGY IN LOPE DE VEGA by Irving P. Rothberg	141
CARA Y CRUZ DE LA NOVELÍSTICA GALDOSIANA by William H. Shoemaker	151
THE CHARACTER OF DON JUAN OF *EL BURLADOR DE SEVILLA* by Gerald E. Wade	167
CALDERÓN'S COMEDY AND HIS SERIOUS SENSE OF LIFE by Bruce W. Wardropper	179

BIOGRAPHY AND PUBLICATIONS

Nicholson Barney Adams was born in Fredericksburg, Virginia, on November 6, 1895. He grew up as "Nic" to friends and relatives, and Nic he is today. Fredericksburg in those days was a rural village, a wonderful place for a growing boy, and the last years of the past century, plus the early years of our own it must have been a pleasant time in which to live. One suspects that it was not a locale particularly equipped to fill a boy's spirit with the love of learning, but Nic was one of those whose mind would turn to books and the magic they contained. His sister, Virginia, now Mrs. Edgar W. Dare of Washington, D. C., recalls that she and Nic grew up in a comfortable old house with their mother and father, and that two grandmothers and five maiden aunts lived right next door. In the evenings the little clan would assemble, often in one of the grandmothers' rooms, to talk and to form, what is so often lacking today, a cozy family group linked with common interests and deep affection.

While the others talked, recalls Mrs. Dare, Nic would sit at a big table in the middle of the room doing his homework, untroubled by the homely conversation, the jig-saw puzzle usually under construction, but often attracted by one or another of the three books always in view — the Holy Bible in English, Hebrew and Greek. But his grandmother, fearful of distraction, often shook her head and wondered aloud if he would ever pass his courses. Consequent events were to prove how baseless were her well-meant fears.

Nic fell in love with languages when he was still a little boy, and at the same time was smitten by a pair of deep brown eyes. Into the neighborhood moved a missionary family which had just returned from Brazil, and Nic's first sweethear was their daughter who spoke a fluent Portuguese. It was she who introduced him into the delights of learning a foreign tongue, but it was the love of language itself that remained long after she had faded into fond memories. His second introduction to a different language came also in Fredericksburg. It came when Nic went to purchase milk at the home of a M. Arnaud who kept a cow and talked to young Nic in the soft French of Avignon.

At the age of seventeen, in 1913, that is, Nic was graduated from Fredericksburg College with the A. B. degree, and his family proudly at first, and then with some embarrassment, saw him receive his diploma and with it all the honors presented at the commencement. But Evie, the Negro cook, when Nic's mother who had returned from the exercises told her of his honors, made only one remark: "I don't care nothin' 'bout all them honors. I'll give him honors if he'll jes keep my woodbox full." In all the years of his life he has never failed at that chore, and may possibly be one of the best wood providers from Sebago Lake, Maine, to Piedmont North Carolina, and probably the best fire-builder.

In the same year as his commencement he became principal of a secondary school in Ottoman, Virginia (1913-14), about one hundred miles down the Rappahanock from Fredericksburg. In this post his versatility emerged in full force, for he was drama coach, athletic director, taught several different subjects and held a Bible class on Sundays. He even managed to save some considerable part of his meager salary of four hundred dollars for the school year to pay part of his tuition at Washington and Lee University, from which he would receive the Lit. D. degree in 1950.

Resident there for one year (1914-15), after he had received his degree, he went to Lynchburg High School to teach French and Spanish, where he served during the school years 1915-17.

In 1917 he entered the Armed Forces of the United States and saw service in the theatre of war in France and Belgium until 1919. His conversations in French with that M. Arnaud who sold the Adams milk suddenly came to his aid, for he became interpreter to Colonel MacArthur, who in later times was to become the famous defender of Corregidor. It is said that

Frenchmen who heard Nic Adams speak French asked him if he was not from Avignon.

After the war, in 1919, he married Agatha Boyd, an Assistant Professor of Botany at Randolph Macon College in Lynchburg and went to Columbia University. There in 1920 he was awarded the degree of Master of Arts, and in 1922 the Doctorate. His dissertation was written under the direction of Dr. Federico de Onís.

Then Agatha and Nic spent a year in Spain at the Universidad Central, returning in 1921 when he went to teach again in the Lynchburg High School. But in 1924 he received a call from the University of North Carolina and went there as Assistant Professor. By 1927 he was named Associate Professor, and in 1930 Professor. Save for an occasional visiting professorship — the University of Wisconsin in 1945, the University of Chicago in 1949 and the University of New Mexico in 1950 — he has spent his academic life in Chapel Hill.

A daughter, Alice Boyd Adams, now Mrs. M. L. Linenthal, Jr., was born here, and Agatha, who had long been his scholarly critic, collaborator in research and helpmate died here in 1949. A scholar in her own right, she was responsible for a considerable part of the cataloguing and classification of North Carolina's collection of Modern Spanish Drama.

At the University Professor Adams for many years has taught graduate courses in Early Prose Fiction, the Spanish Novel from 1605 to 1898, Modern Spanish Novelists, Early Lyric Poetry, Modern Lyric Poetry, a Seminar in Romanticism, and, of course, many of the lower division courses.

Active in professional societies, he has long been a member of the Modern Language Association of America, the American Association of Teachers of Spanish and Portuguese, of which he was president in 1958, and the South Atlantic Modern Language Association, together with a number of others. He was Assistant Editor of *A State University Surveys the Humanities* (Chapel Hill, 1946); has been for many years Associate Editor of *Hispania*; and is a reading consultant for *Publications of the Modern Language Association of America, Hispania, Romance Notes* and *Studies in Philology*. His kind personal advice to students, friends and colleagues in the profession has been always given unstintedly, and his circle of acquaintances and friends in the world and in Academia is one of the largest we know.

In 1955 he married Dorothy Stearns Wilson, whose immense capacity for life and mirth, for culture and gentility, for home-making and companionship, and for deep, true humanity of spirit joined together to make the latter years of his career happy ones indeed. Together they attended the meetings of the language associations, together they traveled in this country, in Canada and in Mexico. And in the spring of the current year, when Nic was on Kenan Leave for the spring semester, they went to Spain. They returned to America toward the end of the summer, but flew back again for two weeks in October, and in Córdoba he received the medallion which conferred upon him the title of Miembro Correspondiente de la Real Academia de Córdoba.

When this *homenaje* to him and to his work went to press, he was still busy at his post in Chapel Hill, teaching his classes and preparing the final redaction of a study on Zorrilla for the Twayne series of great world authors.

John Esten Keller
    Chapel Hill, 1965.

PUBLICATIONS

BOOKS

The Romantic Drama of García Gutiérrez. New York, Instituto de las Españas, 1922.
Edition: *El Abencerraje,* with Gretchen Todd Starck. Boston, Sanborn and Company, 1927.
Spanish Literature in English Translation. Chapel Hill, University Extension Bulletin, 1929.
Edition: José Zorrilla, *Don Juan Tenorio.* New York, Knopf, 1929.
Edition: *Popular Spanish Readings.* New York, Crofts, 1932.
Edition: *Spanish Folktales,* with R. S. Boggs. New York, Crofts, 1932.
Brief Spanish Review Grammar and Composition. New York, Holt, 1933. Revised edition, 1957.
Edition: *Selections from Pérez de Ayala,* with S. A. Stoudemire. New York, Norton, 1934.
Brief French Review Grammar and Composition, with J. C. Lyons. New York, Holt, 1936.
Original and edited: *Lecturas Modernas,* with E. B. Place. New York, Holt, 1959.
The Heritage of Spain. New York, Holt, 1943. Revised edition, 1959.
Edition: *Tales from Spanish America,* with R. L. Grismer. New York, Oxford University Press, 1944.
España (Revised Spanish Translation of *The Heritage of Spain*). New York, Holt, 1947.
Edition: B. Pérez Galdós, *Marianela.* Boston, Ginn, 1951.
Revision and Additions to G. T. Northup, *Introduction to Spanish Literature.* Chicago, University of Chicago Press, 1960.
Spanish Literature: A Brief Survey, with John E. Keller. Paterson, N. J., Littlefield Adams, 1962.
España en su Literatura, with John E. Keller. New York, Norton, 1962.
Breve panorama de la Literatura Española, with John E. Keller (Translation and Revision of *Spanish Literature*). Madrid, Editorial Castalia, 1964.
Spanish for Today, with the collaboration of Herschel J. Frey. New York, Holt, Rinehart and Winston, 1964.
Hispanoamérica en su Literatura, with J. E. Keller, Elizabeth Daniel and John M. Fein. New York, Norton, 1965.

ARTICLES

"Notes on Spanish Plays at the Beginning of the Romantic Period," *Romanic Review*, XVII (1926), 128-42.

"Sidelights on the Spanish Theatre of the Eighteen-Thirties," *Hispania*, IX (1926), 1-12.

"A Note on García Gutiérrez and Ossian," *Philological Quarterly*, VII (1928), 402-4.

"A Little-Known Spanish Adaptation of Dumas' *Don Juan de Marana*," *Romanic Review*, XX (1929), 241.

"A Spanish Romantic Parodies Himself: Los hijos del tío Tronera," *Publications of the Modern Language Association*, XLV (1930), 573-77.

"The 'Grotesque' in Some Important Spanish Plays," *Todd Memorial Volume* I, pp. 37-46. New York: Columbia University Press, 1930.

"Hartzenbusch's 'Sancho Ortiz de las Roelas,'" *Studies in Philology*, XXVIII (1931), 851-56.

"Siglo de Oro Plays in Madrid, 1820-1850," *Hispanic Review*, IV (1936), 343-47.

"Some Recent Novels of Revolutionary Spain," *Hispania*, XX (1937), 81-84.

"Notes on Espronceda's *Sancha Saldaña*," *Hispanic Review*, V (1937), 304-08.

"A Note on Lara's *El doncel*," *Hispanic Review*, IX (1941), 208-21.

Spanish Section of "The Romantic Movement. A Selective Bibliography for the Year 1941," edited by Walter Graham. *E. L. H.*; *a Journal of English Literary History*, IX (1942), 31-4 (yearly in later volumes).

"Notes on Dramatic Criticism in Madrid, 1828-1833," *Studies in Philology*, XLII (1945), 609-616.

"A Note on the Duke of Rivas and Mme. Cottin," *Hispanic Review*, XV (1947), 218-221.

"A Note on Larra's *No más mostrador*," *Romance Studies Presented to William Morton Dey*. Chapel Hill, 1950, 15-18.

The Columbia Dictionary of Modern European Literature, (in press) Articles on Dicenta, Marquina, Linares Rivas, Martínez Sierra, the Quintero Brothers, Tamayo y Baus, A. López de Ayala, Fernández y González.

"French Influence on the Madrid Theatre in 1837," *Estudios dedicados a Menéndez Pidal*, VII, n. 1, 135-151, Madrid, 1957.

REVIEWS

Reviews of books, too numerous to list here, have appeared in *Hispania, Hispanic Review, Modern Language Journal, The Modern Language Quarterly, Revista Iberoamericana, Revista de Estudios Hispánicos, Romanic Review* and *The South Atlantic Bulletin,* to list some of the most important.

ORIGEN Y SEMÁNTICA DE LA PALABRA "CHÉVERE"

by José Juan Arrom
Yale University

Llevada por las alegres notas de una conga, la palabra *chévere* le ha dado la vuelta al mundo. El estribillo de aquella pieza —una de las que gozaban de mayor popularidad internacional hacia los años '30— decía así:

> ¡Uno, dos y tres,
> qué paso más chévere,
> qué paso más chévere
> el de mi conga es!

Chévere se empleaba ahí como uno de esos términos que de cuando en cuando se difunden en un idioma para denotar un alto grado de excelencia. Por aquellos años, en las Antillas todo lo bueno era chévere: chévere un ágil paso de baile, chévere una fiesta animada, chévere una casa agradable, chévere un traje elegante, chévere un hombre simpático, chévere una muchacha bonita, chévere una frase feliz. Pronto cobró, además, un valor afectivo. En Cuba se saludaba a un amigo con un cordial: "¡Qué hubo, chévere!" Y en Puerto Rico he oído a un profesor dirigirse a un colega con un afectuoso: "Oye, cheverón". Y por ese camino hasta se llegó a emplear con valor de interjección afirmativa:

> —Nos vemos mañana?
> —Chévere!

Es decir, "estupendo", "fenómeno", "barín", o cualquier otra de las muchas expresiones que sucesivamente se han puesto de moda en el habla familiar como superlativo de lo bueno, lo bello y lo encomiable.

Mucho antes de que la boga internacional de la música cubana hiciera resonar esa palabra en los más remotos confines del mundo hispánico, *chévere* era ya de uso común y corriente en la ancha zona del Caribe. No ha sido recogida en el Diccionario de la Real Academia Española, pero sí aparece en otros registros lexicográficos más al día. Y es precisamente al consultar esas obras cuando uno encuentra connotaciones diametralmente opuestas a su sentido actual y explicaciones de su origen que convendría examinar y esclarecer.

Comenzando por los diccionarios más recientes de carácter general, en la *Enciclopedia universal Sopena* (Barcelona, 1963), se lee: "*Chévere*. m. En Cuba y Puerto Rico, cheche, valentón. // adj. Amér. En Méjico, magnífico, excelente. *Estar chévere* una cosa, frs. Amér. En Cuba, ser bonita, agradable". Martín Alonso, en su *Enciclopedia del idioma* (Madrid, 1958), la consigna así: "*Chévere*. m. Cuba y Puerto Rico. Cheche, pitre, valentón. // 2. adj. Méj. Magnífico, muy bueno y bonito". El *Diccionario enciclopédico U.T.E.H.A.* (México, 1951), trae lo siguiente: "*Chévere*. adj. y s. En Puerto Rico, cheche. // En México, correcto, elegante". Y Francisco J. Santamaría, en su *Diccionario general de americanismos* (México, 1942), apunta: "*Chévere*. m. En Puerto Rico, cheche.—2. En Tabasco, elegante, correcto".

Siguiéndole la pista al término en registros regionales mexicanos, encontramos que el mismo Francisco J. Santamaría, en su *Diccionario de mejicanismos* (México, 1959), consigna: "*Chévere*. m. En Tabasco, elegante, correcto. // Cuba. Suárez, 177, 'bravucón, perdonavidas. De chéchere, cheche'." Arnulfo Ochoa, en "Regionalismos de uso más frecuente en la parte sureste del estado de Guanajuato" (*Investigaciones lingüísticas*, IV, núms. 1-2, enero-abril 1937, pág. 71), simplemente apunta: "*Chévere*.—Elegante". Y Peter Boyd-Bowman, en *El habla de Guanajuato* (México, 1960, pág. 260): "*Chévere*. Elegante, agradable, divertido, chistoso. SE Gto., Tab., Yuc."

Pasando ahora a las Antillas, Constantino Suárez, en su *Vocabulario cubano* (Madrid, 1921), consigna: "*Chévere*. Cub. m.— El individuo bravucón, perdonavidas. Otros dicen chévere cantúa.

Et. De chéchere, cheche". Fernando Ortiz, en su magistral *Glosario de afronegrismos* (La Habana, 1924), es quien primero estudia la palabra, relaciona filológicamente a *chévere* con *cheche* y sugiere el origen africano de ambos términos. Dice Ortiz:

> *Chévere.* m. Sinónimo de *cheche.*
> Su uso está bastante extendido, principalmente en su acepción de 'elegante', 'bien trajeado', 'guapo', 'petimetre', 'presumido'. Acaso se derive de la misma raíz que *cheche*, lucumí *che*, unida a otra voz lucumí *egberi* 'con la cabeza alzada', o *égbere* 'espíritu o genio maléfico' o *égberi* 'iniciado' o 'compañero'.
> El vocablo úsase comunmente entre los ñáñigos y el hampa, lo que puede justificar el influjo de estas voces lucumíes.
> Sin embargo, este mismo uso por los ñáñigos nos lleva a presumir que *chévere* procede del calabar *sebede* 'adornarse profusamente', que allá en Africa equivale a 'bien trajeado', 'petimetre', etc., o sea a *cheche*, como en Cuba decimos; y también 'desafiar'. (Goldie, p. 266). Así tendríamos *chévere* (calabar) sinónimo de *cheche* (lucumí).
> En Cuba se oye decir a veces "es un cheche muy chévere". También suele oírse *cheveré.*

La misma corriente populista que difundía el término por medio de la música bailable, lo lleva a la llamada poesía afrocubana. Y así, Ramón Guirao lo emplea en su poema *E negro etá basilón* y lo recoge en el Vocabulario al final de su antología *Órbita de la poesía afrocubana* (La Habana, 1938) de la manera siguiente: "*Chébere.* Elegante, bien trajeado, matón. Criollismo de *chevalier*". Y a continuación: "*Cheche.* Pendenciero, matón".

Influido por la tesis africanista de Ortiz, Esteban Rodríguez Herrera resume en su *Léxico mayor de Cuba* (Vol. I, La Habana, 1958): "*Chévere.* s. m. Cheche, valentón; lo mismo en Puerto Rico. — adj. Magnífico, muy bueno o bonito como en México; o elegante y correcto, como en Tabasco: ¡Qué chévere está tu traje! ¡Te queda muy chévere ese sombrero! Es vocablo de origen africano que ha pasado ya al lenguaje vulgar de Cuba, aunque todavía con tono fam. y festivo".

Siguiendo la tesis de Ortiz, Manuel Álvarez Nazario, en su obra *El elemento afronegroide en el español de Puerto Rico* (San Juan, 1961), comenta, primero (pág. 245), sobre *cheche*:

> *Cheche.* com. Valentón, matón, perdonavidas. Por extensión, ha venido a decirse también, en el habla familiar e informal por toda la Isla, de la persona que se distingue o sobresale en la ejecución de algo. El mismo vocablo se aplicó antaño en La Habana, Cuba, según informes de Ortiz, al "negro curro del manglar", extendiéndose más adelante su uso en relación con el blanco bravucón o matón, de donde pasó luego a referirse a la persona pulida, bien trajeada, petimetre. Le parece a dicho autor voz de creación afrocriolla, derivada tal vez, por duplicación enfática, de la palabra lucumí o yoruba *che* 'hacer', 'conquistar', 'vencer', 'sojuzgar', 'castigar'. En Puerto Rico, su procedencia cubana, y específicamente habanera, aparece sugerida en unos versos de Alonso, *El Jíbaro* (1849), que registran el empleo de la variante *chenche*, con el sentido original señalado, y en cuya representación gráfica indica la *n* lo que en apariencia fue una resonancia nasal interna que se ha perdido ya en el derivado moderno de *cheche*:
>
> > Manque no soy de la Bana,
> > tengo mi aquey muy fundao,
> > polque soy de Puelto Rico
> > er chenche más afamao.
>
> La denominación de *chenche* se dio además en la Isla, durante el siglo pasado, quizá por natural asociación con el concepto de 'fortaleza, pujanza, vigor, etc.', a los integrantes de los cuerpos de milicias disciplinadas, disueltos en 1870.

Y a continuación (pág. 246), sobre *chévere*:

> *Chévere.* com. Pitre, cheche. Por extensión, y dejando atrás el anterior uso como sustantivo, hoy raro, ha pasado a significar en el habla popular general, en función de adjetivo o adverbio, que algo es excelente, de calidad superior, muy satisfactorio; que algo está muy bien ejecutado. El aumentativo *cheverón, -a*, que se mantiene en vigencia como sustantivo, con los significados que se indican en primer término, expresa también, como adjetivo o adverbio, las mismas ideas señaladas en relación con el uso más moderno de *chévere*. Al igual que *cheche*, procede este término del habla vulgar de Cuba (donde es vocablo de empleo en el hampa y entre ñáñigos), pero su introducción en Puerto Rico data de fecha más reciente que la de *cheche*; tal vez no se remonte su empleo entre nosotros

más allá del período de la primera guerra mundial. También ha pasado a Venezuela. Su uso en Cuba entre los negros ñáñigos le hace suponer a Ortiz un posible origen carabalí que parte de la voz *sebede* 'adornarse profusamente', equivalente africano —dice— de 'bien trajeado o petimetre'. Acaso las coincidencias semánticas entre esta palabra y *cheche* hayan favorecido el desarrollo en *sebede* del sonido palatal de inicio que tiene *chévere*. El cambio $d > r$ era frecuente, por otra parte, en el habla de los bozales.

Y dando ya por sentado que *chévere* es un término de origen africano, o que suena a africano, G. R. Coulthard consigna en su reciente estudio *Race and Colour in Caribbean Literature* (London, 1962, pág. 28): "In 1924 [Ortiz] published his *Glosario de afronegrismos*, a collection of African or African-sounding words in the popular speech of Cuba and of words of Spanish origen with new Cuban meanings. Many of these words have a markedly African rhythmic sonority (*cumbancha, simbombo, chévere, sandunga, mondongo*, etc.), and are to be found some years later in the compositions of the Afro-Cuban writers".

Hecho el recuento de lo principal que se ha escrito sobre el sentido y el posible origen de esta palabra, debo ahora plantear mis dudas. ¿Es *chévere* en realidad sinónimo de *cheche*? ¿Procede del lucumí *che-egberi*, del calabar *sebede* o acaso del francés *chevalier*? ¿Entró en el habla cubana a través del hampa habanera? Empezando por la primera de esas dudas, debo declarar que he pasado mi juventud en Cuba, he recorrido la isla de un extremo a otro en numerosas ocasiones, y no recuerdo haber oído que se confundiera en la lengua hablada a *chévere* con *cheche*. Todo lo contrario: el chévere es siempre una persona simpática y amistosa. El cheche no: el cheche es un buscapleitos antipático y peligroso. Hay un dejo de cariño y de admiración al comentar: "¡Qué chévere es Fulano!" Pero el tono es de ira o reprobación cuando se le dice a alguien: "¡No te vengas haciendo el cheche!" No acierto a ver por qué afirma don Fernando que sean sinónimos dos términos diametralmente opuestos. La misma frase que cita —"es un cheche muy chévere"— demuestra precisamente que no se trata de dos sinónimos sino de voces con significados bien distintos. De un cheche —matón, perdonavidas— puede haberse dicho que era un chévere por la elegancia en el vestir, la gracia al bailar y aun la destreza al reñir. Pero, a la inversa, un chévere no se sentiría muy halagado de que lo tildaran de cheche, ya que en el fondo esta voz conlleva una connotación peyorativa. Al confundir ambos términos no se ha logrado, pues, sino enturbiar el sentido de *chévere* y despistar al que busque su verdadero origen.

Porque, a la verdad, tampoco me parecen muy convincentes los razonamientos con que se sostiene la posible procedencia africana. A más de la improbabilidad de que hayan ocurrido algunos de los cambios fonéticos que se han sugerido, hay el hecho de que *chévere* se arraigó igualmente en México, y resultaría difícil probar que allá lo llevaron los curros del Manglar. Creo, por consiguiente, que debiera buscarse otra explicación que justificara el arraigo en ambos países y de paso aclarase la cuestión de los contrapuestos sentidos.

A ese fin quisiera proponer una hipótesis totalmente distinta. Si hacemos un poco de historia, remontándonos hasta los primeros años de la conquista y colonización, hallaremos que de 1519 a 1521 —años, precisamente, en que Cortés invade y sojuzga el imperio azteca con gente llevada de Cuba— el personaje más influyente en la corte de Carlos V era un caballero flamenco, ayo, camarero mayor y primer ministro del joven e inexperto emperador. Este caballero era quien decidía las cuestiones americanas de mayor monta, incluyendo las encomiendas y otros asuntos de vital interés para los colonizadores. Y este caballero se llamaba Guillermo de Croy, Señor de Chièvres (1458-1521). El poder e influencia del Señor de Chièvres eran tales que le decían el *Alter Rex*. Las Casas, que lo trató por motivos de la generosa causa que defendía, escribió de él: "Trujo también consigo el rey a su ayo y camarero mayor, que llamaron mosior de Xevres, también de muy autorizada persona y dotado de gran prudencia, de quien confió todo lo que al Estado concernía y las mercedes y todo lo demás que no tocase a justicia". (*Historia de las Indias,* lib. III, cap. 99; en la ed. de México, 1951, vol. III, pág. 168). Otro español, Sancho Cota, apuntó en sus *Memorias*: "Mosiur de Xebres governava y guiava todas las cosas del príncipe, el cual fue muy poco grato a los cavalleros españoles primeros que venimos al servicio del príncipe". (*Memorias de Sancho Cota,* edited with an introduction and notes by

Hayward Keniston, Cambridge, Mass., 1964, pág. 73). La sorda hostilidad que estos renglones revelan no fue óbice para que Cota escribiese estos versos (ibid., pág. 135):

> Allí era residente
> un cavallero notable,
> en virtudes muy loable
> el de Xebres presidente.

A más de su extraordinario ascendiente con el Emperador, había otras causas que hacían a Chièvres "muy poco grato" a la mayoría de los españoles. Para éstos, acostumbrados a la sobriedad de la corte de los Reyes Católicos y a la monacal austeridad de la regencia del Cardenal Cisneros, era chocante el lujo y boato importados por el primer ministro y su séquito flamenco. Y en alto grado Monsieur de Chièvres les irritaba el nervio más sensitivo de todos: el que les iba directamente de la cabeza al bolsillo. En Castilla se hizo popular, al ver un doblón, decir:

> Sálveos Dios,
> doblón de a dos,
> que Monsieur de Xevres
> no topó con vos.

Versos que corrieron también en esta otra versión:

> Doblón de a dos,
> norabuena estedes,
> que con vos no topó
> [Monsieur de] Xevres.

Sabiendo ya quién era y cómo era este Monsieur de Chièvres —o como si dijésemos, el Chévere original, el arquetípico, el más chévere de los chéveres— podemos deducir cómo penetró y evolucionó el término en el habla popular de ambos países. No es posible, desde luego, seguir el proceso paso a paso ya que, justamente por tratarse de un giro circunscrito al habla familiar, no lo he hallado en los textos literarios de la época. Pero, por otra parte, no creo sea necesario mucho esfuerzo para ver que en español *Chièvres* vino a pronunciarse *Chévere,* y que la *v* que se ha conservado en la grafía de la forma españolizada no es más que un evidente vestigio de su olvidado origen. Y en cuanto al sentido, igual que de un hombre cruel se dice que es un Nerón y de un ricacho que es un Creso, así también de alguien influyente, acaudalado o elegante bien pudo decirse que era un Chévere. La posterior trayectoria tampoco sería difícil de explicar: voz de uso netamente popular, el pueblo, careciendo de poder y de riqueza, ha descartado lo de 'influyente' y 'acaudalado'. Y lo que ha conservado, a más de los hiperbólicos 'magnífico' y 'excelente', ha sido 'muy bueno o bonito, correcto, elegante, agradable, divertido'. Y así son, y no matones y perdonavidas, los verdaderos chéveres. Y esos los matices con que el término ha pasado, conllevando siempre un aire de simpatía, a otras regiones de Hispanoamérica.

EL IMPACTO DEL CULTERANISMO EN EL TEATRO DE LA EDAD DE ORO *

by JAMES A. CASTAÑEDA
Rice University

El carácter a menudo polémico de ciertas actividades literarias del siglo XVII es el tema de este artículo, de cuyo título se puede inferir fácilmente el nombre de uno de los protagonistas. La más leve referencia al culteranismo evoca la figura del cordobés don Luis de Góngora. Nuestro propósito en esta ocasión es enfocar la reacción suscitada en España por la aparición y difusión de las nuevas modalidades poéticas del movimiento denominado, ora *cultismo,* ora *culteranismo,* o, sencillamente, *gongorismo*. Intentaremos trazar la trayectoria de dicha reacción desde su génesis hasta el momento en que las referencias al culteranismo pierden su filo tajante y adquieren un tono tan levemente satírico que linda en lo innocuo. También, se esbozarán las diferentes formas que

---

* En una carta del 18 de marzo de 1962, el profesor Adams, *Chairman* de una sección, me invitó a leer un trabajo en la reunión de la SAMLA que iba a celebrarse en Miami Beach en noviembre del mismo año. La presentación de ese trabajo, titulado "Cultismo en el teatro de Lope de Vega", representaba mi primera actuación profesional de este tipo, y la adaptación del informe que se imprimió unos meses después fue mi primer artículo publicado. El presente trabajo, inspirándose en gran parte en esas investigaciones sobre Lope y Góngora, representa una ampliación del tema que abarca también la reacción de otros dramaturgos al culteranismo. Conste, pues, aquí mi profundo agradecimiento, respeto, y afecto al profesor Adams, no sólo por el gran influjo que ejerció al iniciarme en los ritos del mundo académico, sino también por el constante apoyo que me ha brindado con sus agudas observaciones, sus juicios acertados, su crítica sincera, y —sobre todo— su amistad.

toma esta censura, siendo preciso exponer de antemano algunas de las características de la "nueva poesía". Aunque nos interesa principalmente la censura del culteranismo que se manifiesta en la comedia, nos desviaremos de vez en cuando para examinar semejante reacción en otros géneros. Además, notaremos el caso particular de Calderón, dramaturgo que admira y con gran frecuencia utiliza las modalidades de la poesía de Góngora.[1]

Antes de abordar el estudio que nos hemos propuesto, convendría precisar la acepción que asignamos a unos términos que serán a menudo repetidos a lo largo de este trabajo. La palabra "gongorismo" y sus derivaciones "gongorizante", "gongorizar", etc., no admiten ambigüedad. Al contrario, la palabra *culto* tiene un sentido favorable y otro despectivo. Para Góngora y sus secuaces, predomina el sentido etimológico que implica "cultura, pureza, corrección, elegancia, etc.", mientras que los enemigos del movimiento utilizan la palabra con el sólo propósito de denigrar este estilo, calificándolo de una locura literaria en que siempre se busca la oscuridad. Otros términos derivados de *culto* son *culterano, culteranismo* y etiquetas aún más despectivas, tales como *cultería, cultigracia, contracultos, cultidiablesco*, etc.[2]

Para poder llegar a una mayor comprensión de lo que constituye el culteranismo, conviene intercalar unos comentarios sobre las aportaciones de Dámaso Alonso al estudio de Góngora. Debido al carácter difícil y aun hermético de la poesía de Góngora y al análisis bastante superficial que le dedicaron varios críticos, uno de ellos, Francisco de Cascales, en sus *Cartas filológicas* de 1634, inventa la fórmula que hizo fortuna: "príncipe de la luz" y "príncipe de las tinieblas",[3] así estableciendo una interpretación equivocada de la poesía de Góngora, según la cual hay dos períodos,

---

[1] Aunque nos parece una gran exageración la frase que cierra el valioso artículo de Eunice Joiner Gates, "Góngora and Calderón", *Hispanic Review*, V (1937), pág. 258: "Rare indeed is the page in Calderón that is not reminiscent of Góngora".

[2] Para un interesante y bien documentado estudio de esta terminología y las acepciones que le dan los autores y críticos del siglo XVII, véase Lucien-Paul Thomas, *Le Lyrisme et la préciosité cultistes en Espagne: étude historique et analytique* (Halle: Max Niemeyer, 1909), págs. 160-180.

[3] Francisco Cascales, *Cartas filológicas*, I, ed. Justo García Soriano, *Clásicos Castellanos*, Vol. 103 (Madrid, 1961), pág. 189.

el primero, en que las poesías son cortas y fáciles, y el segundo, en que son largas y oscuras. Esta teoría, apoyada por la autoridad de Menéndez Pelayo,[4] perpetúa la leyenda negra de Góngora hasta la revaloración crítica de su poesía, llevada a cabo por la generación de 1927, capitaneada por Dámaso Alonso, quien, con pruebas más que suficientes, refuta esta dicotomía.[5]

Habiendo ya señalado en algún detalle en otro lugar [6] la postura de Lope ante el culteranismo, nos limitaremos ahora a un resumen del papel que éste desempeña en la censura del culteranismo.

Abunda evidencia incontrovertible sobre un hecho: Lope admiraba y temía el prodigioso talento de su rival, don Luis de Góngora. Consta incluso que en obras como *La dama boba*, de 1613, *La Filomena* y *La Andrómeda*, ambas de 1621, y en *La Circe*, de 1624, existe lo que Dámaso Alonso denomina un "Lope gongorino" en "Competencia con el mismo Góngora en un arte formal..."[7] A pesar de esta actitud de Lope, Góngora nunca dejó

---

[4] Se lee en su *Historia de las ideas estéticas en España*, II (Santander, 1947), págs. 328-9: "Góngora... en las tenebrosidades del *Polifemo* y de *Las Soledades*, convertido (como escribió Cascales) de *ángel de luz* en *ángel de tinieblas*". Sobre esta transformación de términos, véase Dámaso Alonso, *La lengua poética de Góngora*, 3ª ed. (Madrid: C.S.I.C., 1961), pág. 9: "Menéndez Pelayo... que probablemente citaba de memoria, atribuye a Cascales la forma 'ángel de luz' y 'ángel de tinieblas', y la mayor parte de los críticos posteriores no han hecho más que repetir, aquí como en tantas otras ocasiones, lo dicho por el gran escritor". Gran parte del segundo tomo de las *Ideas estéticas* (1884) consiste en lo que califica Dámaso Alonso de "una furibunda fulminación de Góngora y del gongorismo" en su libro *Menéndez Pelayo, crítico literario (las palinodias de don Marcelino)*, (Madrid: Gredos, 1956), pág. 69.

[5] Señalado por N. B. Adams en su edición revisada del manual de George Tyler Northup, *An Introduction to Spanish Literature*. Third Edition Revised and Enlarged by Nicholson B. Adams (Chicago: The University of Chicago Press, 1960), pág. 301. Para los principales estudios gongorinos de Dámaso Alonso, véanse *La lengua poética de Góngora. Parte primera*. Tercera edición corregida (Madrid: C.S.I.C., 1961) y *Estudios y ensayos gongorinos* (Madrid: Gredos, 1955). Interesan también, por su agudo análisis de la poesía de Góngora, *Poesía española. Ensayo de métodos y límites estilísticos*. Segunda edición aumentada y corregida (Madrid: Editorial Gredos, 1952), págs. 307-392, y *Góngora y el "Polifemo"*, I-II. Cuarta edición, muy aumentada (Madrid: Editorial Gredos, 1961).

[6] J. A. Castañeda, "El impacto de Góngora en la vida y obra de Lope de Vega", *Romance Notes*, Vol. V, No. 2 (Spring, 1964), págs. 174-82.

[7] *Poesía española*, pág. 466.

de brindarle una hostilidad agresiva. La siguiente cita de Romera-Navarro describe bien las relaciones personales que imperaban entre los dos poetas: "Góngora jamás tendrá un elogio para Lope, ni le dará en modo alguno la más leve señal de estimación literaria o personal. Lope de Vega, en cambio, alabará en ocasiones varias a su enemigo, no mencionará su nombre sino con respeto, y hasta en sus censuras del culteranismo hará a menudo una salvedad honrosa para el ilustre cordobés." [8]

Es bien conocida la trayectoria de la poesía culta que incluye a Garcilaso, Herrera, y Góngora. Se reconoce también el influjo que han ejercido los dos primeros en la lírica del siglo XVII. Ciertas vetas de esta poesía culta se encuentran en la mayor parte de los poetas de la Edad de Oro y es solamente el abuso y la exageración de estas vetas que provocan los ataques anticulteranos.

Para nuestro estudio de la censura del culteranismo, sería posible calificar de año decisivo el de 1613, en que aparecen dos obras de un Góngora maduro, ya seguro de su técnica, el *Polifemo* y la *Primera Soledad*. Este año de 1613 es significativo por señalar el comienzo de la reacción de Lope —y es de notar que cuando las opiniones en la Corte se dividieron sobre el mérito de estas obras, Lope sale a la defensa de Góngora con su soneto laudatorio, "Canta cisne andaluz, que el verde coro". [9]— Sin embargo, por el momento nos interesa la reacción negativa de Lope al culteranismo más que los varios elogios que dedica el Fénix a Góngora y las obras en que se empeña en ser más culto que el maestro.

De todos los elementos del culteranismo, se destacan dos que son satirizados más que otros en la Edad de Oro: es decir, el uso —o, mejor dicho, el abuso— de latinismos y del hipérbaton. Claro que el general carácter oscuro, criticado por todos, deriva por la mayor parte de estos obstáculos lingüísticos.

---

[8] M. Romera-Navarro, *La preceptiva dramática de Lope de Vega y otros ensayos sobre el Fénix* (Madrid, 1935), pág. 152. Para interpretaciones interesantes sobre la actitud refrenada de Lope, véanse Elisha K. Kane, *Gongorism and the Golden Age* (Chapel Hill: The University of North Carolina Press, 1928), pág. 48, y también Emilio Orozco Díaz, *Góngora* (Barcelona, Editorial Labor, S. A., 1953), págs. 58-62.

[9] Lope de Vega, *Obras escogidas. Poesía y prosa* (Madrid: Aguilar, 1953), pág. 931.

Las parodias y sátiras lopescas se dirigen principalmente a la general oscuridad del culteranismo y al abuso del hipérbaton. En varias obras escritas entre 1613 y 1617 hay breves alusiones al culteranismo que no dejan de revelar cierta ligereza.[10] Tal es el caso en *El capellán de la Virgen,* de 1615,[11] donde encontramos en un soneto, la más deliciosa de las parodias satíricas de las violentas transposiciones del hipérbaton, lo que todos los adversarios del culteranismo, no sólo Lope de Vega, señalaron como su más intolerable abuso:

> Inés, tus bellos ya me matan, ojos,
> y al alma, roban pensamientos, mía,
> desde aquel triste, que te vieron, día,
> no tan crueles, por tu causa, enojos,
> tus cabellos, prisiones de amor, rojos,
> con tal, me hacen vivir, melancolía,
> que tu fiera, en mis lágrimas, porfía,
> dará de mis, la cuenta, a Dios, despojos.
> Creyendo que de mí, no, Amor, se acuerde,
> temerario, levántase, deseo,
> de ver a quien, me, por desdenes pierde.
> Que es venturoso si se admite, empleo,
> esperanza de amor, me dice, verde,
> viendo que, te, desde tan lejos, veo.[12]

Otra parodia graciosísima del hipérbaton se encuentra en *Tiempo de regocijo,* novela de Alonso de Castillo Solórzano, uno de los críticos más severos de la "nueva poesía". En esta obra, don Fadrique había solicitado los servicios de un poeta culto para ciertas pretensiones amorosas...:

> Quiso el culto poeta la paga de su trabajo, y una mañana cuando don Fadrique se levantaba, le dio un paje un papel, en que leyó estas razones:
> "Afectuosa puse mente en cuidado en servir a V. S. con los de mi musa meditados versos, séanme intercesores

---

[10] Entre ellas *La dama boba* (1613), *Acad. N.,* XI, pág. 595; *Con su pan se lo coma* (1613 ó 1614, según Morley y Bruerton, *Chronology,* pág. 183), *Acad. N.,* IV, pág. 318; la dedicatoria a *Virtud, pobreza, y mujer* (probablemente de 1615), *B.A.E.,* LII, pág. 212; y *El desdén vengado* (1617), *Acad.,* XV, pág. 425.
[11] Morley y Bruerton, *Chronology,* págs. 178-9.
[12] *Acad.,* IV, págs. 469-70.

con V. S. para que en una que se me ofrece necesidad, se sirva de darme treinta su generosa mano escudos, no por de mi trabajo premio, sino por ser V. S. quien es." [13]

Escasean en el teatro de Lope ataques sobre abusos léxicos, pero contrasta rotundamente con esta actitud la sátira chispeante de Quevedo, incluida en su "Aguja de navegar cultos, con la receta para hacer soledades en un día":

RECETA

Quien quisiere ser culto en sólo un día,
La jeri (aprenderá) gonza siguiente:
*Fulgores, arrogar, joven, presiente,
Candor, construye, métrica armonía;*
 *Poco mucho, si no, purpuracia,
Neutralidad, conculca, erige, mente,
Pulsa, ostenta, librar, adolescente,
Señas traslada, pira, frustra, harpía.*
 *Cede, impide, cisuras, petulante,
Palestra, liba, meta, argento, alterna,
Si bien, disuelve, émulo, canoro.*
 Use mucho de *líquido* y de *errante,*
Su poco de *nocturno* y de *caverna,*
Anden listos *livor, adunco,* y *poro;*
 Que ya toda Castilla
Con sola esta cartilla
Se abrasa de poetas babilones,
Escribiendo sonetos confusiones;
Y en la Mancha pastores y gañanes,
Atestadas de ajos las barrigas,
Hacen ya cultedades como migas. [14]

Aunque tales catálogos de voces cultas no figuran en las obras de Lope,[15] abundan en el teatro de la época. Se encuentran otros

---

[13] Castillo Solórzano, *Tiempo de regocijo,* edición de Cotarelo y Mori (Madrid, 1907), págs. 406-407.

[14] *B. A. E.,* XXIII, pág. 482.

[15] Aunque faltan las burlas en forma de catálogos, Lope no deja de censurar abiertamente la excesiva latinización del lenguaje. Véase, por ejemplo, su "Respuesta a un papel que escribió un señor de estos reinos en razón de la nueva poesía", *Obras escogidas. Poesía y prosa* (Aguilar), págs. 925-31.

en cinco comedias de Tirso [16] y en un romance satírico de Castillo Solórzano. [17] En tres de estas obras de Tirso, *Amar por arte mayor, La celosa de sí misma,* y *Celos con celos se curan,* las censuras o parodias se limitan a parte de una escena en que un criado sencillamente se burla de las complicaciones del nuevo estilo, o bien representa una figura ridícula cuando intercala una serie de cultismos en uno de sus parlamentos. Censura más directa se encuentra en el tercer acto de *Santo y sastre,* donde Tirso incluye en un diálogo entre Dorotea y el gracioso, Pendón, una referencia despectiva a un poeta que "gongoriza", cuya poesía critican los personajes de la manera siguiente:

Pendón. Fiscal cuadrúpedo llama
de las liebres (éste) al galgo;
nieto al amor de la espuma;
alcatifas de tabí
a los prados, y a un neblí
llamó estafetas de pluma.
Dorotea. ¡Qué necio modo de hablar!
Pendón. Estos se llaman poetas
con cáscara, no los metas
en la boca, sin quebrar
sus versos con un martillo;
que si a gustarlos te pones,
por ser poetas piñones
te han de quebrar un colmillo. [18]

Si Lope es un tanto tímido y parco al criticar a la persona de Góngora, hay otros que no lo son. Conocidísimo es el soneto mordaz de Quevedo cuyos primeros versos rezan así:

Yo te untaré mis versos con tocino,
porque no me los muerdas, Gongorilla,

---

[16] *Amar por arte mayor* (I, v), *B.A.E.,* V, pág. 425b; *Celos con celos se curan* (III, ii), *B.A.E.,* V, pág. 375a, b; *La celosa de sí misma* (II, v), *B.A.E.,* V, pág. 138b, c; *La fingida Arcadia* (III, iii), *Obras dramáticas completas,* II (Aguilar), págs. 1420-22; *Santo y sastre* (I, i), *Obras dramáticas completas,* III (Aguilar), págs. 50-51.
[17] En *Donaires del Parnaso,* ed. Gallardo, *Ensayo,* t. II, cols. 293-294 (Citado por Romera-Navarro, pág. 222).
[18] *Loc. cit.,* pág. 51.

>   perro de los ingenios de Castilla,
>   docto en pullas, cual mozo de camino. [19]

Y citamos también el primer terceto, para demostrar hasta qué punto llega Quevedo en su ataque personal:

>   ¿Por qué censuras tú la lengua griega
>   siendo sólo rabí de la judía,
>   cosa que tu nariz aun no niega? [20]

Pero aunque en este campo de la sátira personal reina supremo Quevedo, Tirso no le va muy en zaga en el tercer acto de su comedia, *La fingida Arcadia*, compuesta, es interesante de notar, unos siete años antes de la muerte de Góngora. Habiendo explicado el lacayo Pinzón que el Parnaso se compone de tres lugares: gloria, infierno y purgatorio, Tirso, con alusiones que no dejan duda ninguna, zambulle a Góngora en el Infierno, como fundador de una secta, y en el Purgatorio, a sus discípulos, utilizando para nombres de éstos voces culteranas personificadas:

>   Pinzón.   Pecados veniales
>   son las palabras ociosas,
>   que con fuego han de purgarse;
>   vocablos impertinentes,
>   que fuera de sus lugares
>   están, como carne huida,
>   son los que en nuestro lenguaje
>   posponen los adjetivos,
>   latinizan el romance
>   y echan el verbo a la postre,
>   como oración de pedante.
>   Dicen que está en el infierno
>   su primer dogmatizante,
>   que introducir nuevas sectas
>   no es digno de perdonarse.
>   Penan en el purgatorio
>   sus discípulos secuaces,
>   por no pecar de malicia,
>   que los más son ignorantes.

---

[19] Francisco de Quevedo Villegas, *Obras completas*, Tomo II, *Obras en verso*, pág. 176.
[20] *Ibidem*.

>
> Rogerio. Y ¿quien son?
> Pinzón. Este es *Candor*,
> aquél se llama *Brillante*,
> *Émulo* aquél, y *Coturno*
> el otro; aquél el *Celaje*,
> *Cristal animado* el otro;
> *Hipérbole*, *Pululante*,
> *Palestra*, *Giro*, *Cerúleo*,
> *Crepúsculos* y *Fragantes*,
> murieron con contrición
> y quisieron enmendarse;
> mas no tuvieron lugar.
> Rueguen a Dios que los saque
> de penas de purgatorio,
> que a fe que hay entre ello fraile
> que habla prosa y vascongada
> y versos trilingües hace. [21]

Como queda dicho, faltan en la producción dramática de Lope tales catálogos de vocablos, pero vuelve Lope a censurar la oscuridad del culteranismo en *La amistad y obligación*, escrita probablemente entre 1622-23, [22] en un diálogo ameno entre el lacayo Lope... y Severo, músico:

> Severo. Soy músico, soy poeta.
> Lope. ¿De qué región?
> Severo. No se trata
> de un arte tan celestial,
> señor, con tanta abundancia.
> Lope. ¿Sois vulgar o culterano?
> Severo. Culto soy.
> Lope. Quedaos en casa,
> y escribiréis mis secretos.
> Severo. Tus secretos, ¿por qué causa?
> Lope. Porque nadie los entienda. [23]

De parecidas parodias en comedias posteriores, *Amar, servir y esperar*, [24] *La moza de cántaro* [25] (en que figura una carta culta en

---

[21] *Loc. cit.*, pág. 1421.
[22] Véase Morley y Bruerton, *op. cit.*, pág. 256.
[23] *Acad. N.*, III, pág. 353.
[24] *Acad. N.*, III, pág. 235.
[25] *Acad. N.*, XIII, págs. 647-8.

prosa) y *Acertar errando,* nos limitaremos a citar parte de una escena de esta última obra, en que Tarquín trata de requerir de amores a Julia:

>Tarquín. Yo soy amante de manos;
>no con mirar me contento;
>más gusto de lo que apalpo.
>Julia. ¿Tu sabes amar?
>Tarquín.   Y mucho.
>Julia. ¡Qué groserón! ¡Qué villano!
>Yo quiero muy a lo culto.
>Tarquín. ¿Culto? Pues la vela apago.
>Julia. ¿Qué has hecho, necio?
>Tarquín.   ¿Eso inoras?
>Ya estamos cultos entrambos.
>¿Puede haber obscuridad
>en el limbo culteráneo
>de los versos de un poeta
>como ésta.[26]

La trayectoria de esta posición de Lope frente a las innovaciones del culteranismo nos lleva a *Las Bizarrías de Belisa* que tiene la fecha segura del 24 de mayo de 1634 y que, antes del reciente hallazgo del Profesor Silverman,[27] se consideraba la última comedia de Lope. El hecho de que la obra contenga tres ataques contra el culteranismo demuestra que nunca se reconcilió Lope con los secuaces de Góngora.

El tercero lo citaremos por su valor histórico:

>Aquella que escribe en culto,
>por aquel griego lenguaje,
>que no le supo Castilla,
>ni se le enseñó su madre.[28]

Durante el ciclo de Lope, abundan censuras del culteranismo, unas jocosas como las del mismo Lope, otras de índole parecida a las de Quevedo y algunas de las de Tirso. Pero a medida que trans-

---

[26] *Acad. N.,* III, págs. 48-9.
[27] Véase Joseph H. Silverman, "Lope de Vega's Last Years and His Final Play, *The Greatest Virtue of a King*", *The Texas Quarterly* (Spring, 1963), págs. 174-187.
[28] *Acad. N.,* XI, pág. 457.

curren los años después de la muerte de Góngora, ocurrida en 1627, se van disminuyendo tanto en cantidad como en seriedad, perdido ya el interés polémico en el movimiento.[29] Esto es lo que se refleja en las ligeras burlas del culteranismo que encontramos en *El marqués del Cigarral*,[30] de Castillo Solórzano, comedia escrita probablemente después de 1635, y en *Entre bobos anda el juego*[31] (1638) de Rojas Zorrilla. En *El lindo don Diego*, cuya composición se ha fechado entre 1654 y 1662, el término *culto* le sirve a Moreto tan sólo para un juego de palabras en que se destaca una vez más la ridiculez del protagonista. Despidiéndose Mendo y Diego de su prima, Mendo comienza...

> Señora, no se despide
> quien deja el alma asistiendo
> al *culto* de vuestros ojos
> desde que vive de vellos.[32]

A lo cual añade el lindo don Diego:

> Yo, prima, no sé de *cultos*,
> porque a Góngora no entiendo,
> ni le he entendido en mi vida.[33]

En efecto, y como era de esperar, durante el ciclo calderoniano, el culteranismo ha dejado de ser un vibrante tema de actualidad y, por consiguiente, suscita menos censura.

Acabada ya la militante polémica, algunas de las innovaciones

---

[29] En cuanto al caso específico de Lope, cf. la opinión de Joaquín de Entrambasaguas, *Discurso correspondiente a la solemne apertura del curso académico 1962-1963* (Madrid, 1962), págs. 34-35: "...ya muerto Góngora, el *Fénix*, sin el temor de sus sátiras, y muy por encima de los imitadores topiquistas de su rival, que por entonces comenzaban a multiplicarse, empezó a publicar poemas cultos, de más lograda factura neorrenacentista que, a veces, en muchos fragmentos suyos podrían pasar por obra de don Luis al que, con ellos su rival y admirador se sentía no inferior sino a su altura, si es que no creía superarle".

[30] *B.A.E.*, XLV, págs. 310, 311, 317 y 320.

[31] Ed. F. Ruiz Morcuende, *Clásicos Castellanos*, Vol. 35 (Madrid, 1956), págs. 103, 105 y 122.

[32] Ed. Narciso Alonso Cortés, *Clásicos Castellanos*, Vol. 32 (Madrid, 1937), págs. 65-66.

[33] *Ibidem.*, pág. 66.

de Góngora empiezan a incorporarse al español, autorizadas en muchos casos por Calderón mismo. Según Eunice Joiner Gates, "It has been several times noted that among the dramatists of the Golden Age, none has shown himself to be more gongoristic than Calderón." [34]

Pero en esto como en todo, Calderón se muestra muy ecléctico, utilizando las aportaciones valiosas de Góngora en cuanto a elementos léxicos y a la metáfora [35] pero evitando como regla general las violentas transposiciones sintácticas del hipérbaton. [36]

Estos apuntes nos indican cómo, a lo largo de la literatura teatral de la Edad de Oro, es preciso reconocer la importancia de la prodigiosa figura de Góngora. En la primera época fomenta éste grandes polémicas... durante la última época se puede notar a menudo su influjo. Algunos lo odiaron, otros lo reverenciaron, pero nadie puede negar su impacto tremendo en las letras españolas en la Edad de Oro.

---

[34] *Loc. cit.*, pág. 241.

[35] Milton A. Buchanan, "'Culteranismo' in Calderón's *La vida es sueño*", *Homenaje ofrecido a Menéndez Pidal*, I (Madrid, 1925), pág. 546; "It was in the use of neologisms that Calderón showed his strongest bias toward the new school of poetry"; pág. 548: "In his use of words, Calderón may therefore be included among sane and progressive assimilators of new words that develop the resources of the language"; Eunice Joiner Gates, *loc. cit.*, pág. 256: "...Calderón was very greatly indebted to Góngora for his poetic diction, and most especially for his use of metaphor".

[36] Buchanan, *loc. cit.*, pág. 550: "Nowhere in *La vida es sueño* is there an example of an adjective so far removed from the noun it modifies as to suggest a concession to culteranismo."

RELECCIÓN DE LOS PRIMEROS PÁRRAFOS DE "NIEBLA" DE UNAMUNO

by F. S. Escribano
University of Colorado

I

Uno de los temas más característicos de la supuesta "generación del 98" es el de qué es España, cómo es y qué ha sido España. Este problema tan aparentemente insistente ha sido causa de que no se vea o no se quiera ver que el tema "España" en autores como Unamuno, Baroja, Azorín y Ortega y Gasset, tiene raíces más hondas, que van más allá de las ramas literarias y de un tópico que desvirtúa la preocupación universal de estos escritores. Casi todos nos hemos dejado llevar, un poco ciegamente, por ese tópico de lo español, su paisaje, su historia, su modo de ser en el tiempo y en los tiempos. Esto era natural, porque había una circunstancia, desde Felipe III —definitivamente— hasta hoy, desde los arbitristas del siglo XVII hasta novelas de reciente publicación como *A Villalobos le sienta bien la muerte,* de Fernández Alcántara, que España no sólo iba mal, sino de mal en peor. De ahí los dos frentes de batalla: "la leyenda negra" y "la leyenda áurea"; de ahí, las contemporáneas posiciones extremistas o extremadas de la F.A.I. y de las J.O.N.S. Ante este barullo, ha sido posible el cultivo del tópico "España" y sus sucedáneos ("españolismo", "realismo", "individualismo"), cerrando la vía a un pensamiento superior a la lavada de la ropa sucia de casa. Ha sido y es todavía un modo de escatimar y menguar el sentido universal de la literatura española, sentido que no hay que confundir con el internacional y el cosmopolita. Si en algo sufre la literatura española es, a mi modo de ver, precisamente en ser reacia a buscar la aceptación y el aplauso internacionales. El otero tenía que ir a Mahoma, porque Mahoma no iba al otero. Dicho de otro modo, los críticos extranjeros son los que a menudo han "descubierto" los valores universales de la literatura española, mientras los críticos nacionales se lo han pasado lavando la ropa intelectual con la esperanza de que todo saldría en la colada. De ahí que la crítica extranjera haya visto con mayor altura la categoría universal del pensamiento del grupo del 98, que ha sobresalido, inadvertidamente para muchos de nosotros, más y con más ahinco en la busca del hombre, del hombre a secas, pero no seco, del hombre con toda su humanidad. En realidad, cuando los escritores de esta "generación" se preguntaban "¿qué es ser español?", en la mayoría de los casos la pregunta se desplazaba metafísicamente a qué es ser hombre, a qué es el ser humano. Este pasar de una limitada zona personal y tradicional a otra universal es discernible, si nos damos cuenta de que el autor bucea más hondo de lo que a primera lectura parece. Al leer con más cuidado analítico aquellos párrafos en que el autor está hablando de España, se descubre un salto mortal a un más allá universal. Aduzco algunos ejemplos muy significativos, en que subrayo el desplazamiento a lo universal.

Pío Baroja, en *Las inquietudes de Shanti Andía,* novela que da la impresión de ser facilona, muy a menudo se sirve de lo circunstancial para revelarnos lo universal: "El viejo Yurrumendi, un extraño inventor de fantasías, le dijo a Zelayeta que aquella cueva era un antro, donde se guarecía una gran serpiente con alas, la *Egan suguía*. Esta serpiente tenía garras de tigre, alas de buitre y cara de vieja. Andaba de noche, haciendo fechorías, sorbiendo la sangre de los niños, y su aliento era tan deletéreo que envenenaba./ Desde que supimos esto, la cueva nos imponía respeto. A pesar de ello, yo propuse que quemáramos la maleza del interior. Si estaba la *Egan suguía,* se achicharraría, y si no estaba, no pasaría nada. A Recalde no le pareció bien la idea. *Así se consolidan las supersticiones.*"[1]; "Esta impresión de la

---

[1] *Obras completas* (Madrid: Biblioteca Nueva, 1947), II, 1018.

escuela, fría y húmeda, donde se entumecen los pies, donde recibe uno, sin saber casi por qué, frases duras, malos tratos y castigos, esa impresión es de las más feas y antipáticas de la vida./ *Es extraño; lo que ha comprendido el salvaje, que el niño, como más débil, como más tierno, merece más cuidado y hasta más reposo que el hombre, no lo ha comprendido el civilizado,* y, entre nosotros, el que sería incapaz de hacer daño a un adulto martiriza a un niño con el consentimiento de sus padres./ *Es una de las muchas barbaridades de lo que se llama civilización.*" [2]; "Eustacio Yurrumendi había viajado mucho; pero era un hombre quimérico a quien sus fantasías turbaban la cabeza. *Todos tenemos un conjunto de mentiras que nos sirven para abrigarnos de la frialdad y de la tristeza de la vida;* pero Yurrumendi exageraba un poco el abrigo." [3]

No es afirmar nada original el que Azorín sea un autor que con tanta insistencia, unida a una enorme delicadeza de fino cristal, ha dado una universalidad a las cosas y a las personas más ínfimas y más cotidianas. En "La lucecita roja" termina el lector contemplando la perdurabilidad de las acciones humanas. No es posible destacar ahora, renglón por renglón, la inefable técnica que nos lleva a esa continuidad de los hechos del vivir de la humanidad. En otro esbozo filosófico, el de "El buen juez" de *Los pueblos,* don Alonso, juez de un pueblo manchego, dictamina una sentencia judicial que alborota al ínfimo pueblo. Azorín se ha inventado un pueblo ínfimo para dar realce a la filosofía de la Justicia. Azorín relata, con insospechada malicia, todas esas pequeñeces de lo humano cotidiano. (¿Se habrá notado ya que Azorín es nuestro Proust?). Uno del pueblo, don Luis, ha comentado: "—Es una sentencia rara". [4] Cuando don Alonso vuelve a su casa, también doña María, Lola y Carmencita están alebrestadas. Pero don Alonso las tranquiliza: "'Ya sé, ya sé que a vosotras os preocupa lo que las gentes van diciendo. No se me oculta que la ciudad está alborotada; pero esto no es extraño. Sobre la Tierra hay dos cosas grandes: la Justicia y la Belleza. La belleza nos la ofrece espontáneamente la Naturaleza y la vemos también

---

[2] Ed. citada, II, 1015-1016.
[3] Ed. citada, II, 1020.
[4] *Obras completas* (Madrid: M. Aguilar, Editor, 1947), II, 139.

en el ser humano; mas la Justicia, si observamos todos los seres grandes y pequeños que pueblan la Tierra, la veremos perpétuamente negada por la lucha formidable que todas las criaturas, aves y mamíferos mantienen entre sí. Por esto la Justicia, la Justicia pura, limpia de egoísmos, es una cosa tan rara, tan espléndida, tan divina, que cuando un átomo de ella desciende sobre el mundo, los hombres se llenan de asombro y se alborotan. Este es el motivo por lo que yo encuentro natural que si hoy ha bajado acaso sobre esta ciudad manchega una partícula de esa Justicia, anden sus habitantes escandalizados y trastornados'./ Y don Alonso ha sonreído, por última vez, con esa sonrisa extraordinaria, inmensa, que sólo le es dable contemplar a la Humanidad cada dos o tres siglos..." [5]

En el caso de Ortega y Gasset, frente a *España invertebrada* y otros temas de España y sus circunstancias están *El tema de nuestro tiempo*, *La deshumanización del arte* y muchos ensayos que sobrepasan la condición humana de España y van a una trascendencia metafísica. Si Ortega y Gasset se hubiese mantenido en una constante filosófica sería, hoy por hoy, una de las más altas cumbres de la filosofía europea. Pero una ingénita comezón de estilizar muy elegantemente el pensamiento, que le llevaba a veces a ser más superficial de lo que era, y un noble quehacer por rehacer a una España ñoña, le restaron méritos genuínamente filosóficos. (En cambio, Xavier Zubiri, su mejor discípulo, con poca producción literaria, con silencio de pensador, sin interesarle España, ha llegado a una categoría filosófica de hondo pensar. Pero, ¿es que a Platón interesó Grecia, o a Santo Tomás de Aquino Italia, o a Kant Alemania? Dejemos a los pocos auténticos pensadores en paz y con vida.)

En Antonio Machado, su *Juan de Mairena* y *Abel Martín* son obras henchidas de un valor metafísico que llegan a las soledades de existencialistas como Camus y Sartre, pero con un "duende" que aterra por su tajante verdad y al mismo tiempo nos hace intuir una fuerte voluntad humana para no hundirse en el cieno de los instintos.

---

[5] *Obras completas* (Madrid, M. Aguilar; Editor, 1947), II, 141. No subrayo los renglones de los dos párrafos citados por su evidencia trascendental, arrancada de un insignificante pueblo manchego.

Valle-Inclán, el del brazo de las mentiras y las verdades, convierte sus duendes célticos en esperpentos, en que la humanidad se mira reflejada ante la invisible magia de un espejo cóncavo y ve sus absurdos con toda la profundidad de un Goya y de un Solana.

Y, ¿Unamuno? A pesar de todo su "casticismo", siempre fue más allá del ambiente histórico del hombre que evolucionó del tartesio al contemporáneo. Unamuno, como los otros escritores del 98, se revolvía contra la ñoñería de las llamadas fuerzas vivas de la época en que le tocó vivir y pensar. Todas esas fuerzas vivas, de un extremo al otro, cuando gobernaban o estaban en la oposición, las consideraba muertas; muertas, porque no daban con la metafísica del vivir del hombre. Por eso fue el peor catedrático de griego que ha habido en España. Declinaciones, desinencias, conjugaciones y todo lo demás de la gramática griega se lo aprendía uno mismo, sin maestro ni niño muerto que le valiese. Lo importante era pensar en la filosofía griega para irse a la filosofía de la vida. Unamuno fue intachable enemigo de la burocracia, de eso que se llama pomposamente "administración". Sentía que todo burócrata era en el fondo un cretino; no distinguía entre el cretino de buenos instintos, afable, servicial y con ganas de servir y el cretino de bajos instintos, charlatán, arrogante y con más complejos que los que descubrió Freud en su clínica. Su intenso pensar en la muerte y en la inmortalidad humana y su lucha con la fe y la razón fueron la manifestación más honda de elevarse del hombre de carne y hueso, del que tanto gustaba aludir, a asentar las bases de una filosofía de la existencia humana. Lo confiesa en su "Historia de *Niebla*". Cuando en 1935 preparaba reeditar *Niebla*, vuelve la memoria a los años que mediaron entre la publicación de su nivola en 1914 y la venida de la República en 1931; es entonces, en 1935, cuando resume su angustia filosófica: "Es cuando me sentí envuelto en la niebla histórica de nuestra España, de nuestra Europa y hasta de nuestro universo humano".[6] Antes de *Niebla*, tenemos *Paz en la guerra* (1897), y después de *Niebla* su drama *El otro* (1932), o sea la línea recta y ascendente del tópico "España" al tema del problema del hombre.

---

[6] *Obras completas* (Madrid: Afrodisio Aguado, S. A., 1951), II, 187.

Entre estas dos obras a cada extremo, las hay en que el tópico español no tiene ni querencia ni vigencia de interés personalmente unamunianos. Su gran obra *Del pensamiento trágico de la vida en los hombres y los pueblos* nada tiene de españolismo, como la *Summa Theologica* de Santo Tomás nada tiene de preocupación italiana o la *Crítica de la razón pura* de Kant quiere ser un análisis del problema "Alemania". Es axiomático que el pensamiento filosófico es metafísico cuando se desprende de las ataduras nacionales, mezquinas y bajas. En el caso de Unamuno, lo universal a menudo se consigue desde el trampolín de lo humano cuotidiano hacia la abstracción. La metafísica para Unamuno era un pensar no de lo abstracto a lo abstracto. Por eso cambió la fórmula cartesiana de "pienso, luego soy" a "soy, luego pienso". Gran parte de sus obras mantienen esta fórmula técnica, en que del hombre vestido, comido y bebido, se ascendia a qué es ser hombre. En realidad, toda su obra es un ensayo, sea novela, sea teatro, sea cuento, sea artículo de periódico. Dentro de esta técnica del ensayo, el diálogo es la expresión de su hondo pensar. Unamuno repetía con frecuencia "diálogo" o "mucho diálogo". O sea: "Hay aquí toda una metafísica. O una metahistoria". [7]

II

Niebla, 1914, es obra pensada y trabajada entre los dos polos de los primeros años de Unamuno en que se vislumbra ya el problema de la existencia y los últimos de ese desgarrador problema. En *Niebla* se cuaja definitivamente el problema epistemológico de la existencia del hombre. Es *La vida es sueño* de Calderón en otras coordenadas. En Calderón, la duda se basa en una escatología católica. En Unamuno, ha desaparecido ese destino cristiano para plantearse el problema de la existencia y su último conocimiento. A Calderón le venía la metafísica hecha y acabada, en que sólo existía el problema de acatarla y realizarla para la mayor gloria de Dios. A Unamuno la metafísica de la existencia le venía envuelta en una inexorable niebla que había que disipar para llegar

---

[7] *Obras completas*, II, 688.

a la última realidad del hombre. Es sintomático que al final de la nivola, Augusto, muerto ya, se aparece a su autor en sueños y cuando terminan de polemizar y Augusto le dice: "¡Y ahora adiós!", Unamuno explica: "Y se disipó en la niebla negra./ Yo soñé luego que me moría, y en el momento mismo en que soñaba dar el último respiro me desperté con cierta opresión en el pecho." [8] También Segismundo seguirá soñando al final de la obra, pero su sueño será vivir de tal modo, que luego alcance la contemplación eterna de Dios. Para Unamuno será vivir "con cierta opresión en el pecho." Esa "opresión en el pecho" está explicada en otro párrafo de *Niebla*: "Al separarse uno de otro, Víctor y Augusto, iba diciendo éste: 'Y esta mi vida, ¿es novela, es nivola o qué es? Todo esto que me pasa y que les pasa a los que me rodean, ¿es realidad o es ficción? ¿No es acaso todo esto un sueño de Dios o de quien sea, que se desvanecerá en cuanto Él despierte, y por eso le rezamos y elevamos a Él cánticos e himnos, para dormecerle, para acunar su sueño? ¿No es acaso la liturgia toda de todas las religiones un modo de brezar el sueño de Dios y que no despierte y deje de soñarnos?" [9]. Calderón continuaba con la idea bíblica que Dios hizo al hombre a su imagen; para Unamuno, Dios "o quien sea" sueña al hombre.

En realidad, *Niebla* es un ensayo sobre el hombre, sobre su ser o no ser. La escribió como novela, porque en la técnica expresiva de Unamuno el diálogo es imprescindible, primordial como expositor del pensamiento. Este dialogar se encuentra en Montaigne, con lo cual dio a sus ensayos esa difícil explicación de su inefable atracción. De Montaigne a Unamuno, la mayoría de los ensayistas se ha dedicado a una explicación narrativa de su pensamiento y lo íntimo se nos ha esfumado. En este tipo de ensayo lo que nos baila ante los ojos es el academiquismo; en Montaigne y Unamuno, es su ensimismamiento para extraer y abstraer la realidad del hombre y sus cosas. Para dar toda la vitalidad que precisa el ensayo, Unamuno inventó un nuevo género: la nivola, en consonancia con el problema y ajustándose apretadamente, sin dejar resquicio alguno, al contenido y propósito. Unamuno explica el origen de este nuevo género literario: "—Pues le he oído contar a

---

[8] *Obras completas*, II, 864.
[9] *Obras completas*, II, 777-778.

Manuel Machado, el poeta, el hermano de Antonio, que una vez le llevó a don Eduardo Benot, para leérselo, un soneto que estaba en alejandrinos o en no sé qué otra forma heterodoxa. Se lo leyó, y don Eduardo le dijo: 'Pero ¡eso no es soneto!...' 'No, señor —le contestó Machado—, no es soneto, es ...*sonite*.' Pues así con mi novela, no va a ser novela, sino..., ¿cómo dije?, *navilo*..., *nebula*, no, no, *nivola*, eso es, ¡*nivola*! Así nadie tendrá derecho a decir que deroga las leyes de su género... Invento el género, e inventar un género no es más que darle un nombre nuevo, y le doy las leyes que me place. ¡Y mucho diálogo." [10]. Unamuno no nos dice que *nivola* se relaciona sutilmente con *niebla*, voz repetida con marcada intención a todo lo largo de la nivola, pero los últimos renglones de su "Historia de *Niebla*" fijan la relación etimológica: "Y por eso os digo, lectores de mi *Niebla*, soñadores de mi Augusto Pérez y de su mundo, que esto es la niebla, esto es la nivola, esto es la leyenda, esto es la historia, la vida eterna." [11]

Toda esta nivola de *Niebla* es una transmigración de lo real a lo ficticio y vice-versa, exposición de una serie de antinomias neokantianas, que son la constante de la filosofía unamuniana. [12]

Los primeros cinco párrafos de *Niebla* son como un prólogo-síntesis de la novela y presentan simbólicamente su sentido filosófico. Argumento y narración se funden y armonizan para presentar el ensayo sobre la existencia del hombre. Dicho de otro modo, vida y metafísica se plasman en sí mismas con tal artificio, que desaparecen las diferencias entre una y otra, entre lo cotidiano particular y lo existencial general, universal. Unamuno soldó la fábula y la metafísica de *Niebla* en una unidad vital. En esos cinco primeros párrafos nos cuenta el creador de la nivola de Augusto Pérez cómo el protagonista echó a andar a modo de un hombre, de todo un hombre que había creado: "Al aparecer Augusto a la puerta de su casa extendió el brazo derecho, con la palma abajo y abierta, y, dirigiendo los ojos al cielo, quedóse un momento parado en esta actitud estatuaria y augusta. No era que tomaba posesión del mundo exterior, sino era que observaba si llovía. Y al recibir

---

[10] *Obras completas*, II, 777.
[11] *Obras completas*, II, 694.
[12] Preparo un libro sobre *Las antinomias de Kant en el pensamiento y estilo de Unamuno*.

en el dorso de la mano el frescor del lento orvallo, frunció el sobrecejo. Y no era tampoco que le molestase la llovizna, sino el tener que abrir el paraguas. ¡Estaba tan elegante, tan esbelto, plegado y dentro de su funda! Un paraguas cerrado es tan elegante como es feo un paraguas abierto./ 'Es una desgracia esto de tener que servirse uno de las cosas —pensó Augusto—; tener que usarlas. El uso estropea y hasta destruye toda belleza. La función más noble de los objetos es la de ser contemplados. ¡Qué bella es una naranja antes de comida! Esto cambiará en el cielo cuando todo nuestro oficio se reduzca, o más bien se ensanche, a contemplar a Dios y todas las cosas en Él. Aquí, en esta pobre vida, no nos cuidamos de servirnos de Dios; pretendemos abrirlo, como a un paraguas, para que nos proteja de toda suerte de males.'/ Díjose así, y se agachó a recogerse los pantalones. Abrió el paraguas por fin, y se quedó un momento suspenso y pensando: 'Y ahora, ¿hacia dónde voy? ¿Tiro a la derecha, o a la izquierda?'. Porque Augusto no era un caminante, sino un paseante de la vida. 'Esperaré a que pase un perro —se dijo—, y tomaré la dirección inicial que él tome.'/ En esto pasó por la calle, no un perro, sino una garrida moza, y tras de sus ojos se fue, como imantado y sin darse de ello cuenta, Augusto./ Y así una calle y otra y otra." [13] Reducidos a esquema estos párrafos, se sobrentienden cinco premisas: 1. presencia del hombre; 2. teoría del conocimiento; 3. escatología o destino del hombre; 4. teoría de lo bello y de su antinomia, lo pragmático; 5. teoría de lo fortuito en la vida del hombre.

Un análisis detenido —o medianamente detenido por falta de espacio— nos llevará a vislumbrar el sentido simbólico que Unamuno ha querido dar al comienzo de su nivola con la aparición de Augusto Pérez y el problema vital que supone la existencia del protagonista. Nombre de pila y apellido nos revelan que es un hombre, "augusto" porque no es un ser irracional, y Pérez, porque es como nombre genérico o sea nombre común a muchos hombres, es decir al hombre. Tenemos la sensación de un hombre adámico que tiene ante sí el mundo entero. Augusto hace un primer gesto de conocimiento de la naturaleza, como mundo real y verdadero ante sí. Es una acción que nos hace sentir la realidad

---

[13] *Obras completas*, II, 695.

que nos rodea y que impone límites. Es quizá una insinuación de que lo real circundante nos lleva a creer en nuestra propia realidad, ya que Unamuno en *Niebla* plantea el problema de lo real y lo irreal. Pero en seguida, ante ese mundo exterior, Augusto reacciona desde dentro de sí, al ver que tiene que hacer uso del paraguas. La vida de Augusto ha comenzado a complicarse, a enredarse. Entre el mundo "Augusto" y el otro —ese *otro* que es la antinomia constante del pensar unamuniano que llega a la cima atormentadora de su drama *El otro* — "no-augusto" se interponen otras cosas, otras ideas, que son la niebla que tenemos que traspasar para llegar a la última realidad de las realidades. Los artefactos, como un paraguas, tienen su uso necesario, pragmático, pero esto destruye la belleza de las cosas. Cuando no sirven, no están en uso; es cuando cobran su verdadera belleza. Lo hermoso es así. Piensa Augusto: "la función más noble de los objetos es la contemplación". Y de todo lo bello, la contemplación de Dios es la máxima belleza. Desgraciadamente, inclusive esta acción, como acción humana, se reduce en esta vida a menoscabar la total exaltación de Dios, reduciendo nuestro sentido religioso a costumbres y actos utilitarios, como si Dios fuese también un paraguas, un paraguas más. En la incredulidad de Unamuno hubo siempre esta insistencia en una credulidad en Dios, limpia y sin nigromancias. Era la lucha entre la razón y la fe o sea la lucha entre la *Crítica de la razón pura* y la *Crítica de la razón práctica* de Kant, antinomias que nunca pudo desechar de su pensamiento y hasta de su estilo. La paradoja en Unamuno —y su tragedia— fue eso. Las antinomias kantianas corren por toda la nivola, como en todas sus obras.

Este Pérez, después de recapacitar sobre el significado de su acto utilitario, contrapuesto con otro que no lo tiene, o no debe tenerlo, como creer en Dios, continúa saliendo al mundo. Antes de abrir el paraguas ha hecho otro gesto utilitario, de hombre "Pérez": agacharse para arremangarse los bajos de los pantalones. Luego viene esa tremenda pregunta del destino del hombre: "Y ahora, ¿hacia dónde voy?" O sea: ¿adónde me lleva la vida?, ¿adónde me llevo yo? Augusto musita y vacila en busca del sentido de la vida. Susurro y vacilación compendian la incógnita —nuestra incógnita— de la ecuación "vida". Como hombre que es, le queda el remedio de esperar. Toda la vida es esperar, y es esperar entre dos haceres: esperar a hacer o esperar a no hacer. Ahí está el quid. Augusto todavía no ha sentido el golpe más hondo de la vida, por eso piensa en un ser que está equidistante entre el ser y no ser, entre lo nuestro y lo que no es nuestro. Augusto Pérez remite su decisión de ir adonde sea, siguiendo a un perro. Nada más natural y apropiado. Además, es un anticipo de Orfeo, ese perro fiel que recoge el protagonista de entre unos matorrales, como, quien dice, de la nada: ese perro que será como un espejo de sus pensamientos, que le devuelve con fidelidad la imagen de sus buceos. Así, en el compás de una sala de espera es donde Augusto despierta totalmente. Al ver pasar "a una garrida moza" cuyos ojos golpean como mágicos mazos su ser de hombre, "imantado y sin darse de ello cuenta". Unamuno hace que su protagonista cometa un acto puro: no la conoce, no sabe quién es, tampoco sabe si es rica o pobre. El interés utilitario no ha intervenido en ese acto volitivo de Augusto Pérez. Entonces comienza el "sueño de carne"[14] de Augusto... hasta que se muere o más exactamente se suicida, que parece ser el único acto volitivo que su creador le permitirá hacer. El médico, ante el cadáver de aquel Pérez, dice "entre dientes y cual hablando consigo mismo: '—¿Quién sabe si existía o no, y menos él mismo...? Uno mismo es quien menos sabe de su existencia... No existe sino para los demás...'"[15]

Niebla es un ensayo con técnica de novela sobre la existencia del hombre. En ella ha revelado su autor la última realidad del hombre: Dios o "quien sea", creador del universo, es a Unamuno, creador de la nivola, como Unamuno es creador de Augusto Pérez y éste es creador de su niebla. Oyendo discutir a dos de sus personajes "creados", exclama Unamuno: "¡Cuán lejos estarán estos infelices de pensar que no están haciendo otra cosa que tratar de justificar lo que yo estoy haciendo con ellos! Así, cuando uno busca razones para justificarse no hace en rigor otra cosa que justificar a Dios. Y yo soy el Dios de estos dos pobres diablos nivolescos."[16]

Y con esto quería hacer Unamuno triunfar la *Crítica de la razón práctica* sobre la *Crítica de la razón pura*.

Niebla, pues, alcanza categoría universal.

---

[14] *Obras completas*, II, 688.
[15] *Obras completas*, II, 860.
[16] *Obras completas*, II, 824-825.

MELANCHOLY AND DEATH IN CERVANTES

by OTIS H. GREEN
University of Pennsylvania

In 1925 it seemed clear to Américo Castro that Cervantes, guided by the Stoic principle of *sequere Naturam,* implacably condemned to death those of his characters who through an error, an act of folly, failed to follow Nature. This principle Castro called *muerte post errorem.*[1] His argumentation is well known. In a series in publications beginning in 1949,[2] I have shown that the source of the widespread belief that any infinite sadness produces (or tends to produce) death is to be referred to the medieval ideas of the time (in large part derived from Hippocrates and Galen), and to the proto-psychology of Juan Huarte de San Juan in his *Examen de ingenios para las ciencias* (1575). In the present article I propose to examine *every* occurrence of *muerte post melancholiam* in the corpus of Cervantes' works and to refer these occurrences, not to the Stoic idea of *sequere Naturam* but rather to the Graeco-Medieval-Renaissance theory of the passions. It will be convenient to quote at this point convincing texts from the fifteenth and sixteenth centuries.

ALFONSO DE MADRIGAL (El Tostado): "...dice Ipocrás: —El amor es cobdicia que se face en el coraçón, por causa de la cual

---

[1] *El pensamiento de Cervantes* (Madrid, 1925), pp. 127 f., 131, 347.
[2] "Courtly Love in the Spanish *Cancioneros,*" *PMLA*, LXIV (1949), p. 270, n. 98 *et alibi*; *Courtly Love in Quevedo* (Boulder, Colorado, 1952), pp, 62-69; "El *ingenioso* hidalgo," *HR*, XXV (1957), 180 and n. 15, 187 and n. 46, 188, and *passim*; "Realidad, voluntad y gracia en Cervantes," *Ibérida*, III (1961), 123 f., and *passim*.

interviene(n) algunos accidentes de que por ventura muere el enamorado." [3] MIGUEL SABUCO DE NANTES (writing under the name of his daughter Oliva): "Síguese ahora el afecto del amor y deseo. El amor ciega, convierte al amante en la cosa amada, lo feo hace hermoso y lo falso perfecto, todo lo allana y pone igual; lo dificultoso hace fácil, alivia todo trabajo, da salud cuando lo amado se goza. También mata en dos maneras: o perdiendo lo que se ama, o no pudiendo alcanzar lo que se ama y desea". [4] FRAY LUIS DE GRANADA: "...la hermosura de alguna criatura... basta muchas veces para transtornar el seso del hombre, y para hacerle caer en cama, y a veces perder la vida". [5]

The point to be established in this article is, therefore, that Don Quijote, El Celoso Extremeño, and their congeners are not "executed" by Cervantes for an act of folly; they die of their own broken hearts. Even Camila, the guilty wife of *El Curioso Impertinente*, on learning of the death of her lover Lotario "acabó en breves días la vida, a las rigurosas manos de tristezas y melancolías" (*DQ*, I, 35).

All readers remember (though few have understood) Sancho's lament at the deathbed of his master: How can a man be so foolish as to let himself die, "sin más ni más, sin que nadie le mate, ni otras manos le acaben que las de la melancolía?" (II, 74). Fewer will recall, on the other hand, that even Teresa Panza understands these matters. She writes to her husband (after learning that he is now governor of the promised island): "me pensé allí caer muerta de puro gozo, que ya sabes tú que dicen que así mata la alegría súbita como el dolor grande" (II, 52). [6]

---

[3] *Tractado que fizo ... el Tostado ... como al ome es necessario amar....* in *Opúsculos literarios de los siglos XIV a XVI*, ed. A. Paz y Melia (Madrid, 1892), p. 228.

[4] Cited by Florencio M. Torner, *Doña Oliva Sabuco de Nantes, siglo XVI* (Madrid, 1935), p. 101.

[5] *Introducción del Símbolo de la Fe*, I, xxii, 2. See my *Courtly Love in Quevedo*, p. 63.

[6] See Lawrence Babb, *The Elizabethan Malady: A Study of Melancholia in English Literature from 1580 to 1642* (East Lansing, Michigan, 1951), p. 15: "Any passion, if it is very sudden and violent, may kill outright." See the Index of this work, s. v. joy. On the killing power of sudden joy, see also the *Persiles* (I, 12): "pero como los desmayos que suceden de alegres y no pensados acontecimientos, o quitan la vida en un instante o no duran

We are now prepared to follow the theme sadness-death as it appears in Cervantes' complete works. In the opening scene of *La Entretenida,* in a give-and-take dialogue not unworthy of Tirso, a *fregona* says to a *lacayo*:

> Siempre la melancolía
> fue de la muerte parienta,
> y en la vida alegre asienta
> el hablar de argentería.   (454a)

In the first Book of *La Galatea* Lisandro is warned: "...la amistad de Carino te costará la vida, pues no es posible sino que te la acabe el dolor de haberla yo por ti perdido!" (621b). In Book II Timbrio, "tan pobre de esperanza cuan rico de pensamiento," finds himself in a state of near despair because of frustration in love: "falto de salud y en términos de acabar la vida sin descubrirlos" (650b). In Book IV: "resucitó Rosaura de la muerte de su tristeza a la vida de su alegría" (685b). She relates the vicissitudes of her love: "Considerando, pues, que si mi remedio se dilataba había de dejar por fuerza en las manos del dolor la vida" (688a).

In *El amante liberal* Mahamut tells of the grief of Leonisa, whose beloved Ricardo, as she says, had been lost at sea: "cuya muerte siempre lloraba... hasta que le trajo a término de perder la vida, que yo no le sentí enfermedad en el cuerpo, sino muestras de dolor en el alma" (819ab). In *La española inglesa* the Queen says to Recaredo: "...pues sabemos que así suele matar una súbita alegría como mata una tristeza" (864a). It is scarcely necessary to mention *El celoso Extremeño*: "...siento no sé qué en el corazón... y temo que brevemente me ha de quitar la vida" (917a).

In *Don Quijote,* the *cabrero* says of Guillermo, Marcela's father: "De pesar de la muerte de tan buena mujer murió su marido, Guillermo" (1070b). In *El curioso impertinente* there is a double case of heartbreak: that of Anselmo: "...comenzó a

---

mucho, fue pequeño espacio en el que estuvo Transila desmayada" (Miguel de Cervantes, *Obras completas,* ed. Angel Valbuena Prat [Madrid], 1956, p. 1554b). All references hereafter will be to this edition.

cargar tanto la imaginación de su desventura, que... conoció que se le iba acabando la vida"; and that of Camila, whose "tristezas y melancolías" have already been noticed (1195ab). Sometimes frustration and disappointment produce not death but only illness: "Cayó malo [el mozo de mulas], a lo que yo entiendo, de pesadumbre" (1231b). Don Quijote tells the story of the "licenciado en cánones por Osuna" who, recovering his wits after a long illness, is reported to have said: "el decaimiento en los infortunios apoca la salud y acarrea la muerte" (1276a).

In II, 39, La Trifaldi tells "su estupenda y memorable historia": "...de lo que recibió tanto enojo la reina doña Maguncia, madre de la infanta Antonomasia, que dentro de tres días la enterramos" (1406a). In Chapter 48 doña Rodríguez tells how she was left a widow: "Divulgóse la cortesía de mi esposo, tanto, que los muchachos le corrían por las calles, y... mi señora le despidió, de cuyo pesar, sin duda alguna, tengo para mí que se le causó el mal la muerte" (1436b). In Chapter 59 — after the *descomedimiento* of the trampling bulls— "no comía Don Quijote, de puro pesaroso, ni Sancho no osaba tocar a los manjares..., de puro comedido". "Come, Sancho amigo," his master tells him, "sustenta la vida, que más que a mí te importa, y déjame morir a mí, a manos de mis pensamientos y a fuerzas de mis desgracias... pienso dejarme morir de hambre, muerte la más cruel de las muertes" (1474b). So un-Christian a temptation could not last long, of course. There is even a brief rebirth of hope as the Knight and Squire contemplate momentarily the possibility of a new life under a bucolic sky as *el pastor Quijotiz* and *el pastor Pancino*. Then comes the reversal. A sudden attack of fever and a long, brain-cooling sleep achieve the psychological restoration of Don Quijote to his former self; but it is melancholy — "la melancolía que le causaba el verse vencido" (1521a) — that produces the death which Cervantes has been preparing since II, 8 and, very especially, since II, 58. [7]

The *Persiles* contains some dozen references to heartbreak, the first in Chapter 9 of Book I. A personage heard singing in

---

[7] See the section "Voluntad y gracia" in the *Ibérida* article referred to in note 2, especially pp. 126-127.

Portuguese is transferred from one *barca* to another by interested listeners, to whom "en medio portugués y en medio castellano dijo: 'Al Cielo y a vosotros, señores, y a mi voz, agradezco esta mudanza y esta mejora de navío, aunque creo que con mucha brevedad le dejaré libre de la carga de mi cuerpo, porque las penas que siento en el alma me van dando señales de que tengo la vida en sus últimos términos'" (1549b). His premonition is a true one: "Y dando un gran suspiro, se le salió el alma" (1552a). In Chapter 21 of the same Book the victim is Rosamunda: "...estaba tal que por momentos llamaba a las puertas de la muerte.... Con los continuos desdenes, vino a enflaquecer, de manera que una noche la hallaron en una cámara del navío sepultada en perpetuo silencio" (1571a). In Chapter 20 of Book Two we have a near-victim in the person of Renato, defeated in a duel: "tomáronme por muerto... me dejaron solo, en poder del quebranto y de la confusión, con más tristeza que heridas, y no con tanto dolor como yo pensaba, pues no fue bastante a quitarme la vida, ya que no me la quitó la espada de mi enemigo" (1621). In the following book (Chapter 9) Antonio, returning home, explains to his companions that "pensaba darse a conocer a su padre, no de improviso, sino por algún rodeo que le aumentase el contento de haberle conocido, advirtiendo que tal vez mata una súbita alegría, como suele matar un improviso pesar" (1652a).

Chapter 21 bears the heading: "Llega Andrea Marulo, descúbrese la ficción de Isabela, y quedan casados". The union of Andrea and Isabel Castrucho is more than the bride's uncle can bear: "¿y es posible que así se deshonren las canas de este viejo?" The validity of the marriage is confirmed, "oyendo lo cual su tío, se le cayeron las alas del corazón... y, dando un profundo suspiro... dio muestras de haberle sobrevenido un mortal paroxismo." Two days later he is buried (1684a-1686b).

Near the end of the *Persiles* Auristela, moved by self-love rather than by the love of God, temporarily decides that she will realize herself in life most fully by remaining a virgin rather than by marrying Periandro. On learning of her intention, Periandro leaves her presence with "un volcán en los ojos y una mordaza en la lengua" (1708ab). Addressing his Auristela in the rustic solitude he has sought, Periandro cries out in a soliloquy: "quisiera que advirtieras que no sin escrúpulo de pecado puedes ponerte en el camino que deseas, sin ser mi homicida." The suddenness of the revelation has been too great for him to bear (1709a).

He does bear it, however, as events bring to light the falsity of Auristela's whim and make possible the union of the lovers: Periandro finds it necessary to return to Auristela to inform her of a danger that threatens her safety, after which the normal course of the long love story is resumed. Two sentences at the beginning of the penultimate chapter give the physiological explanation: just as in the heat of battle fresh wounds give no pain, but later, when the blood cools off, can overcome the endurance of the wounded man, so "en las pasiones del alma..., en dando el tiempo lugar y espacio para considerar en ellas, fatigan hasta quitar la vida" (1711b). That Periandro would have suffered death is implied but not stated; a sudden peripeteia interferes with the action of "tiempo, lugar y espacio" and his life and happiness are restored.

Quod erat demonstrandum: from 1585 to 1616 Cervantes followed current medical teaching ("como dice Ipocrás," according to El Tostado) in his treatment of the passions of joy and sorrow — a doctrine known and understood by all, including the peasant's wife Teresa Panza. The numerous deaths presented as the result of emotional shock or of more prolonged psychological dejection are not a function of some failure of the dying persons to "follow Nature." They are simply the end-product of physiological changes: any infinite sadness tends to produce death.

One should stress the verb *tends*. Periandro does not instantly collapse into a coma on learning suddenly of Auristela's "mystical" whim and temporary decision never to marry; the author still needs him. Prolonging of his despair would surely have brought him to the grave — we may believe — had the reconciliation not occurred. Cervantes simply chose not to prolong it.

So it is in the other cases that have been presented: the degree of each character's susceptibility to the onrush of joy or of sorrow depends upon the author's literary plan.

This was true in contemporary England. Katherine, in John Marston's *Jack Drum's Entertainment,* cries out:

> Black sorrow, nurse of plaints, of teares, and grones,
> Evaporate my spirit with a sigh,
> That it may hurrey after his sweet breath,
> Who made thee doate on life, now hunt for death;

as does Helena in Shakespeare's *All's Well that Ends Well*:

> I am undone! There is no living, none,
> If Bertram be away....
> The hind that would be mated by the lion
> Must die of love.

Such attitudes are always subject to parody (even the sacred is). In *As You Like It* a rejected lover who has announced his approaching demise is brought up sharply by the object of his affections: "This poor world is almost six thousand years old... Men have died from time to time, and worms have eaten them, but not for love." Yet in *Romeo and Juliet* the hero and heroine die as a result of separation in love.

William G. Meader, from whose *Courtship in Shakespeare*[8] all these examples are taken, says of the poet of Avon (as we may say of Cervantes): "It seems that the general tendency in Shakespeare is to view with quite an unjaundiced eye the proceedings of lovers who, through terrific emotional stress, may be led to such a condition as might possibly cause madness or death or both." It is ever a case of *muerte post melancholiam,* not *post errorem.*

---

[8] *Courtship in Shakespeare: Its Relations to the Tradition of Courtly Love* (New York, 1954), pp. 123-125 and corresponding notes, p. 245.

ATTACKS ON LOPE AND HIS THEATRE IN 1617-1621 *

by RUTH LEE KENNEDY
University of Arizona

The very eloquent defense of the Lopean *comedia* that one finds in Tirso's *Los cigarrales de Toledo* (1621)[1] did not come out of the blue. It was inspired by attacks on Lope and his formula in 1617 and 1620, attacks which aimed at closing the theatres — or, that being impossible — at bringing under strict control the *comedias* and such ecclesiastics as were writing or attending them.

The besiegers — and they numbered among their forces Aristotelians, theologians, and stern laymen — were in 1620 working against a double background: 1) the literary war which Suárez de Figueroa[2] and Torres Rámila had launched in 1617 against

---

* This study is background for two further articles: 1) "Reappraisal of Tirso's Relations to Lope and the New Comedy," *Bull. of the Comediantes* (1965-66; 2) "Tirso and the Aristotelians," as yet in ms.

[1] No copy of the 1621 edition is known today, and its very existence has been questioned. It *did* exist, however; concerning this point, see my study, "On the Date of Five Plays by Tirso", *HR, X,* 205-206; also notes 61, 62.

[2] Lope's attitude toward the Aristotelians in 1620 may be judged from Maestro Burguillos' poem (ed. princeps, 132v) which asks: ...¿Cómo, que siendo yo poeta ilustre,/ gloria y honor de Navalagamella/ el cortesano aplauso me deslustre?/ Suerte infeliz de cornucopia estrella,/ no quedará pilastra o balaustre [sic]/ del sacro templo de la fama bella/ *sin sátira que diga cuán confusas/ de perro tan mortal están las musas./* Si yo por dicha hubiera traducido/ con mala prosa libros de Toscano.... This reference to the *perro,* as well as others in that same poem, are to Suárez de Figueroa. We shall, when dealing with "Tirso and the Aristotelians," have occasion to study at length the *sátiras* of 1620 and the figures involved. For the two

Lope, a war which was still being fought bitterly in 1620; 2) the cry for moral change, which would find its crystallization in the so-called *Gran Consulta* that was sent to the King in February of 1619 by the Council of Castile.[3] There were, in 1620, those who were hoping that the *premáticas* which this report implied would include decrees against the theatre. This attempt has, for the most part, been overlooked by students of Spanish literature, even though it is one which has left not inconsiderable resonance in the polite literature of the time. The literary satire in Tirso's *Cigarrales de Toledo*, as well as that found in certain plays of his, can be fully understood only if seen against this background.

On March 31, 1621 young Philip IV ascended the throne, and it must soon have been evident to reform elements that they could expect from their theatre-loving young King no encouragement in this matter of the *comedia*. Nevertheless, Pedro Fernández de Navarrete's gloss of the *Gran Consulta*, termed *Conservación de monarquías y discursos políticos sobre "La Gran Consulta" que el Consejo hizo al señor rey Felipe III* (1621), makes quite certain that the reform group was now pressing the new government for broad reform. In the matter of change in the theatre, these elements would have to bide their time; but by March 7, 1624, they were able to get the attention of the *Junta de Reformación*, which had been reconstituted by Philip IV. This *Junta* had, by March 1st, 1625, consulted the problem of the *comedias* with the Conde-Duque de Olivares, and by the 7th of that same month, it would condemn Tirso for his "comedias... profanas... de malos incentivos y ejemplos;" what is more, it would banish him from Madrid for ten years and would forbid him to write more plays. The present study is concerned only

---

which Lope wrote against Torres Rámila and Suárez de Figueroa, see J. de Entrambasaguas, *Estudios sobre Lope de Vega* (Madrid, 1946-47), II, 239-411.

[3] Sempere y Guarinos' *Historia del lujo* (Madrid, 1788, II, 115-116) has analysed this *Consulta*. It may be read in the *BAE* (XXV), together with Pedro Fernández de Navarrete's gloss of it: *Conservación de monarquías y discursos políticos sobre "La gran consulta" que el Consejo hizo al señor Rey don Felipe III*, put out in 1621 (Barcelona, Sebastián de Cormellas) for the benefit of the new King, Philip IV.

with the earlier manifestations of that movement, for A. González Palencia has already made known its later development in his "*Quevedo, Tirso, y las comedias ante la Junta de Reformación.*" [4]

We shall have to go back to 1617 to get some perspective. The *Spongia*, written in the summer of 1617, as Señor Entrambasaguas has pointed out,[5] was levelled primarily against Lope's long poems (in particular, the *Jerusalén conquistada*), not against his theatre. This deficiency Suárez de Figueroa would remedy ere the year was out in his *El Pasajero*[6] (1617). Therein, he devotes a large part of the third *aviso* to the *comedia*. Young Luis, who contemplates writing a play, opens the discussion by declaring (p. 75): "...fáltame por saber ahora el estilo que tengo de seguir en la comedia." The Doctor of Jurisprudence (i.e., Suárez de Figueroa), hoisting high immediately his classic banner in the names of Plautus and Terence, outlines for that brash young man the demands of Aristotelian art with regard to comedy: 1) unity of time ("veinte y cuatro horas o cuando menos de tres días"); 2) characters of lowly estate ("personas ciudadanas, esto es comunes, no reyes ni príncipes"), who should, nevertheless, offer examples ("que os ministraran ejemplos para cualquiera de las personas que se suelen introducir"); 3) unity of action ("un cuerpo solo... de muchas partes, [las cuales] deben todas mirar

---

[4] S. Aguirre, Madrid, 1946 (cien ejemplares numerados).

[5] *Op. cit.*, I, 301. The only real defense of the Lopean theatre there included is that of Alfonso Sánchez de Moratalla, found not in the *Expostulatio Spongiae* proper, but rather in the "Appendix ad Expostulationem Spongiae." See Sr. de Entrambasaguas' (*op. cit.*, I, 569-571) high opinion of this defense. Sánchez de Moratalla —whom Menéndez y Pelayo has termed "el mayor revolucionario artístico que vio España en el siglo XVII dentro de los principios de la escuela *naturalista*"— defends Lope and his theatre in dithyrambic terms. His basic thesis is that art must imitate nature, *but it must imitate the spirit of the period in which the dramatist is writing, not that of the classic past.* He sums up: "Tenemos arte, tenemos preceptos que nos obligan, y el precepto principal es imitar a la naturaleza, porqué las obras de los poetas expresan la naturaleza, las costumbres y el ingenio del siglo en que se escribieron." See Menéndez y Pelayo, *Ideas estéticas* (Santander, 1947), II, 305-307.

[6] Madrid, Luis Sánchez, 1617 —with *Tasa* dated Nov. 16, 1617. Page references in this study are to the edition of Francisco Rodríguez Marín (without place or date), 75-81.

a un blanco y estar entre sí tan unidas que de la una verisímil o necesariamente se siga la otra"); 4) natural dialogue that is in keeping with the character speaking ("lenguaje familiar [que dé] a cada uno el lenguaje y afecto conforme a la edad y ministerio, y [que sea] en verso por la suavidad con que deleita"); 5) didactic in general purpose ("la comedia... mira principalmente a las costumbres y es un espejo de la vida"), and even sprinkled liberally with maxims ("...fuera de la tragedia, a quien más sirven las sentencias [7] es a la comedia"). He accepts as definition of the *comedia* that found in Francisco Cascales' *Tablas poéticas*: [8] "...imitación dramática de una entera y justa acción, humilde y suave, que por medio de pasatiempo y risa, limpia el alma de vicios."

Young Luis, appalled at the mere thought of writing a *comedia* in accordance with the rules of art ("en diez años no aprendiera yo el arte con que decís se deben escribir"), states bluntly (pp. 79-80): "lo que pienso hacer es seguir las pisadas de los cuyas representaciones adquirieron aplauso, escríbanse como se escribieren." He then sketches, in broadest terms, what Suárez de Figueroa evidently intended as a satirical composite of Lope's many *capa y espada* plays (pp. 79-80):

---

[7] He had spoken in even clearer terms on the doctrinal when writing his *Plaza Universal* (Discurso xci, f. 321 v., ed. 1615): "...los autores de comedias que se usan hoy ignoran, o *muestran ignorar totalmente el arte*... componen farsas casi desnudas de documentos, moralidades y buenos modos de decir.... No se acaban de persuadir estos modernos que, para imitar a los antiguos, debrían llenar sus escritos de *sentencias morales,* poniendo delante los ojos *aquel loable intento de enseñar el arte de vivir sabiamente, como conviene al buen cómico,* no obstante tenga por fin mover a risa."

In his *Varias noticias importantes* (Madrid, 1621, f. 146r.), he touches but little on matters literary, but he does insist that writers "pueden con el medio de sus eruditos discursos introducir algún honesto recreo, *mas no del todo sin provecho.* Later (f. 244v.), he announces a book, *Residencia de talentos,* in which he may have intented to deal with the literary scene.

[8] Ed. príncipe: Luis Beros, Murcia, 1617. Quotation taken from Menéndez y Pelayo, *Ideas estéticas,* II, (1940), X, pp. 239-247. Cascales insists much on the differences between the historian and the poet; the former's role must be that of narrator; the latter's that of *imitator*. He also rejects the role of teacher for the poet: "No se pueden sufrir aquellos que enseñando Agricultura, o Philosophía, u otras artes y ciencias, quieren ser tenidos por poetas, en lo que no hay imitación ninguna."

> Sacaré al tablado una dama y un galán, éste con su lacayo gracioso y aquélla con su criada, que le sirva de requiebro. No me podrá faltar un amigo del enamorado que tenga una hermana, con que dar celos en ocasión de riñas. Haré que venga un soldado de Italia y se enamore de la señora que hace el primer papel....

In his *comedia* as planned, he finds a place, too, for the punctilious hidalgo (father to the heroine), a sister with whom to "accommodate the friend", and (he had almost forgotten him!) an old *escudero* who is natural enemy to the lackey. In the end, don Luis will pair them all off: four marriages, no less!

Even before attacking the *comedia* of *capa y espada*, Suárez de Figueroa had paid his respects (pp. 75-77) to the *vidas de santos*, in which the first act is given over to the childhood of the saint; the second to his virtuous acts; and the third to his miracles and death. And "abuse, not use," has come to permit in them "algunos episodios de amores, menos honestos de lo que fuera razón." These *vidas de santos*, which he terms "espantavillanos," ordinarily make use of *tramoyas* or *apariencias* to attract the mob and to fill the coffers of the box-office, but the Doctor advises Luis to watch these mechanical effects, lest they break down and bring on him the noisy disapproval of those in the pit. Moreover, he begs him not to introduce in such plays "cosas en demasía torpes con fin de que hayan de resultar milagros dellas."

The extremely low esteem in which Suárez de Figueroa held the Lopean comedy is summed up in the following words (p. 75):

> Plauto y Terencio fueran, si vivieran hoy, la burla de los teatros, el escarnio de la plebe, *por haber introducido quien presume saber más cierto género de farsa menos culta que gananciosa*.... Ahora consta la comedia... de cierta miscelánea donde se halla de todo. Graceja el lacayo con el señor, teniendo por donaire la desvergüenza. *Piérdese el respeto a la honestidad y rompen las leyes de buenas costumbres el mal ejemplo, la temeridad, la descortesía*. Como cuestan tan poco estudio, hacen muchos muchas.... *Todo charla, paja todo, sin nervio, sin ciencia ni erudición*. Sean los escritos hidalgos, esto es, de más calidad que cantidad; que no consiste la opinión de sabio en lo mucho sino en lo bueno.

In short, Lope's *comedia* sinned in every direction: it was inartistic in form; in characters and content, false and repetitive of plot, i.e., without variety; in moral purpose, frivolous and dangerous to social customs. In 1620, the stress would be primarily on the last two considerations; nevertheless, the ecclesiastics and stern laymen who led the fight in that year would be thoroughly cognizant of all that was going on in the war of the Aristotelians against Lope. And Tirso, when making his defense of the Lopean comedy in *Los cigarrales* and elsewhere, would answer the charges of the three groups.

By October, 1618, Dr. Manuel Valle de Moura, Inquisitor of Evora, would, in his *De incantationibus seu ensalmis*,[9] be listing Suárez de Figueroa among the *tratadistas* of the theatre and would be insisting on the dangers of the *comedia*, "especialmente representando mujeres." Those attending such functions may well be risking mortal sin for themselves:

> —Si en las comedias se mezclan cosas o palabras torpes, gestos o movimientos lascivos de mujeres, o cosas semejantes, parece cosa indubitable que hay peligro; y consiguientemente, por razón de tal peligro, al cual todos éstos, en especial los que miran, se exponen libremente y sin causa suficiente que los excuse... se exponen a caer en pecado mortal.

He will, moreover, with meaningful intention, recall the decrees against the theatre which had been promulgated in Philip II's reign:

> ...según decían, aquel insigne prelado, D. Fr. Diego de Yepes, confesor de Felipe II, viéndose cercano a la muerte y para dar cuenta a Dios, de ninguna cosa se dolía más, ni le causaba tanto temor como el haberse vuelto a introducir en España, y con su permisión, las representaciones del teatro...

This opinion, which did not come off the Lisbon press until 1620, presumably reached Madrid in that same year, there to

---

[9] See E. Cotarelo y Mori, *Bibliografía de las controversias sobre la licitud del teatro en España*, (Madrid, 1904), 583.

add its small waters to the broader stream of the reform movement which was asking for action against the theatre. "Premáticas" had come out in late October of 1619, [10] but they were far less inclusive in nature than the stern moralits had wished. Limited as they were to a few matters which concerned masculine appearance (*pantorrillas, petos, guedejas,* and *azul*), they seemed to the grave "catones" the mouse which the mountain had brought forth after heavy labour. Sumptuary decrees were again in the making during the first months of 1620, [10] but when they were issued in late March of that year, they merely reaffirmed those of late 1619. As we shall see presently, there were those who were hoping that officialdom would include in those 1620 decrees regulatory measures both against the theatre and against the dramatists who were writing and attending them.

Among those of 1620 who have left on record their disapproval of Lope and his theatre were: Antonio de Liñán y Verdugo, [11] Diego de Ágreda y Vargas, and the anonymous author of the *Diálogos de las comedias.* Of the three, it is Liñán y Verdugo, in his *Guía y avisos de forasteros,* who has the more tempered approach, perhaps because he was tremendously impressed by Lope's genius. [12] Even and so, the *casa de la comedia*

---

[10] See Góngora's letter, included in M. Artigas' *Don Luis de Góngora y Argote* (Madrid, 1925), 308. Góngora will record also the second *premáticas* on the last day of March, 1620. See *Obras poéticas de don Luis de Góngora,* ed. Foulché-Delbosc, (New York. 1921), III, 171.

I have traced official action in matters of costume in "Certain Phases ot the Sumptuary Decrees of 1623 and their Relation to Tirso's Theatre", *HR,* X (1942), 91-115. Therein I had occasion to mention these decrees of 1619 and 1620, pp. 91-92.

I looked, without success, for the official decrees of 1619-20 in the archives of Spain. However, from Góngora's letter of March, 1620 and from a document, dated Jan. 9, 1620, "Consulta del Consejo [Real] acerca de cuellos y trajes, con repetición de otra consulta, que se copia," it is evident that the decrees of March merely proclaimed anew those of Oct., 1619: "que se ejecute lo que está mandado en razón de las guedejas y rizos, pantorrillas y bigoteras." See González-Palencia, *La Junta de reformación* (Valladolid, 1932), 34-37.

[11] Father Zarco has argued that Liñán y Verdugo is Fray Alonso Remón, fellow Mercedarian to Tirso. See *Bol. Ac. Esp.,* XVI (1929), 185; also Sarrailh's article in *RFE,* VI and VIII.

[12] The author, speaking of one Feliciano who had studied in Alcalá, says (p. 47): "escribía algunos versos, latinos y castellanos, con erudición

was, for him, indissolubly linked with the *casa del juego* and the *mujercilla deshonesta*. It is a trinity of evil that is destroying the young men of the day, one used so often that it becomes a set phrase. Commenting on the frivolous existence of one of the young *cortesanos* who get up at 11 or 12 o'clock, he will lament (pp. 142-43):

> Puestas las mesas, no se ha comido el primer bocado cuando ya se previene la casa de la conversación y juego donde se ha de ir, *el aposento de la comedia que se ha de oír,* y la casa de la mujercilla deshonesta que se ha de visitar....

Again, (pp. 143-144), "ese mismo tiempo... *lo gasta en la comedia,* en la casa de juego, o con la mujercilla deshonesta;" for a third time (p. 224):

> Levántanse con el libro de las comedias, acuéstanse con haber visto en la representación de ellas lo que leyeron escrito; de la casa del juego se va a la de la mujercilla liviana....

and on the very next page: "toda la noche en la casa del juego, toda la mañana en casa de la mujercilla deshonesta, y *toda la tarde en la comedia.*"

And when one of the interlocutors asks at one point: "¿Qué sentís de las comedias?", D. Antonio will answer in the following terms (p. 146):

> Materia es ésa... que no quisiera que hubiérades tocado en ella; porque *hallo tan encontrados los pareceres de hombres, no sólo buenos cortesanos pero muy doctos,* que es apretar mucho al señor Maestro obligarle a que resuelva una cosa, en que, si se muestra contrario, ha de quedar odioso y, si favorable, en opinión de no muy cuerdo.

But the Master feels no such hesitancy. Rather, he is glad of the opportunity to give an opinion on the matter, and he pro-

---

y gala, no como nuestros castellanos, Virgilio y Terencio, Lucano y Enio: ya entenderéis por quien digo, don Alonso de Arcila [sic] y Lope de Vega Carpio, monstruoso ingenio de estos siglos y edades..."

ceeds to answer the question in the measured tones of one who has been asked for an official judgment (pp. 146-48):

> Las comedias, de suyo, ni son buenas ni malas, porque la recreación, si es honesta, lícita es; ...entretenimientos honestos y comedias honestas permisibles son a una república; pero ¿sabéis lo que siento de las comedias? Lo que de los coches, que si fueran menos, fueran menos dañosos... Las comedias, en su principio cuando no sólo los emperadores y césares romanos sino los bárbaros las desterraron de sus repúblicas, eran muy deshonestas, muy torpes, y muy obscenas (y de *obscenas* a *scenas* pocas letras hay); ahora en nuestros tiempos, nuestros españoles habían admitido, o permitido, una manera de comedias honestas y ejemplares; pero, de unos días a esta parte, han abierto la puerta a unos bailes tan deshonestos que parece que vuelven las aguas por do solían ir: *hartos ojos tiene la república cristiana para mirarlo; a ellos toca vedarlo o permitirlo; lo que me duele es que sean mantenimiento de cada día; que pienso que bastara que las hubiera en los días que no son de hacer algo,* porque llevan camino de envejecer la costumbre y hacerla ley, *y que después no baste el mundo a quitarlas por ninguna ocasión en España,* tan indomable en observar sus antigüedades.

Diego de Ágreda y Vargas, in his *Novelas morales, útiles por sus documentos* [13] (1620), has recorded the views of a group of young idlers on matters of the *comedia*. In outlining the daily schedule of one these young blades of 1620, he will state (pp. 321-322):

> Se vistió y fue a misa al monasterio de la Santísima Trinidad y, al entrar por su vistosa lonja..., vio algunos de sus amigos que esperaban a las once misa, hora propia de los que haciendo de la noche día, son sus más virtuosas ocupaciones comedias, Calle Mayor, y Prado.... Llegóse a ellos, tratóse de las novedades, gobernóse el mundo...,

---

[13] Tomás Junti (Madrid, 1620) — with "*aprobación del ordinario*" dated February 1st and *erratas,* May 26 of the same year. All page references are to the princeps. "Documentos" are the explanations that follow each story, in which Ágreda y Vargas points out exactly what may be learned from the conduct of each character.

ordenaron la república... *Llegaron a los teatros, que hay pocas conversaciones de mozos que no lleguen a ellos,* donde primero, *discurriendo por las comedias, vituperaron su poca inventiva, la frialdad de lo yocoso* [sic], *la falta del argumento y suspensión,* más ocasionada del corto trabajo que de cortedad de ingenio, diciendo que parecía que se acertaban acaso, pues *los que más había que las profesaban, hacían más conocidos yerros.* Reprobaban las divinas, por no ser decente que ocupen tan indigno lugar, como, *porque valerse de apariencias y historias* arguye poco caudal.

Todas ellas no han menester mucho —replicó otro— pues hemos visto algunas de hombres ignorantes, que sin saber leer ni escribir, [14] llevaron tras sí el vulgo, que es el fin de los que las escriben.

Estos acertaron acaso —dijo otro, a quien respondió uno de los circunstantes: —Lo mismo les sucede a todos, si bien no hay ninguno que, aunque se lo diga a gritos y silbos el pueblo, le dé crédito y se desengañe...; por diversos caminos hay en el mundo infinitos "vinorres" de capa negra; y por el cómico innumerables y que podrían vender a gruesas éstas que, como ellos dicen conforme al arte se han de llamar "papeles" y [que] los no tan entendidos artistas llaman "farsas." [15]

Even though these young loungers can not use the arms of the Aristotelians with the precision of a Suárez de Figueroa, nevertheless they are borrowing arrows from his quiver when they complain of the comedia's lack of "invention" (i.e., the lack of variety in plot), its plebeian qualities, the ignorance of those who compose them, the use of *apariencias* in *vidas de santos*.

---

[14] Suárez de Figueroa, in his *Pasajero*, (p. 76), had mentioned the *sastre de Toledo* who had written plays that lasted on the boards 15 or 20 days: "Ese fue el que llamaron de Toledo. Sin saber leer ni escribir, iba haciendo coplas hasta por la calle..." The recollection would, no doubt, plague Lope, who had written a play with him! See F. de B. San Román, *Lope de Vega, los cómicos toledanos, y el poeta sastre* (Madrid, 1935), prólogo, pp. c-cviii.

[15] These young men would teach a thing or two even to Aristotelians such as Suárez de Figueroa, or to the author of the *Diálogos de las comedias*, both of whom use the term "farsas." Apparently Ágreda y Vargas was an independent, for he has satirized the Aristotelians, as well as the *Lopistas*. With his satire of the former group we shall be concerned on another occasion.

But Ágreda y Vargas' chief quarrel with the theatres is that even the priests are writing plays and are attending their presentation (pp. 321-322):

> ...y esta desdicha [de las comedias] no sólo se ha apoderado de los de la capa y espada *sino de muchos eclesiásticos que pudiendo, si le tienen, emplear el ingenio en cosas decentes a su profesión, le ocupan en cosa tan indigna como es fomentar con la materia de sus escritos los teatros,* con irrisión del vulgo y aprobación y sangre, si lo es el dinero de aquellos miserables, cuya ignorancia puede sólo disculpar su vida.

He will then call on antiquity for a meaningful parallel that could impress the authorities of 1620 (pp. 321-22):

> Acuérdome que oí al propósito a un hombre docto... que un sacerdote de aquellos falsos dioses escribió en Roma una comedia y con mucho secreto hizo que la representasen los histriones. Tuvo aviso el Senado y haciendo cuidadosas diligencias, aunque no pudo jurídicamente probarlo, se enteró que era verdadera la relación, y confiriendo el caso, resolvió de absolverle. Dejó un Senador su asiento y, puesto en pie, dijo: "Oh, padres conscriptos ¿por ventura estáis olvidados de vuestra justicia? O, por la desdicha desta república, ¿falta de vuestros pechos la antigua piedad? Si en la casa de César no es bien que haya la más pequeña sospecha, ¿será justo que se halle en la de los dioses que dedicaron y admitieron en la suya a estos hombres?" Obraron de modo en ellos estas palabras que, de común acuerdo, le mandaron enterrar vivo.

Replicó [uno de los jóvenes de la lonja], (pp. 321-2):

> *¡Ay, si lo que durase el mundo se executase entre nosotros tan justa ley,* pues tenemos más obligaciones! Por la piedad con que veneraban su religión, por la rectitud de sus juicios, les concedió Dios el imperio del mundo. *Juzgaron rectamente [los senadores], que no es bien que los que han de exemplificar al pueblo hagan lo contrario, ni [que] sirva el respeto que se debe a la dignidad de reprimir el brazo de la justicia para que no castigue los escandalosos defectos de quien con solo ese fin se valió de ella. ¿Qué dijéramos de algunos de los*

[*eclesiásticos*] *de nuestros tiempos, cuyas costumbres son tan depravadas que lo más loable dellas fuera el escribirlas?*

Ágreda y Vargas was evidently asking punishment *for Lope*, even if he does add: "...pero quédese aquí, que son amigos y dirán que somos ignorantes, y que nos meterán en alguna farsa o entremés,[16] o nos dirigirán algún papel, que es lo mismo, pensando armarnos caballeros...." Lope will (in a play of 1620) promptly realize Ágreda y Vargas' fears: through Tello, lackey of *La discreta venganza*, he will parallel the structure that Maestro Burguillos had used to belabour his enemies in the *Justa poética*[17] of May, 1620, in order to avenge himself against the unresponsive Leonor[18] (I, iv, 304):

> Si te viere más, Leonor,
> plega al cielo que me canse
> un necio con sus visitas...
> con sus versos un poeta,
> *con sus prosas un pedante*
> *destos que cuentos de viejas*
> *llaman "Novelas morales".*

---

[16] The reference could be to *Los corcovados*, in which Ruiz de Alarcón was satirized cruelly—or to some which either the Aristotelians were writing against Lope or which he was writing against them. The author of the *Diálogos de las comedias* will say (p. 220a): "Díchome han que estos días... los que componen las farsas han dado en hacer en ellas unas sátiras atrevidas en que por vía de pasquines sacan en público las cosas que se murmuran en la corte... ya de algunos señores envidiados, ya de otros señores envidiosos..." The reference could be to the pleasantries which Lope was exchanging with either Alarcón or with Suárez de Figueroa!

[17] The *Justa poética*, (Viuda de Alonso Martín, Madrid, 1620) carries an *aprobación* of June 5, 1620 but did not come off the press until after August 18th.

Lope, through Burguillos, would there challenge every possible enemy ("Reto a..."). He would even curse "Lope": "Oh, tú, si acaso lo supiste Lope/ ... jamás llegues al trote ni al galope/ a la difícil cumbre del Parnaso;/ trasgo poeta con sus musas tope/ ... pues el proverbio de tu nombre borras/ con él se llamaran las cosas malas..."

[18] Morley and Bruerton (*The Chronology of Lope de Vega's* "Comedias" [N. Y., 1940], 188) date this play: "1615-22 (probably 1620-22)." This reference confirms once more the fantastic accuracy of that remarkable study. Ed. used: *BAE, XLI*.

Tirso, too, will answer in kind, as we shall see on another occasion.

That the author of the *Diálogos de las comedias* likewise feared reprisals from the Lopean camp is probably to be inferred from the fact that his attack on the *comedia* is anonymous, although it is a truly remarkable one which quite merits Cotarelo's praise (p. 210): "...estos diálogos difieren mucho de otros farragosos papeles que nos hemos visto obligados a extractar en este catálogo bibliográfico." The author of these *diálogos* was an older scholar of broad background, one acquainted with both canonical and lay sources. He had been in Valladolid, which he twice mentions. He knew the theatre well, both that of the classic school and of Lope: of "los Lupercios, López y Leonardos" he speaks (p. 230) approvingly whereas Lope de Vega is for him: (p. 225) "Lope o lobo carnicero de las almas, tan celebrado de los críticos." This latter phrase makes evident that, like Ágreda y Vargas, he was keeping up with the fight that the Aristotelians were waging against Lope. His summation of the *capa y espada* play, "todo es nada y todo es aire" may be compared with Suárez de Figueroa's "todo charla, paja todo...."

The two characters who take part in these six dialogues are a "teólogo" and a "regidor:" the former acts in the role of a teacher, the latter in that of student. These dialogues were clearly directed to official ears, and at a time when new sumptuary decrees were under consideration since the Theologian speaks of "...las premáticas que ahora se trazan" (p. 230a). Cortes was still in session (p. 217a) and the Teólogo hopes to bring action through this body: "...*y es que yo me resuelvo, pues hay ahora cortes y os cabe ir a ellas, que muy seriamente se tratase de que se quitase este modo que se usa de comedias.*" These dialogues were clearly written in the early months of 1620.[19] Moreover, the *regidor,* in asking for his master's opinion

---

[19] Cotarelo says of the date (*op. cit.,* p. 210b)): "...se escribió en tiempo de Felipe III... después de hecho su viaje a Portugal [1619]; estando celebrándose Cortes; y después de la beatificación de San Francisco Javier [1619] y antes de su canonización [1622]. Y como Felipe III murió el 31 de marzo de 1621, sólo queda el año de 1620 para que en él pudiese ser

on this matter of the *comedias,* states (p. 211) that he desires it "para saber de una vez y de raíz la verdad *y dar mi voto cuando allá en nuestro regimiento se tratare.*"

He asks for a well-thought-out, practical plan (220a), one that will not ask that the theatre be forbidden completely, for he fears (p. 219) that the protectors of the *comedias* ("los valedores") "han de persuadir a los magistrados de la república que no hay tanto mal en ellas, como se encarece, porque son gente que lo mira así a poco más o menos y se deja llevar del sentir común y del dicho de la gente...."

We can not here concern ourself with the "practical remedy" that they work out between them in great detail, other than to say that it is essentially the little theatre movement as we have known it here in America, with these important differences: it would all be carried out under the strict supervision of the church; and the subject matter of the *comedias* would be limited to Biblical themes or to those taken from the *Flos santorum,* from history, from exemplary literature, etc. For our particular purpose, we must of necessity limit ourselves to the charges that the author was bringing against the *comedia* and against those dramatists (particularly Lope) who were filling the public theatres by supplying romantic literature to Spain's young people.

Conceding (with Saint Thomas) that (p. 211) "las comedias, en general, no pueden reprehenderse; antes hay y ha habido muchas muy buenas y compuestas por personas muy doctas y aún santas," he nevertheless, insists that, historically speaking, they have throughout time enjoyed a bad reputation (p. 213): "los santos llaman a los teatros "escuelas de vicios, universidad de maldades, peste de la república, hornos de Babilonia, oficinas de pecados, ferias de los demonios, y otros nombres semejantes, todo por la infinidad de pecados que allí se cometen." As for

---

escrito este opúsculo." As the Cortes was dissolved at the end of March, 1620, and as there is a reference (p. 230a) to "las premáticas que ahora se trazan," there is every reason to believe that the *Diálogos* were written in the first months of 1620. This is further confirmed by what is almost certainly a contemptuous reference (p. 225b) to Salas Barbadillo's *El sutil cordovés, Pedro de Urdemalas,* (whose *erratas* are dated Jan. 6, 1620): "...estotros conterillos de Pedro de Urdemalas..."

those of the moment, they are pernicious in their effect on public customs. He asks (pp. 213-4):

> ¿Qué se puede seguir de ver un enredo de amores lascivos y deshonestos; otro de marañas y embustes y testimonios de un criado revolvedor y urdidor de males; otro de venganzas, pundonores vanos, enormes crueldades y todo esto azucarado con la agudeza del dicho, la sutileza y artificio del verso, adornado con el aparato y riqueza de vestidos, honrado y autorizado con la multitud de oyentes, que algunas veces son personas calificadas; ver unas mujercillas de vida peligrosa y muchas de mala vida conocidamente, salir allí como unas reinas, aderezadas con lo mejor y más rico y precioso que se halla en el mundo...? ¿Qué han de aprender allí las doncellas que en su vida tal vieron ni oyeron? ¿Qué, las casadas que se criaron con vergüenza y recogimiento? ¿Qué, los mancebos que les está hirviendo la sangre...? Ver allí alabada la maldad, reprehendida la virtud, solemnizado el engaño, y el verse honrado el que tomó la venganza; tenida por dichosa la atrevida y por grande aventura la de aquélla que por ser liviana vino a casarse con el príncipe y la otra que salió vestida de hombre de casa de su padre y tuvo tales y tales aventuras por donde conseguir casamientos de príncipes, y fue celebrada de los grandes señores: todo aquello lo creen algunas bobillas locas y muchos mancebitos que abren ahora los ojos al mundo.

Elsewhere he contrasts the insubstantial, essentially false, deleterious fare which Lope was offering his audiences in the *capa y espada* play with the dramatic material which is available in the Bible. He asks bluntly (p. 225):

> ¿Dónde vuestro Lope, o lobo carnicero de las almas, *tan celebrado de los críticos,* llegó a ingeniar o inventar amores como los de Jacob y Raquel, dónde aventuras y valentías como las de David? Lléguense a fingir gallardías como las de Judith y Esther y bravezas como las de Sansón. Todo es nada y todo es aire y cosas de ingenuelos captivos, rateros habilitados.

He will insist with Suárez de Figueroa that Lope's plots are repetitive, lacking in variety (p. 225):

> ...y esas comedias de ese autor que he nombrado, aunque el verso y los conceptos, por la mayor parte, son de ingenio (y mal empleado); pero lo uno, con la representación y aparato y con el verso y los afectos mugeriles que brindan la sensualidad y parecen más de lo que son; lo otro, los enredos, todos se parecen unos a otros; todos tienen unos mismos fines: todos se casan y todos se conciertan; y para esto sufren unas impropiedades que, allende de ser *disparatadas mentiras,* tienen brava dureza consigo. Fuera de esto *son semejantes en todas,* que a pocas tretas se alcanzan y se ve a do van a parar: ya es el criado que urde los enredos y la dama que salió con hábito disfrazada de casa de sus padres; ya el rey que se perdió en la caza y topó con una pastora a la cual buscaba; ya de la reina que se aficionó al criado que vió desenvuelto o al soldado que oyó cantar sus valentías; una ama al que le aborrece y es amada del que es aborrecido. De manera que un buen ingenio bien alcanza presto que *todas aquellas cosas son engaña-niños,* como las oyen éstos o idiotas, que es todo uno...; los ingenios, hechos a mayores intentos, se ríen de ello *como de cosa sin sustancia y aún para ficción, desproporcionada.*

And as for the dramatists who are writing them, the Regidor points out that they had better be thinking of God's judgment and of penitence (p. 215): "los poetas que ahora viven y han hecho y impreso estas farsas tienen bien que temer el juicio de Dios y bien por qué hacer penitencia." The Theologian will go even further (p. 215):

> Y fuera deso están obligados en consciencia a hacer penitencia pública, desdiciéndose y reclamando contra sus propios libros, procurar que se veden y no se hagan tales comedias, porque los que siempre están haciendo el daño deben cesar dél y cuanto pudieren restaurar el que han hecho; piensen estos ingenios depravados, contagión general de la república, parricidas de su patria, traidores, enemigos secretos de la cristiandad, que hacen satisfacción bastante con cesar, ya cansados de componer tales comedias, sino que pues con su poesía e ingenio luceferino realzaron tanto esta diabólica invención. Empleen sus agudezas en procurar como pudieren deshacer el daño, impedir al mal que, como cáncer, cada día va cundiendo.

Indeed, ecclesiastics are not only writing and publishing such plays; they are even *attending* them, to the horror of the Regidor; and the Theologian, in hearty agreement with this point of view, will call on the Bishops to take action against them (p. 215ab):

> ...me ha ofendido tanto ver entrar religiosos en las comedias que me parece ha sido uno de los mayores escándalos públicos de la república y que han deshonrado en grande manera sus religiones, y que aunque no fuera sino por el mal ejemplo y escándalo que dan, no sé cómo puede nadie excusalles de pecado mortal, ni como pueden absolverse, si no se enmiendan; y que ya que sus superiores no les corrigen, habían de tomar los obispos la mano y usar de la potestad que les da el Concilio Tridentino para enmendarles. [20]

The Regidor is, moreover, distressed that so many noblemen should be moving in the orbit of "estas mujercillas comediantes" (p. 215):

> ...uno que se va con una; otro que lleva a otra a sus lugares; uno que les da las galas y trata como a reina; otro que la pone casa y estrado y gasta con ella, aunque lo quite de su mujer e hijos, y él ande tratándose infamemente; otro que con publicidad celebró en iglesia pública el bautizo de un hijo de una destas farsantes, colgando la iglesia y haciendo un excesivo gasto con música de capilla y con convite. No hay compañía destas que no lleve consigo cebados de la desenvoltura muchos destos grandes peces o cuervos que se van tras la carne muerta...; es una de las mayores infamias de nuestra nación. Oímos decir que el otro señor salió desterrado por la otra Amarilis; [21] otro por la otra Maritardía o

---

[20] He goes ahead to indicate (p. 214a) that even the nuns are hearing comedias: "Las religiosas encerradas, que en su vida supieron si aquéllas son mentiras o verdades ¿qué han de sacar de oír estas comedias que por cosa muy cudiciada apetecen verlas y se las llevan sus devotas o parientes?"

[21] Presumably Amarilis de Córdoba, who was the *querida* of the Duque de Osuna. See Cotarelo y Mori, *El conde de Villamediana* (Madrid, 1886), 73-74, n. 1. Villamediana will satirize her in a poem beginning "Atiende un poco, Amarilis / Mari-*quita* or Mari-*caza*..." See Cotarelo y Mori, *op. cit.*, 250-251.

Maricandado, que le dieron un faldellín que costó mil ducados, un vestido que costó dos mil, una joya de diamantes rica; y todo esto se escribe y gacetea en otros reinos y se pierde mucha honra y aún se descredita la cristiandad. *Más valdría poner la segur a la raíz y quitallo todo...* que lo demás es andar por las ramas, pues se conoce cada día la eficacia deste veneno que saca de sí a los hombres, aunque sean principales y de grandes prendas.

From the above quotations it is evident that Lope and his romantic comedy were, in the year 1620, under very heavy fire indeed; that this fire came from both lay and clerical forces; that these forces were bringing all possible pressure to close the public theatres, or, that failing, as they feared it would, to bring the *comedia* and such ecclesiastics as were writing and attending plays under rigid control. The Lopean comedies were for this group, "engaña-niños" without substance, filled with "disparatadas mentiras," which even for fiction were "desproporcionadas." The dramatists who wrote them (of Lucifer-like talent) were parricides of the fatherland, secret enemies of Christianity; their invention was a diabolic one that was so efficaciously evil that it could "take men out of themselves, even those of high station and great talent."

After the death of Philip III on March 31st, 1621 and the accession of Philip IV, with his special devotion and that of his wife for the theatre, the stern of spirit must have felt for the time being that their cause was a lost one. There is on record, between 1621-24, but a single voice which was decrying the theatre. Alonso de Ribera finished before November 17, 1621 his *Historia sacra del Santíssimo Sacramento contra las heregías destos tiempos,*[22] but he apparently could not get it printed until 1626. Therein he makes an appeal to the bishops and prelates to remedy the situation. In the second *tratado* (vi) of his book, entitled "De la institución de la fiesta del Corpus Christi y sus indulgencias," he seeks to demonstrate "cuán pernicioso, ilícito

---

[22] Information taken from E. Cotarelo y Mori's *Bibliografía de las controversias sobre el teatro*, pp. 519-521.

y indecente sea hacer en la fiesta del Corpus comedias profanas, danzas y bailes de mujeres...." He cries out (p. 520):

> ¡Oh, ceguera grande de cristianos que quieren hacer culto divino la destrucción y infierno de almas! No tienen la culpa sino los eclesiásticos que, como interesados, y por entrar a la parte de los gustos, lo favorecen y llevan adelante, con daño manifiesto de sus conciencias. *Sírvase Dios de abrir los ojos a los obispos y prelados por cuya cuenta corre para que lo remedien.*

And having decried what happened in the case of an actor and married actress ("con quien era público que estaba amancebado") who were playing St. Joseph and the Virgen, he ends by quoting el maestro Fr. Antonio de Arce who years before had written:

> de mi parecer... no solo se habían de derribar los teatros y desterrar los poetas destas cosas sino cerrar las puertas de las ciudades y pueblos a los comediantes, como a gente que trae consigo la peste de los vicios y malas costumbres.

But in 1621 his was a voice that was crying in the wilderness.

By March 7, 1624, however, the forces of reform had mustered sufficient strength to bring consideration of this problem before the *Junta de reformación*. Angel González Palencia has, (in his study "Quevedo, Tirso, y las comedias ante la Junta de Reformación,") studied all minutes of this Junta's sessions which pertained to the theatre between March 10, 1624 and April 7, 1627. In the meeting of March 6, 1625, *which follows immediately after the decree against Tirso*, it is stated (pp. 78-79) under the heading, *No se escriban comedias*: "Hablóse que *se representó a 1.º de marzo con el Señor Conde-Duque [de Olivares]* y pareció a S. E. que el Presidente [de la Junta, i.e., Francisco de Contreras], mi señor y el Consejo, de su oficio, lo hiciesen y que su Ilma. [el nuncio, i.e., Julio Monti] lo podrá mandar así." In the decree itself against "Maestro Téllez, por otro nombre Tirso que hace comedias," (dated March 6, 1625), it is evident that the matter was even taken to the King:

Y, por ser caso notorio, se acordó que se consulte a S. M. de que el confesor diga *al Nuncio* [23] le eche de aquí a uno de los monasterios más remotos de su Religión y le imponga excomunión mayor *latae sententiae* para que no haga comedias ni otro ningún género de versos profanos. Y esto se haga luego.

The Junta apparently became (willingly or otherwise) the agency through which Olivares could take action against such bitter enemies of his regime as were Quevedo and Tirso. [24] Lope would go unscathed.

---

[23] This, according to a note of González Palencia, was marked out and in its place written "que mande a su provincial." Given the dedication of Tirso's *Tercera parte* to Julio Monti and the Mercedarian's words "Tempestades y persecuciones invidiosas procuraron malograr los honestos recreos de mis ocios; y yo sé de alguna borrasca que, a no tener a V. S. por San Telmo, diera con él a pique," I believe we may take it for granted that the Junta, when it failed to get the support of the Papal Nuncio, then turned to the Provincial of Tirso's order, over which it would have some control.

[24] I have had occasion to deal with Tirso's antagonism to the Conde-Duque and the new King in such studies as "*La prudencia en la mujer and the Ambient that Brought It Forth*", *PMLA*, LXIII (1948), 1173-1175; "Notes on Two Interrelated Plays of Tirso: *El amor y el amistad* and *Ventura te dé Dios*", *HR*, XXVIII (1960), 208-213; "Literary and Political Satire in Tirso's *La fingida Arcadia*," printed in "*The Renaissance Reconsidered, Smith College Studies in History*, XLIV (1964), 91-110.

RELIGIOUS HISPANISMS IN AMERICAN INDIAN LANGUAGES

by LAWRENCE B. KIDDLE
University of Michigan

Spain's discovery, conquest, and colonization of the Americas has inspired a centuries-old debate between passionate defenders of the behavior of Spaniards in the New World and equally passionate critics of that behavior. This polemic began with the publication in 1552 of Fray Bartolomé de las Casas' *Brevísima relación de la destruición de las Indias* and has continued up to our day. Truth in this long and heated controversy lies undoubtedly between the two extremes. It is not my intention in this note to add to the lengthy bibliography on the question of Spain in the Americas, but rather to call attention, through linguistic evidence, to the great role played by Spanish-speaking people in the transfer of European cultural institutions to the New World. Until the middle of the sixteenth century the Spanish nation and people alone acted as agents in an historic diffusion of culture traits between the Old World and the New. I refer to new and exotic products, such as corn, tomatoes, chocolate, potatoes, and tobacco; to useful domestic animals, such as horses, pigs, donkeys, cows, sheep, turkeys, and guinea pigs; and to social practices, customs, and institutions, such as the use of steel needles in sewing, metal coinage, and religion. The mark of Spain and the Spaniard is often preserved in the interchange of these products, traits, and institutions by the Spanish stamp of the name, a loan word, that non-Spanish speakers apply to the borrowed trait or by terms used within the complex of a borrowed institution, such as religion.

The present study of the religious acculturation of the American Indian is divided into three parts. I shall first discuss the nature of cultural and linguistic borrowing in order that the linguistic terminology used in this fascinating aspect of the study of language may be clearly understood. Then, I shall consider the role of the Church in the Spanish Indies in order to present the historical and cultural background for the borrowing of religious terms by Amerindian groups with Spanish contacts. The last part of the paper offers illustrations of actual loans discovered in selected New World indigenous languages. In this part I cite examples of religious hispanisms used by speakers of approximately fifty Indian languages spoken in areas extending from the home of the Wappo tribe located northeast of San Francisco, California, to that of the Araucanians who live in southern Chile.

The study of loan words in languages tells us what a culture group has learned from its neighbors. The borrowing situation may be contiguous, that is between culture groups sharing a common border, such as the United States and Mexico or Germany and France. Another borrowing situation obtains when two groups occupy the same geographical area, such as the Norman French and the English in Medieval England or the Arabs and the Spanish in Medieval Spain or the Spaniards and the Indians in the New World. This last type of ethnolinguistic exchange is called intimate borrowing.[1] In the study of loan words it is possible to distinguish those borrowings that reflect the form of the original language either completely or partially by calling the former *loanwords and the latter loanblends*. Our English words, *chair* and *chauffeur*, are loanwords from the French which we borrowed at two different periods, as may be seen in the differing pronunciation of the initial consonant represented by *ch* in our orthography. *Chair* is an early loan and *chauffeur* is a more recent borrowing. The Guaraní word *kiritó* 'Christ' is a loanword whose original is the Spanish *kristo* and its distorted shape tells us that it was an early borrowing, dating from a period when the Guaraní Indians had not yet learned to pronounce the Spanish initial cluster, *kr*. Turning now to loanblends, the type of borrowing in which only part of the

---

[1] Bloomfield 1933, 458

new word is foreign and the rest of the form is native, I can cite the Pennsylvania German *blaumepai* 'plum pie', compounded of the native morpheme *blaum* 'plum' and the borrowed form *pai* taken from American English. From the religious hispanisms cited in this paper, I give the Keresan *mi.sakay* 'church', a blend of the Spanish *misa* 'Mass' and the Keresan *kay* 'the inside'. In the case of borrowings that do not retain any of the shape of the original morpheme the term *loanshift* is used. Loanshifts may be classed as extensions, in which a native morpheme acquires a new or extended meaning due to its similarity to the term in the original language, such as the Texas-Mexican word, *ganga,* which is addition to meaning 'bargain', now means 'gang'.[2] Another class of loanshift is called a creation and here native terms are combined in a new way to express the new idea. These creations are also known as stimulus loans. A good illustration of this type of loan is the native Wappo term for 'priest' used alongside of the loanword *pádre*.[3] The native term literally translated means 'the person who gives out names'. The function of name-giving belonged in this California tribe to the grandmother and the impact of the Spanish priest's prerogative of name-giving may be appreciated in the borrowing.

The indigenous loans referred to above and those mentioned from now on belong to the intimate borrowing category previously mentioned and defined. In this case the dominant culture, Spanish European, and the prestigious language, Spanish, have given words to the Indian tongues. The borrowings began during the earliest conquest period when the Spaniards sought to adjust the Indians to European ways, especially in the fields of government and religion. These borrowings continued throughout the colonial period. This study is limited to the consideration of loanwords and loanblends, that is to Indian words that show retention of Spanish morphemes. Extensions and creations are almost impossible to treat unless one is thoroughly familiar with the native languages.[4]

The Spanish conquest of America was a religious conquest, perhaps the only one our planet has known. The Church was the

---

[2] Cerda 1953, 112
[3] Sawyer 1964, 175
[4] Haugen 1953, II, 383-391

strong right arm of the conquistador and it supported unequivocally the Spanish government throughout the colonial period. The missionary zeal and the piety of Queen Isabella were so convincing that the papacy granted unusual and far-reaching powers to the Spanish monarchs for the purpose of conquering and christianizing the New World. From the very beginning the welfare of the Indian was paramount. The *encomienda* system developed in the sixteenth century contained strong provisions for protecting and indoctrinating the Indians. The first Church Council held in the Spanish Indies in 1535 in Mexico City was deeply concerned over the problem of caring for the Indian. It would have been relatively easy to have considered the Indians to be vicious and stubborn pagans on a par with the Protestant heretics of Europe and to proceed to exterminate them as far as possible but the Catholic Church found the Indian and later the Negro to be possessed of a soul and worthy of acceptance into the same church as the conquistador himself. [5]

The shock of the conquest on the American Indian must have been profound. The Indian was a mystical, deeply religious being who was sensitive to the powerful external forces that control the destiny of man. He peopled the landscape with spiritual beings whom he sought to propitiate in countless ways. In advanced religious centers such as those of Mexico and Peru he had established priesthoods and sisterhoods whose members acted as his mediators in his relations with supreme beings. His religious development was, in fact, strikingly similar to that of Europe and this led the Spaniards to consider that the Indians were misguided apostates or original Christians who had fallen away from the faith. This explains why the mission stations in the Americas were called *reducciones* because, in the belief of the churchmen, it was necessary to lead back or "reduce" the Indian to the fold from which he had strayed. The Spanish conqueror was brutally irreverent. He destroyed the holy images, he banished forcefully the respected religious leaders, and he scorned the religious faith and values of the conquered Indian. Cortés' action in destroying the Aztec idols, in cleansing the bloody altars, and in substituting Christian rites

---

[5] Williams 1944, 179-192; Service 1954, 42-43

and symbols for the older and revered symbols of the faith of his fathers must have affected profoundly the Indian of ancient Tenochtitlan. Fortunately the Church was wise and it knew how to effect the transfer in a slow and patient way. It provided a safe haven for the disoriented Indian. It gave him the Christian Mass for the human sacrifice, it rebuilt the destroyed temples and it provided new altars frequently in the very places where the old temples and altars had existed. Christian saints replaced the supreme beings that had influenced the Indian's life. In all this adjustment the Church was deeply involved in lessening the shock of christianization, in preserving for the bewildered Indian some part of what he had revered before. All the intimate aspects of the Indian's life were controlled by the Church. Through the sacraments his contacts with his spiritual guardian were continuous from the cradle to the grave. He was protected by legislation and by the Inquisition from unhealthy influences from Europe. He was protected in the mission stations by zealous Franciscans, Dominicans, Augustinians, and Jesuits, who frequently taught the Indian the Christian doctrine in his own indigenous language. When churchmen were not with the Indian in his long journeys by foot, roadside chapels and crosses reminded him of the Church's eternal presence. The Church was school, hospital, orphanage, old folks home, and center for village festivals. The clergy, in short, were the best friends of the aborigines during the Spanish period.[6]

An interesting quotation that describes an activity of the Guaraní missions of the colonial period illustrates admirably the acculturation process of the Indian:

> "Cada domingo, después de rezadas todas las oraciones del catecismo y los misterios, los dos que de pie en medio de la iglesia llevaban la voz decían: estos son los nombres y el orden de los números: *uno*. Y respondía el pueblo: *uno*. Y seguían ellos: *dos*. Y todos a su vez: *dos*; continuando *tres, cuatro* y así sucesivamente hasta *ciento* y *mil*. Después de esto decían los dos que guiaban: estos son los nombres de los días de la semana: *domingo*, repitiendo todos *domingo*. Seguían ellos: *lunes*; y

---

[6] Tannenbaum 1959, 24-29

todos repetían, *lunes*; y así contaban hasta *sábado*. Luego pasaban a los meses: estos son los nombres de los meses del año: *Enero*; y repetían todos, *Enero*. Luego *Febrero, Marzo,* etc. hasta *Diciembre*. Con lo cual se lograba que a los indios, desde niños, se hiciesen familiares estos nombres, y usasen con expedición de aquel modo de contar que falta en su lengua..." [7]

That the Indians not always understood the religious concepts and behavior imparted to them by the Spaniards may be seen in the meaning of two borrowings the Spanish words, *gloria* and *ayuno,* as reported by Nida. [8] The word *gloria* acculturated as *gluria* in the Nahuatl dialect of Teltelcingo, Mexico, means 'a religious drinking bout' as a result of the constant association of religious festivities and the consumption of great quantities of liquor. In the Quechua dialect of Bolivia the word *ayuno* signifies a fiesta characterized by riotous eating and drinking. This is, as Nida explains, probably due to the fact that fasting lasts generally until noon and after the fasting the remainder of the day is given over to the heavy consumption of liquor and food.

The final division of this study offers hispanisms found in selected Amerindian languages. They illustrate well the penetration of Spanish words in the religious terminology used by American Indians with Spanish contacts. It is to be noted that this section treats religion broadly in the manner of an anthropologist as a cultural complex that covers not only the rites, symbols, and practices of the faith but also attendant aspects, such as ritual kinship or the system of baptismal sponsors and the names of the days of the week, which among American Indians centers around Sunday, the Christian day of rest. The observance of Sunday as the sacred day of the week is evidence of the great unity that exists in Euro-American culture.

The first category of hispanisms concerns members of the Christian celestial hierarchy: God, the Virgin, Christ, the Holy Ghost, angels, saints, and one member of what could be called the "lower" archy, the devil.

---

[7] Hernández 1913, I, 255
[8] Nida 1950, 224

I. Celestial (and Infernal) Hierarchy and Symbols.
  a. Spanish **djós** 'God'.
    djus, djós Tepecano, Mexico (Mason 1917-18, 94 *et passim*).
    yúʔus, yúʔušt Keresan, USA (Spencer 1947, 137).
    diuži Zapotec, Mexico (Velma Pickett, personal communication).
    landyós (May Morrison, p. c.).
    njógšì Tewa, USA (Harrington 1947, 112).
    njósì Mixteco, Mexico (Kenneth Pike, p. c.).
    yó·sí Tewa, USA (Harrington 1947, 112).
    yó·s Chiricahua, USA (Hoijer 1939, 111).
    líos, díos, líosnóoka 'to pray', *lit.* 'to speak to God' Yaqui, Mexico (Spicer 1943, 412, 419).
    dios Nahuatl, Mexico (Boas 1920, 13).
    djoselopáge formula for thanking for alms Guarani, Paraguay (Morínigo 1931, 292).
    djós Kayuvava, Bolivia (Créqui-Montfort et Rivet 1920, 265).
    ndios Huave, Mexico (Radin 1929, 22).
    dyos Zoque, Mexico (Wonderly 1946, 93).
    dios Araucano, Chile (Lenz 1893, 205).
    diox Matlaltzinco, Mexico (Canfield 1934, 186).
    rrióš Ttotzil, Mexico (Ethel Wallace, p. c.).
    yos Amuesha, Peru (Mary Ruth Wise, p. c.).

  b. Spanish **bírxen** 'Virgin'.
    wiruhén Keresan USA (Spencer 1947, 138).
    m'ilixina Taos USA (Trager 1944, 146)
    virjena tayca Aymará, Peru (Vocabulario 1905, 470).
    virghen Araucano, Chile (Lenz 1893, 206).
    virgen Kayuvava, Bolivia (Créqui-Montfort et Rivet 1920, 253); Mure, Bolivia (Créqui-Montfort et Rivet 1913, 169); Rokorona, Bolivia (Créqui-Montfort et Rivet 1913, 170); Takana, Bolivia (Créqui-Montfort et Rivet 1922, 160).
    wirxina, virxina Uro-čipaya, Bolivia (Métraux 1935, 328, 348).
    birjen Katio, Colombia (Santísimo Sacramento 1936, 110).

  c. Spanish **espíritu sánto** 'Holy Ghost'.
    spilito xanto Nahuatl, Mexico (Canfield 1934, 180).
    espiritú santú Mixteco, Mexico (Kenneth Pike, p. c.).
    spiritu santo Araucano, Chile (Molina 1809, II, 364).

espíritu santo Itonama, Bolivia (Créqui-Montfort et Rivet 1916, 24); Mure, Bolivia (Créqui-Montfort et Rivet 1913, 169); Rokorona, Bolivia (Créqui-Montfort et Rivet 1913, 170); Takana, Bolivia (Créqui-Montfort et Rivet 1922, 158); San Blas, Panama (Prince 1913, 300).

d. Spanish **sánto** 'saint, holy'.

sánto Kayuvava, Bolivia (Créqui-Montfort et Rivet 1920, 247).
santú Mixteco, Mexico (Kenneth Pike, p. c.).
sánto Yaqui, Mexico (Spicer 1943, 419); Nahuatl, Mexico (Boas 1930, 86); Guaraní, Paraguay (Morínigo 1931, 297).
sanantóni 'St. Anthony'. **sant'yá·k** 'St. James', **sáw** 'St. John', **sapér** 'St. Peter', **sarorénus** 'St. Lawrence' Keresan USA (Spicer 1947, 148).
sančyak Amuesha, Peru (Mary Ruth Wise, p. c.).

e. Spanish **kristo** 'Christ'.

krístu Zapotec, Mexico (Velma Pickett, p. c.).
kiritó, krísto Guaraní, Paraguay (Morínigo 1931, 293).
kuri·st Keresan USA (Spencer 1947, 137).
kristú Chontal, Mexico (May Morrison, p. c.).
cristo Cakchiquel, Guatemala (Townsend 1960, 25).

f. Spanish **krús** 'cross'.

krús Tepecano, Mexico (Mason 1917-18, 122).
kurú·s 'large cross of a church' Keresan USA (Spencer 1947, 134).
krú Zapotec, Mexico (Velma Pickett, p. c.).
kús 'Holy Cross' Yaqui, Mexico (Spicer 1943, 419).
ankrús Chontal, Mexico (Waterhouse 1957, 244).
curus Pocomchí, Guatemala (Mayers 1958, 138).

g. Spanish **djáblo** 'devil'.

dia'bilo Huave, Mexico (Radin 1929, 3).
djablú Mixteco, Mexico (Kenneth Pike, p. c.).
yawló Maidu, USA (Preston 1950, 191).
dyablo Zoque, Mexico (Wonderly 1946, 95).
diablo Nahuatl, Mexico (González Casanova 1933, 730).
diaflo Araucano, Chile (Augusta 1903, 350).
yáwlo' Wappo USA (Shipley 1962, 19).

The second category of religious loanwords is centered on the sacrament of baptism, the baptismal sponsors, and on the use of Christian names, of which only two are cited: 'John' and 'Mary'. The system of baptismal sponsors or the compadrazgo was eagerly accepted by American Indians.

II. Baptism, baptismal sponsors, and proper names.

a. Spanish **bautízmo** 'baptism', **bautisár** 'to baptize'.

báto 'baptism', **báto⁷áčai** 'godfather', **báto⁷áe** 'godmother' Yaqui, Mexico (Spicer 1943, 416).
pautisa Uro-čipaya, Bolivia (Métraux 1935, 388).
bautisay Quechua, Peru (Vocabulario 1905, 82).
bautisaipara Katio, Colombia (Santísimo Sacramento 1936, 104).

b. Spanish **komádre** 'godsib (female)'.

komádre, kumár Keresan, USA (Spencer 1947, 138).
kamái Yaqui, Mexico (Spicer 1943. 416).
kumáre, kumádre, kumajli⁷ina Tiwa, USA (Trager 1943, 562).
comalle, comagre Nahuatl, Mexico (González Casanova 1933, 729; Ochoa Lobato 1937, 103).
kumáni Popoluca, Mexico (Foster 1949, 333).
mále Zapotec, Mexico (Velma Pickett p. c.).
komále Tzeltal, Mexico (Ethel Wallis, p. c.).
kumá·dre⁷ Wappo USA (Sawyer 1964, 175).
comadre Uro-čipaya, Bolivia (Métraux 1935, planche XIV).
komáre Amuesha, Peru (Mary Ruth Wise, p. c.).

c. Spanish **kompádre** 'godsib (male)'.

kŭmbü'ĕ Huave, Mexico (Radin 1929, 2).
kumpaléu Nahuatl, Mexico (Boas 1917, 40).
kompádre, kumpár Keresan, USA (Spencer 1947, 138).
kómpai Yaqui, Mexico (Spicer 1943, 416).
kump,ajli⁷ina, kumpale, kumpare, kumpadre Tiwa, USA (Trager 1943, 562, 565, 570).
kompágre Zoque, Mexico (Wonderly 1946, 93).
mbáà Mazateco, Mexico (Pike and Pike 1947, 79).
kūpe Carib, Central America (Taylor 1948, 193).
kumpalé Quiché, Guatemala (Bunzel 1952, 156).
kumpáni Popoluca, Mexico (Foster 1949, 333).

wilu gumpáli 'turkey buzzard' Tarahumara, Mexico
(Bennett and Zingg 1935, 124).
kumpá·dreʔ Wappo, USA (Sawyer 1964, 175).
kompáre Kahuapana, Brazil (Rivet 1931, 249).
kompáre Amuesha, Peru (Mary Ruth Wise, p. c.).

d. Spanish **maría** 'Mary'.

maría Tepecano, Mexico (Mason 1917-18, 129).
mali·nci 'Miz Mary' Nahuatl, Mexico (Pittman 1948, 236).
maryá Chontal, Mexico (May Morrison, p. c.).
ma'liah Popoluca, Mexico (Elson 1948, 191).
mar Quecchi, Guatemala (Selis Lope 1937, 47).
maliki-ca 'little Mary' Quechua, Peru (Yokoyama 1951, 55).
mariaè 'Holy Mary' Tecuexe, Mexico (Dávila Garibi 1939, 347).

e. Spanish **xwam** 'John' (XVI cent. šwan).

hwan Zoque, Mexico (Wonderly 1946, 93).
swano Nahuatl, Mexico (Canfield 1934, 180).
šiwan Popoluca, Mexico (Elson 1961, 423).
šun Ttotzil, Mexico (Ethel Wallis, p. c.).
xuguán Quecchi, Guatemala (Selis Lope 1937, 47).
kwan Araucano, Chile (Lenz 1893, 207).
xwan Cakchiquel, Guatemala (Townsend 1960, 9).
wan Amuesha, Peru (Mary Ruth Wise p. c.).

The last category of loanwords refers to the church calendar (fast days, religious holidays, the Christian week).

III. Church calendar and religious holidays.

a. Spanish **ayúna** 'fast', **ayunár** 'to fast'.

ayūna Coahuilteco, USA (Swanton 1940, 13).
enaẙúna 'fasting', aẙuná 'to fast' Guaraní, Paraguay (Morínigo 1931, 134, 137).
ayunana ppunchau 'religious holiday' Quechua, Peru (Vocabulario 1905, 159).
ayunaltma Allentiac, Argentina (Schuller 1913, 241).
ayuno 'a fiesta characterized by heavy drinking' Quechua, Bolivia (Nida 1950, 224).

b. Spanish **fjésta** 'religious holiday'.

piéhta Yaqui, Mexico (Johnson 1943, 431).
pí'iasto Taos, USA (Trager 1944, 148).

fiesta Tarahumara, Mexico (Bennett and Zingg 1935, 270); Millcayac, Argentina (Schuller 1913, 240); Allentiac, Argentina (Schuller 1913, 241).
piesta Katío, Colombia (Santísimo Sacramento 1936, 103).
fiesta yunag 'holiday' Quechua, Peru (Vocabulario 1905, 215).
fista Kahuapana, Brazil (Rivet et Tastevin 1931, 253).
piésta Itonama, Bolivia (Rivet 1921, 188).
pistikis 'at the time of the religious holiday' Uročipaya, Bolivia (Métraux, 389).

c. Spanish **glórja** 'glory'.

glúria 'a religious drinking bout' Nahuatl -Tetelcingo, Mexico (Nida 1950, 224).

d. Spanish **mísa** 'Mass'.

mižá·ʔ 'holiday' Zapotec, Mexico (Velma Pickett, p. c.).
mi·s Keresan, USA (Spencer 1947, 133).
misa Chontal, Mexico (May Morrison, p. c.); Comecrudo, USA (Swanton 1940, 83); Chibcha, Colombia (Grammática 1887, 277).
m,esotu?'una 'church' Taos, USA (Trager 1944, 147).
mixà Otomí, Mexico (Neve y Molina 1767, 148).
mixa Pocomchí, Guatemala (Mayers 1958, 143).
misa uru istahaña 'holiday' Aymará, Peru (Vocabulario 1905, 215).
misa 'Sunday, week' Warau, Guiana (Williams 1929, 235).

e. Spanish **domingo** 'Sunday' (Only one day of the week is chosen to represent the entire Christian week.)

ta'mi·k Keresan, USA (Spencer 1947, 143).
da'migo Navajo, USA (Franciscan Fathers 1910, 60).
to'miku Taos, USA (Trager 1939, 52).
'taingo Mazateco, Mexico (Eunice Pike, p. c.).
domingos mayege Moseteño, Bolivia (Bibolotti 1917, 37).
domingú Mixteco, Mexico (Kenneth Pike, p. c.).
domíngu Quichua, Ecuador (Santiago Chanchay, p. c.).
lóominko Yaqui, Mexico (Spicer 1943, 420).
temenko Amuesha, Peru (Mary Ruth Wise, p. c.).

Many tribes do not use a Spanish morpheme for the word for 'Sunday' but rather use a loanshift creation that translated means 'day when Mass is said' (Quechua, Peru; Aymará, Peru) or 'day of rest' (Wappo, USA; Quechua-Ancash, Peru; Tonkawa, USA).

This study represents nothing more than an introduction to the study of Spanish loanwords in American Indian languages. Investigations in this fields are easier today because of the dedicated field work of members of the Summer Institute of Linguistics, several of whom served me as informants for this study. For those of us who are Spanish teachers the present study makes us aware of the great civilizing role of Spain in the age of discovery and of the peculiar role of the Spanish language as a culture carrier.

---

[9] Hoijer 1944

REFERENCES

Augusta 1903. Fr. F. J. de Augusta. Gramática araucana. Valdivia.
Bennett and Zingg 1935. W. C. Bennett and R. M. Zingg. The Tarahumara. An Indian Tribe of Northern Mexico. Chicago.
Bibolotti 1917. Benigno Bibolotti. Moseteño Vocabulary and Treatises. Evanston.
Bloomfield 1933. Leonard Bloomfield. Language. New York.
Boas 1917. Franz Boas. "El dialecto mexicano de Pochutla, Oaxaca". IJAL 1.9-44 (1917)
Boas 1920. Franz Boas. "Cuentos en mexicano de Milpa Alta, D. F.". JAF 33.1-24.
Boas 1930. Franz Boas. "Spanish Elements in Modern Nahuatl". Todd Memorial Volumes I.85-89. New York.
Bunzel 1952. Ruth Bunzel. Chichicastenango. A Guatemalan Village. PAES 22. New York.
Canfield 1934. D. L. Canfield. Spanish Literature in Mexican Languages as a Source for the Study of Spanish. New York.
Cerda 1953. Gilberto Cerda, Berta Cabaza y Julieta Farias. Vocabulario español de Texas. Austin.
Créqui-Montfort et Rivet 1913. G. de Créqui-Montfort et P. Rivet. "Linguistique Bolivienne: La famille linguistique čapakura". JSAP 10.119-171.
Créqui-Montfort et Rivet 1916. G. de Créqui-Montfort et P. Rivet. "La Langue Itonama". Extrait des Memoires de la Société de Linguistique de Paris, tomes XIX et XX. Paris.
Créqui-Montfort et Rivet 1920 G. de Créqui-Montfort et P. Rivet. "Linguistique Bolivienne: La Langue Kayuvava" IJAL 1.245-265.
Créqui-Montfort et Rivet 1922. G. de Créqui-Montfort et P. Rivet. "La famille linguistique Takana". JSAP 14.141-182; 15.121-167.
Dávila Garibi 1939. J. Ignacio Dávila Garibi. "Un interesante manuscrito en una de las lenguas desaparecidas de Jalisco." Vigesimoséptimo Congreso Internacional de Americanistas. Tomo II. 337-353. México.
Elson 1961. Benjamin F. Elson. "Person Markers and Related Morphemes in Sierra Popoluca." A William Cameron Townsend en el XXV aniversario del Instituto Lingüístico de Verano. 421-430. Norman.
Foster 1949. G. M. Foster. "Some Popoluca Kinship Terminology and its Wider Relationships." SWJA. 5.330-394.
Franciscan Fathers 1910. The Franciscan Fathers. An Ethnologic Dictionary of the Navajo Language. St. Michaels.

González Casanova 1933. P. González Casanova. "Los hispanismos en el idioma azteca". Anales del Museo Nacional de Arqueología, Historia y Etnografía. 25.693-742.
Grammática 1887. Grammática, frases, oraciones, cathezismo, confesionario y bocabulario de la lengua chibcha. Bogotá. 1620. Congreso internacional de americanistas. Actas de la cuarta reunión. II.279-295. Madrid.
Harrington 1947. J. P. Harrington. "Three Tewa Texts." IJAL 13.112-116.
Haugen 1953. Einar Haugen. The Norwegian Language in America. 2 vols. Philadelphia.
Hernández 1913. Pablo Hernández. Organización social de las doctrinas guaraníes. 2 vols. Barcelona.
Hoijer 1939. Harry Hoijer. "Chiricahua Loan-Words from Spanish." Language. 15.110-115.
Hoijer 1944. Harry Hoijer. An Analytical Dictionary of the Tonkawa Language. Berkeley.
Johnson 1943. Jean B. Johnson. "A Clear Case of Linguistic Acculturation." AA 45.427-434.
Lenz 1893. R. Lenz. "Die spanischen Lehnwörter im Araukanischen." ZRPh 17.204-207.
Mason 1917-18. J. Alden Mason. "Tepecano Prayers." IJAL 1.91-153.
Mayers 1958. Marvin Mayers. Pocomchí Texts with Grammatical Notes. Norman.
Métraux 1935. A. Métraux. "Les Indiens Uro-čipaya de Carangas." JSAP 27.111-128, 325-415.
Molina 1809. J. I. Molina. The Geographical, Natural, and Civil History of Chili translated from the original Italian of the Abbé... 2 vols. London.
Morínigo 1931. M. A. Morínigo. Hispanismos en el guaraní. Buenos Aires.
Neve y Molina 1767. Luis de Neve y Molina. Reglas de Orthografia, diccionario y arte del idioma othomi, breve instrucción para los principiantes que dictò... Madrid.
Nida 1950. E. A. Nida. Learning a Foreign Language. New York.
Ochoa Lobato 1937. José Ochoa Lobato. "Versos en dialecto mexicano". Investigaciones Lingüísticas. 4.103-104.
Pike and Pike 1947. Kenneth L. Pike and Eunice Victoria Pike. "Immediate Constituents of Mazateco Syllables." IJAL 13.78-91.
Pittman 1948. Richard S. Pittman. "Nahuatl Honorifics." IJAL 14.236-239.
Preston 1950. W. D. Preston. "Maidu Morphophonemics." IJAL 16.185-192.
Prince 1913. J. Dynely Prince. "A Text in the Indian Language of Panama Darien." AA15.298-326.
Radin 1929. Paul Radin. "Huave Texts." IJAL 5.1-56
Rivet 1921. P. Rivet. "Nouvelle Contribution à l'étude de la Langue des Itonamas." JSAP 13.173-195.
Rivet et Tastevin 1931. P. Rivet et C. Tastevin. "Nouvelle Contribution à l'Etude du Groupe Kahuapana." IJAL 6.227-271.
Santísimo Sacramento 1936. Fr. Pablo del Santísimo Sacramento. El idioma katío. Medellín.
Sawyer 1964. Jesse Sawyer. "The Implications of Spanish /w/ and /rr/ in Wappo History." Romance Philology 18.165-177.
Schuller 1913. R. R. Schuller. "Discovery of a Fragment of the printed copy of the work on the Millcayac Language by Luis de Valdivia." Papers of the Peabody Museum of American Archaeology and Ethnology. 3.223-258.

Selis Lope 1937. Mario Selis Lope. Vocabulario Español-Quecchi. Coban.
Service 1954. Elman R. Service. Spanish-Guarani Relations in Early Colonial Paraguay. Ann Arbor.
Shipley 1962. William Shipley. "Spanish Elements in the Indigenous Languages of Central California." Romance Philology 16.1-21.
Spencer 1947. Robert F. Spencer. "Spanish Loanwords in Keresan." SWJA 3.130-146.
Spicer 1943 E. H. Spicer "Linguistic Aspects of Yaqui Acculturation." AA 45.410-426.
Swanton 1940. John R. Swanton. Linguistic Material from the Tribes of Southern Texas and Northeastern Mexico. Smithsonian Institution Bureau of American Ethnology. Bulletin 127. Washington.
Tannenbaum 1959. Frank Tannenbaum. "Toward an Appreciation of Latin America." The United States and Latin America. 5-57. New York.
Taylor 1948. Douglas Taylor. "Loanwords in Central American Carib." Word 4.187-195.
Townsend 1960. W. Cameron Townsend. "Cakchiquel Grammar." Mayan Studies I.9-13. Norman.
Trager 1939. G. L. Trager. "The Days of the Week in the Language of Taos Pueblo, New Mexico." Language. 15.51-55.
Trager 1943. G. L. Trager. "The Kinship and Status Terms of the Tiwa Languages." AA 45.557-571.
Trager 1944. G. L. Trager. "Spanish and English Loanwords in Taos." IJAL 10.144-158.
Vocabulario 1905. Vocabulario polígota incaico. Comprende más de 12.000 voces castellanas y 100.000 de Keshua del Cusco, Ayacucho, Junín Ancash y Aymará. Compuesto por algunos religiosos franciscanos misioneros de los colegios de Propaganda Fide del Perú. Lima.
Waterhouse 1957. Viola Waterhouse. "Two Oaxaca Chontal Words." IJAL 23.244-245.
Williams 1929. Rev. James Williams. "The Warau Indians of Guiana and Vocabulary of their Language." JSAP 21.201-261.
Williams 1944. Mary W. Williams. The People and Politics of Latin America. Madison, USAFI.
Wonderly 1946. William L. Wonderly: "Phonemic Acculturation in Zoque." IJAL 12.92-95.
Yokoyama 1951. Masako Yokoyama. "Outline of Kechua Structure I Morphology." Language. 27.38-67.

CRACKS IN THE STRUCTURE OF CALDERÓN'S
EL ALCALDE DE ZALAMEA

by Sturgis E. Leavitt
University of North Carolina

Not for a moment would we deny the validity of the many dramatic scenes in Calderón's *El Alcalde de Zalamea,* such as the clashes in each act between Pedro Crespo and Lope de Figueroa, Pedro Crespo's farewell to his son, the arrest of the Captain, and the generous acceptance of defeat by Lope de Figueroa at the end of the play. Nor would we question the splendid characterization of the two excentric old men—except for one instance mentioned later in this study—nor that of the minor characters, Juan, Rebolledo and Chispa.

The construction of Act I of *El Alcalde de Zalamea* is of a very high order. The play begins with a curse that sets the tone of lawlessness that characterizes the play. In the early scenes we see the soldiers griping at their lot, and note their distrust of the officers. Later, the sergeant's effort to keep on good terms with the Captain by billeting him in the house of the prettiest girl in town, his snooping around to find out where the girl is, the Captain's "conspiracy" with a subordinate to see her—all this shows that discipline is anything but well maintained in the army. And yet, back of it all is the stern figure of the general of the army, Lope de Figueroa, clearly a man not to be trifled with, as is seen when he interrupts the conflict in Isabel's room, and is ready to deal out cruel punishment to Rebolledo. In this same scene Pedro Crespo is seen to be a man of strong character, ready to risk his life when his honor is in jeopardy. He, too, is no man to be trifled with. He is, indeed, a worthy counterpart in civilian life to Lope de Figueroa in the military.

Almost all the other characters are no less adequately presented, although some have fewer lines. There is Rebolledo, the trouble-maker; there is Chispa, free and easy camp follower; Pedro's son, Juan, something of a ne'er-do-well; and Isabel, the obedient daughter. These characters are clearly drawn. They are interesting. They are individuals, not types.

However, two characters in Act I could well be dispensed with, Don Mendo and Nuño. They add nothing, whatever to the act. In an explanation that accompanies the RCA recording of this play we find this statement: "...se suprimen los personajes del hidalgo Don Mendo y su criado Nuño, por considerar que su intervención, ajena a la línea directa del drama, es menos comprensible si no se pueden ver sus dos figuras, trasunto de las de Don Quijote y su escudero Sancho." With this assertion we are in agreement, except for the reference to Don Quijote and Sancho. The only reason for the appearance of Don Mendo and Nuño in the play in our opinion, is that someone, Calderón or the manager of the company to whom the comedia was sold, felt that there should be a comic part in the play. As a matter of fact, the scenes in which these two characters appear are far from funny, although no doubt they were intended to be. Don Mendo and Nuño hardly appear in Act II, and they fortunately disappear altogether in Act III.

And one more thing is wrong with Act I—no conflict is presented at the end. With Lope de Figueroa's decision to stay in Pedro Crespo's house, everything is settled. That is, everything is settled, unless the Captain persists in his designs upon Isabel. The audience has to wait until the beginning of Act II to learn that the Captain is going to try to see Isabel again, regardless of the orders of Lope de Figueroa.

And here is where the play begins to fall apart. Of course, Rebolledo is necessary to the action later on, but, even so, how can one possibly believe that the Captain would get chummy with Rebolledo after the latter has let him down in the scene with Lope in Act I? Rather, one would expect the Captain to make

Rebolledo's life utterly miserable from then on. And this objection is multiplied when Rebolledo says that Lope cannot sleep on account of his game leg and therefore will not be disturbed by a serenade. Furthermore, we are dumfounded when Rebolledo says:

> ....la culpa,
> si se entiende, será nuestra,
> no tuya....

A second offense on the part of Rebolledo would be fatal, and he knows it full well. Not only this, but would the Captain risk offending Lope by making a disturbance outside the house where he is quartered?

Other minor points. How can one believe Pedro Crespo so indifferent to the election of town officials that Isabel has to remind him of it? And how is it that Juan could wound the Captain and not be cut down by the Captain's henchmen?

In Act III Isabel could tell her sad story in four lines, if not in four words. Instead, she has sixty-seven lines of soliloquy and one hundred and seventy-five more lines in telling her father what has happened. The only explanation possible is that the author has to build up the part of Isabel in order to make it satisfactory to the actress. Up to then she has only a minor part, that of a dutiful daughter, and how can she (the actress), anxious to get her share of the applause, consent to have the two actors who take the roles of Pedro Crespo and Lope de Figueroa get all the good moments? No, that will not do. The author has to give her a considerable number of good lines, and some emoting, or else she will not play ball.

The wound that the Captain receives is tricky business. He must be wounded badly enough to be unconscious. Otherwise, he would never have permitted the soldiers to carry him back to Zalamea. He must be well enough to stand up to Pedro Crespo when confronted by him. This last is especially necessary, since the audience must not be permitted to take the side of the Captain and have Pedro Crespo seem to be taking an unfair advantage of a severely wounded man. It is, then, far from clear how serious the Captain's wound really was.

In a previous article (*Hispania*, XXXVIII (1955), 430-431) we have attempted to prove how empty the scene is when Pedro Crespo begs the Captain to marry Isabel. Pedro Crespo cannot but know that the Captain will positively refuse to take him up on any proposition he makes. Pedro Crespo can, therefore, make all kinds of extravagant promises with the certainty that they will be refused. The explanation is that the author is "conditioning" his audience to accept without protest the death of an officer in the King's army at the hands of a civilian who has absolutely no jurisdiction in the case—and who knows it.

And while we are on the subject of the execution, is it likely that a peaceful little town like Zalamea would have such a complicated instrument as a garrote to put an end to the career of the Captain?

AN UNNOTICED COMPLEMENT TO "CONCOLORCORVO"

by JOHN KENNETH LESLIE
Northwestern University

One of the gems of American Spanish colonial literature is the *Lazarillo de ciegos caminantes,* the sparkling account of the journey from Montevideo and Buenos Aires overland to Lima made during the years 1771 to 1773 by the mysterious person who called himself Calixto Bustamante Carlos Inga, "Concolorcorvo." There is a complement to this book in the form of a journal entitled *Viaje muy puntual y curioso de Don Miguel de Santistevan: desde Lima a Caracas por tierra en 1740.* Written some thirty years earlier, this work complements "Concolorcorvo" in the sense that it portrays travel and other conditions in the northern reaches of South America, beginning at the point where the *Lazarillo* was to leave off. A manuscript of it consisting of 180 folios was in the possession of the Spanish historian Juan Bautista Muñoz and is now in the Rich Collection of the New York Public Library.

In May 1740 the author and two friends, Don Domingo Vicente de Guisla and Don Miguel de Cáceres, were in Lima bound for Spain, having set out from Cuzco the previous September. Because of the war with England they could not go by way of Panama, Portobelo being at that time in the hands of the English. They decided, instead, to travel overland to Caracas and to take ship at La Guaira. They well knew that the journey would not be easy. As Don Miguel pointed out to his companions: "Verdad es, señores, que el camino que se propone es tan dilatado que pasa de mil leguas y gran parte de ellas es de tierras desiguales en que hay sierras muy frías, valles ardientes, selvas muy intrincadas, bosques muy espesos y llenos de malezas, suelos inconstantes, sendas pantanosas y ríos caudalosos." But there were mitigating circumstances. Since the country through which they would pass was inhabited, the prospect should not deter men who had already experienced the difficulties of the trip from Cuzco. The company would be congenial. On the way they would make interesting new acquaintances, and their observations on the towns and various climatic regions would be instructive. Instead of waiting out the war in Lima, with each new day they would be closer to their ultimate destination. Moreover, financial considerations were of importance: they would avoid the expense of an extensive stay in Lima, which they found excessive, while by sailing from La Guaira they would eliminate the hazardous crossing of the Bahama Channel and at the same time save more than half the cost of passage from Portobelo. So persuasive were Don Miguel's arguments for this course that a fourth man, Don Matías de Angles, proposed to accompany them.

Though June 6 had been agreed upon as the date of departure, the author was not ready by that time. Guisla and Angles set out as planned, but Don Miguel and Cáceres determined to go by water to Guayaquil and join the others in Quito. The latter two sailed from El Callao in July 10 aboard a vessel carrying wine and *aguardiente*. On the twelfth a raging storm forced them to lighten ship by jettisoning part of the cargo, an incident not considered unusual, since the boats plying these waters were customarily overloaded. Reaching the island of Puna on the twenty-first, they hired a *balsa* for the remaider of the trip to Guayaquil. From this port they ascended the river, again by *balsa*, to Taguache, where they procured mules for the climb to Quito, arriving in this city on the twenty-seventh of August. On November 22, having been joined by their two friends, they proceeded north from Quito, accompanied by two other travelers, Don José Matheu y Villamayor and Don Agustin de Merisalde y Chacón, who were traveling to Cartagena.

Their route took them through Tulcán, Pasto, Popayán, and La Plata. At Anchique, in the Magdalena Valley, Guisla took the road to Santa Fe de Bogotá, as planned, but the others, having learned of the arrival in Cartagena of the squadron commanded by Diego de Torres, continued towards Honda, which they reached on March 7. On the twelfth they embarked in canoes for the trip dowm the Magdalena. At Monpox, nine days later, receiving a report that the English fleet was now at Cartagena, they hesitated to continue further down the river. Here they stayed until May 5, when despite the news of the defeat of the English, and for fear of vengeful British corsairs in the Caribbean, the author and Cáceres resolved to return to Honda, a twenty-day journey upstream, and thence to follow the original plan of going to Caracas. On June 3 they were in Santa Fe. A week later they set forth again, and by way of Tunja, Pamplona, Mérida and Barquisimeto, reached Caracas on the twenty-first of September, 1741.

Don Miguel de Santistevan was obviously a man of substance who had excellent connections and commanded respect. The journal does not explain what he had been doing in Cuzco nor how long he had been there. He may have been a native of Quito, since he had relatives and old friends in that city and the surrounding territory. His brother José, whom he tells us he had not seen for many years and with whom he held a reunion in Riobamba, was curate of Guasuntos, in the Province of Alausi. In his youth Don Miguel had been a captain of infantry and a naval lieutenant and had seen service in several campaigns. Along the route of this journey of 1740-41 he was warmly received by numerous important personages: the Corregidor of Guayaquil, the *Contador de la Real Hacienda* of the same city, the commander of the fleet at Puna, under whom he had earlier served, the Alcalde of Quito, the Governor at Caracas, and many others.

The expedition was equipped like an African safari. At the time when all the friends were traveling together they had more than fifty mules, one or more guides (*prácticos*), muleteers, and personal servants. They carried commodious tents, portable cots with mattresses and other folding furniture, mosquito nets, and a plentiful supply of provisions, including even luxury items. Most of the travelers usually headed the line of march, preceded by a guide, while one of their companions brought up the rear to watch over the convoy.

Santistevan's account is really a better guide for the eighteenth-century traveler than the *Lazarillo de ciegos caminantes*. Not only does the author record methodically the distances from place to place, as does "Concolorcorvo"; he carefully details all manner of information: the character and condition of the roads or trails, the state of the fords across the rivers, the points where provisions could be obtained and the nature of them. He gives us a vivid impression of the arduous travel conditions in the northern Andes. It was frequently necessary to have Indians precede the convoy, cutting steps in the trail on the steep mountain sides. By this means they were able to climb in a matter of hours the Alto de Aranda, near Pasto, whose ascent during the rainy season required three to four days. In some places, over swampy terrain, they had the benefit of *calzadas,* one of which is described thus: "Anduvimos cuatro leguas y media por una que llaman Puente de Guanacas y es una calzada de troncos de árboles de poco más de dos varas, que sigue el camino sobre un suelo muy pantanoso y desigual, y en muchas partes tan pendiente que aun teniendo cuidado de colocar a proporcionadas distancias unos más gruesos que otros en forma de escala, es con todo eso digno de admiración que las mulas que trajinan por ella trepen estos escarpes, sin que sean más frecuentes los precipicios. Y observé con espanto el primero, y aunque vi a los primeros de la comitiva que subían, no me atreví a seguirlos, y apeándome de mi mula, lo monté a pie hasta que me resolví a imitarlos, viendo la firmeza con que se aferraban de los sobresalientes troncos y la incomodidad que había de padecer en esta jornada." Somewhat north of this place they came upon a stretch of four *cuadras* of trail so swampy that at times the baggage had to be carried on men's shoulders, for the loaded mules could not lift their feet out of the mud. On the heights the force of the wind was almost irresistible. The author describes the crossing, north of Pamplona, of "la Mesa de Laura, que así llaman una gran loma escarpada de mucho pasto, de donde se sube una cuesta donde el viento norte suele soplar impetuosamente con alguna frialdad. Este día fue tan recio que temí muchas veces que me arrancase del camino, y más de una sacó la mula las manos del sendero, en que trabajaba para montar cuando iba contra el viento."

Such conditions were hard on the mules, which tired and had to be rested on occasion for days at a time. They stayed seven days in Pamplona, for example, resting some of the animals and finding replacements for others. The hire of mules was often difficult to arrange, at times owing to their scarcity, in some places because of the heavy traffic between Honda and Quito, and sometimes, as in Barquisimeto, because the owners, learning that the travelers were from Peru, tried to exact a heavier price than was customary.

Where there were no bridges and the rivers could not be forded, they crossed by means of *tarabitas*, which greatly impressed the author, who describes one of them as follows:

> Se compone de ocho a diez vetas de cueros torcidos que cada uno tiene de grueso poco menos de una pulgada y están atadas en cada lado del río a tres o cuatro maderos fuertemente clavados en la tierra y puestos en fila, de manera que quedan estas cuerdas casi unidas y tirantes, en la forma que están las de una guitarra, para que si se rompe una o más, como acontece muchas veces, sirvan las otras de resguardo. Sobre estas vetas se pone una horqueta de madera muy fuerte, de una pieza gruesa, más que la muñeca, que suele ser de árbol de guayaba, cuyos lados serán cada uno de tres cuartas, y de sus extremos están atados dos o tres correones de cuero de ancho de una pulgada y largas tres o cuatro varas, de que forman un columpio sobre que se sienta el que ha de pasar. Y con las puntas de las mismas cuerdas le ligan por la cintura y muslos a los lados de la horqueta, puesto en esta forma. Como en este paraje están las cuerdas oblicuamente puestas porque el barranco de la parte de Pasto es muy alto y el opuesto sea de una baja playa, en menos de medio minuto se halla en la otra banda, aun teniendo el río más de una cuadra de ancho. Cuando se pasa al contrario, atan la veta que pende de la horqueta y sirve de tirar la cosa que se pasa, o de repararla para que no se precipite, a la cola de un caballo, que la tira hasta ponerla de esta otra parte. Págase al que cuida de este simple artificio, que en aquellas partes llaman tarabita, un real por cada carga.

The author describes the cities and towns along the route, though not with as much detail as the reader might wish. He pictures all manner of other things that caught his attention: the *potreros* near Quito, surrounded by deep ditches to keep the cattle in, the canoes and water trafic on the Magdalena River, the houses without walls at Valencia, the levee at Monpox. Reminiscent of "Concolorcorvo's" description of the *carretas* on the pampa is his picture of the *balsas* at Guayquil:

> Aquí, pues, fletamos esta tarde una de aquellas fluctuantes casas que llaman balsas, porque se forman sobre palos que tienen este nombre, largos más de veinte varas, de figura circular de diámetro hasta una vara, y leves como el corcho, que unidos unos a otros con maderos delgados y más fuertes, que atraviesan y atan con cierta especie de sarmientos, a manera de sogas, de que hay abundancia de todos gruesos en aquellas selvas y llaman de bejucos, se hace el pavimento de ancho que se quiere en solándolo con guaduas aplanadas, de las cuales se sirven para pies derechos, y como tablas, para división del dormitorio, dejando una gran sala con sombra y sin paredes para la ventilación, y sirve de corredor espacioso para el paseo y de bodega para la carga. A los lados las ponen balustradas de una vara de alto de la misma caña o de otra madera labrada más o menos curiosa a proporción del destino que le dan, dejando fuera de ella los palos colaterales, tanto para la comunicación de los marineros de un extremo a otro, que llaman popa y proa, como para el uso de los remos, que no son otra cosa que una pala de una tercia de ancho y dos varas y media de largo, que fijados en los atravesaños, que sobresalen como media vara, los meten perpendiculares haciendo el movimiento y a fuerza de la boga, hacia la proa.
> Para suplir la falta de la güella y darlas alguna sugestión que las desvía de la línea de la dirección del viento y la corriente cuando van al remo o a la vela, meten a popa y proa entre la juntura de los palos del medio una tabla de dos tercias de ancho y tres varas poco más o menos de largo que cala más de media vara de la que fondean aquéllos, y como entran ajustadas entre dos atravesaños y el hueco de los palos, no se llega a ellos sino para levantarlas más o menos cuando hay poca agua o se da fondo. Su gobernalle a remo o a la vela consiste en cuatro hombres que bogan en los extremos cuaternales más o menos a un lado o a otro, según lo dispone uno de ellos, que es el piloto. Y estos mismos necesitan cuando menos para su manejo en el río, porque como en él no se navegue de otro modo ni en otro tiempo que con la marea que es favorable, bastan éstos para su

dirección. Pero cuando salen a la mar (donde se aparten poco de la costa) o navegan por el río en diligencia con alguna persona de distinción, llevan por banda cuatro o más bogas a proporción del tamaño de la balsa. Y si van a la vela, para arrimarse algo más al viento calan algunos de sus remos, que llaman canaletes, a continuación de las dos tablas que sirven de güella, de que resulta que prolongada más ruede la balsa menos.

Don Miguel was continually delighted by the beauties of the natural scene. He rhapsodizes over the region around the estuary of the Guayas, which he calls a veritable paradise. He enumerates and extols the products of the land in terms that foreshadow Andrés Bello's "Silva a la agricultura de la zona tórrida." The wildlife interests him and draws his comments: flocks of parrots and other birds, for example, near the Río de Zárate, the anthills six to eight feet high which they discovered in great numbers near Cucharo and which they opened, and the numerous monkeys observed nearby, of which he says: "...en los montes de frondosos y elevados árboles que guarnecen los márgenes de estos ríos y quebradas tuvimos hoy, como los días antecedentes el risible entretenimiento de haber (como si estuvieran reducidos a rebaños) tan copioso número de monos de pelo alazán tostado que podían, si faltasen hojas, hacer sombra."

Conditions of life and customs of the people elicit the author's commentary. He mentions such things as domestic life in the tropical regions of what is now Venezuela, conditions in the mines in Colombia, the former treatment of the Indian miners and the present treatment of the negro slaves, the obligation of the Indians to repair roads. He reports on the prevalence of leprosy in the Valle de Patia and the frequency of goiters at Mérida and other places. From time to time he records the nature of local fiestas: fireworks, *máscaras* and the performance of *loas* to celebrate the election of an abbess at San Miguel de Ibarra, bullfights on foot and on horseback, the sport of *gallos* (like the *pato* of Argentina), the victory celebration at Turmero for the success of Spanish arms at Cartagena.

One of the most significant aspects of the journal for a revealing picture of the times is the author's continual preoccupation with economic conditions. He records the prices of innumerable products and services. He gives the price of staples in many places: sugar, rice, bananas, cacao; the cost of *aguardiente, añil,* even of *coca.* He tells what he paid along the way for provisions such as mutton, chickens, and eggs. He reports the cost of passage from Lima to Puna; the hire of mules, canoes and *balsas*; the toll rates over bridges, causeways and *tarabitas*; freight rates on the Magdalena; the wages of oarsmen and guides; the salaries of officials and the income of priests. Going beyond such concrete details, he discusses the value of gold production, the decline in the mining of this metal, and the virtual cessation of silver mining. He investigates the volume of coinage at the mint in Bogotá and the methods of operation of this establishment. He comments on the effect of war on prices. He even theorizes on methods of fomenting commerce and on ways to increase the productions of minerals. Moreover he has important recommendations to make concerning the reduction of restrictions on trade and the appointment of *criollos* as administrative officials to deal with economic matters.

Akin to Don Miguel's preoccupation with economics was another of his qualities. He was imbued with at least a modicum of the eighteenth-century spirit of investigation. From time to time his curiosity led him to perform experiments of various kinds. His contemporary, Voltaire, might have mocked some of them, like those on the blood temperature of turtles. This "experiment" took the form of dipping his hands in the blood of some of these creatures at the moment when they were slaughtered. His conclusion was that their blood was of the same temperature as the water of the Magdalena River at the spot where the incident took place. This investigation was to be repeated on other occasions with tortoises and iguanas in order to test blood temperature under varying conditions and led him to a logical conclusion. Incidentally he gives as good a description of a *morrocoy* which was one of his subjects as Darwin was to do in the case of other fauna nearly a century later while on the voyage of the "Beagle." Having heard oral reports and seen published accounts that the water level in the bamboos bore a relationship to the moon and the tides, he carefully experiments on various sizes of these cut in different types of terrain and on series of the same size growing in the same place and concludes that the report is a *patraña*. His curiosity leads him to measure the dimensions of bridges and *tarabitas*. When he reaches the Piedra Pintada, near the Río de Aipe, he measures the size of the rocks, while one of his companions sketches the hieroglyphics chiseled in them.

The *Viaje muy puntual y curioso* is a methodical and sober journal which lacks the liveliness, the picaresque flavor, and the vivid descriptions of "Concolorcorvo's" account and has none of the amusing anecdotes like the latter's story of the "PPPP." Yet it gives a more realistic, objective, and at the same time more personal report of travel and other conditions in the regions through which the expedition passed. Taken together the two works complement each other in painting a fascinating picture of many aspects of the Spanish-speaking territories from Montevideo to Caracas in the colorful period of the eighteenth century.

THE SPANISH SOURCES OF PAUL SCARRON'S
JODELET DUELLISTE

by RAYMOND R. MACCURDY
University of New Mexico

Of the many seventeenth-century French dramatists who borrowed plots from Spanish *comedias* none was more flattering in his constancy than Paul Scarron, eight of whose nine full-length plays are known to be based on Spanish models.[1] Following the popular success of his first play, *Jodelet ou le maître valet* (1643), an adaptation of Francisco de Rojas Zorrilla's *Donde hay agravios no hay celos y amo criado* (1640), it was natural that Scarron should adhere to the same dramatic formula on writing his second play: a plot of complicated intrigue set in a Spanish background, with prominent roles for the servants so that the dramatist could give free rein to his talents for burlesque. It could also be expected that on writing the servants' parts Scarron would provide a special role for the actor Julien Bedeau (also known as Julien Lespy), who made such a hit in the earlier comedy and whose stage name, Jodelet, was incorporated in the title.

The first version of Scarron's second play, *Les trois Dorothées ou le Jodelet soufleté,* was performed at the Marais in 1645 but not printed until 1647.[2] Its complicated plot concerns the rivalry of four young men, Diègue, Félix, Juan and Gaspard, for the love of two sisters, Hélène and Lucie. Although Félix

---

[1] The only one of Scarron's plays which has not been traced to Spanish sources is *Le prince corsaire,* published posthumously in 1663.

[2] For editions of the play, see the bibliography in Emile Magne, *Scarron et son milieu* (Paris, 1924).

professes to be in love with Lucie, he has a mistress, Dorothée, by whom he has had two children. Lucie, who loves Diègue, appears in the guise of the abandoned Dorothée in order to discredit Félix in the eyes of her father who has favored his suit. Suffice it to say that Félix loses out, while Diègue wins his Lucie and Juan gets Hélène. Having little to do with the main action are the scenes involving the valets, Jodolet and Alphonse, who serve Dom Félix and Dom Diègue respectively. Jodolet insults Alphonse and is beaten by him, and later, when he seeks to avenge himself, he is beaten again.

Apparently dissatisfied with the first version of his comedy, Scarron rewrote sections of it and changed the title in 1651 to *Le Jodelet duelliste*. In the new form of the play, the roles of *suivantes*, Béatrix and Gillette, are combined into one; and Dom Juan is eliminated, his role being given to Gaspard, who wins Hélène. Above all, however, Scarron was concerned with giving sharper focus to the enemity of the two lackeys, Jodelet and Alphonse, whose antics provide much of the humor.

Professor Lancaster, who did so much to clarify the literary relations between France and Spain in the seventeenth century, has correctly identified two of the Spanish sources of *Jodelet duelliste*.[3] Scarron's principal source was Tirso de Molina's *No hay peor sordo*, from which he borrowed seventeen scenes. He also borrowed three scenes for his first act from Rojas Zorrilla's *La traición busca el castigo*, first printed in 1640 in the *Primera parte de las comedias de Don Francisco de Rojas Zorrilla*. Lancaster then states that seven scenes of *Jodelet duelliste* have no connection with either Tirso's or Rojas' play, and concludes that Scarron invented them.[4] These seven scenes have to do with the enemity of Jodelet and Alphonse which leads to a challenge to a duel. In short, these are the scenes which led Scarron to change the title of his play to *Le Jodelet duelliste*.

---

[3] Henry C. Lancaster, *A History of French Dramatic Literature in the Seventeenth Century* (Baltimore, 1929), Part II, Vol. II, p. 459. The play has also been studied by Ernest Martinenche, *La comedia espagnole en France de Hardy à Racine* (Paris, 1900), pp. 378-381, and by Paul Morillot, *Scarron et le genre burlesque* (Grenoble, 1888), pp. 279-284.

[4] Op. cit., p. 460.

The fact of the matter is that all these scenes derive from, or were suggested by three scenes in another of Rojas' plays, *No hay amigo para amigo*, which was also included in his *Primera parte* of 1640. In Scarron's play the initial encounter between Jodelet and Alphonse takes place in Act II, scene 2, when Alphonse comes to inquire about the lodgings of Don Félix. Jodelet, who is bantering with Béatrix, provokes him by answering his questions impudently, and Alphonse slaps him. Rather than take offense, Jodelet makes light of the matter, but after his offender leaves, he explains that he did not avenge himself because Alphonse is a stranger:

> Je suis jaloux d'honneur autant ou plus qu'un autre.
> Je suis un vrai démon lorsqu'il y va du nôtre,
> Et lorsque d'un soufflet il n'est venu charger,
> Si ce n'est que j'ai vu qu'il était étranger,
> Je n'aurais pas tourné la chose en raillerie... [5]

This scene derives from Act II of *No hay amigo para amigo* (which is not divided into scenes). Moscón is talking to the maid servant, Otañez, when Fernando arrives to inquire about the domicile of Don Lope, Moscón's master. When Moscón does not give him satisfactory answers, Fernando slaps him. Moscón admits, "Un poquito me he enojado," but when Fernando says that he will defend his act, Moscón offers to serve him.

Scarron then adds three scenes which have no exact counterpart in the Spanish play. In Act III, scene 1, Jodelet pronounces a monologue in which he resolves to avenge his outraged honor. In scene 2 the last part of his speech is overheard by Alphonse who confronts him, but Jodelet greets him as "cher ami" and assures him that his friendship will endure. Again in Act IV, scene 7, Jodelet pronounces another monologue in which he lets it be known that he has distributed cartels about the city challenging Alphonse to a duel, but his soliloquy concludes,

> Oh! qu'être homme d'honneur est une sotte chose,
> Et qu'un simple soufflet de grands ennuis nous cause!

---

[5] All quotations from *Jodelet duelliste* are from the edition of Edouard Fournier, Scarron. *Théâtre complet* (Paris, n. d.).

In the following scene (IV, 8) Don Félix scolds his servant for not having avenged his honor, and asks him how Alphonse struck him. Jodelet, who believes that actions are more effective than verbal explanations, slaps him. The similar scene (Act III, pp. 95-96) in *No hay amigo para amigo* is much longer, funnier, and more satirical of the follies of the gentleman's code of honor. Here, Moscón also slaps his master to show how Fernando had offended him. Then, persuaded by Don Lope that he has no alternative but to kill Fernando, Moscón says:

> Si por valor o por suerte,
> El me diera a mí la muerte,
> ¿Cuál quedará mejor puesto?...
> Pues por Dios, que si me mata
> Que me he de quejar de vos [6]

The most amusing scenes in both plays have to do with the preparations that the lackeys make for their duel. Moscón's resolution to avenge himself weakens when he reflects on the vulnerability of the human anatomy (Act III, pp. 98-99):

> Demos que a las hojas llego;
> Demos también que me dan,
> ¿Por qué parte me darán
> Que no haya responso luego?
> Ello hay heridas mortales
> En todas las ocasiones:
> El hígado, los riñones,
> Los muslos, los atabales,
> Un corazón, dos tetillas,
> En la boca un paladar,
> Y en el arca del cenar
> Treinta varas de morcillas;
> Dos sienes y dos orejas
> Cuatro lagartos después.
> Dos ojos, si no son tres,
> Toda una frente, dos cejas;
> Una garganta vacía,
> Todo un estómago abierto;

---

[6] The quotations from Rojas' *No hay amigo para amigo* are from the edition of R. Mesoneros Romanos, *Comedias escogidas de don Francisco de Rojas Zorrilla*, vol. 54 of the *Biblioteca de Autores Españoles* (Madrid, 1866).

> ¿Y con ser esto tan cierto,
> Hay quien riña cada día?

But Moscón screws up his courage and enacts a duel in which he takes both parts. It is needless to say that he "kills" his enemy.

Similarly in Scarron's play Jodelet has misgivings about the duel when he recalls the many parts of the body that are susceptible to injury (V, 1):

> Si tant d'endroits en nous peuvent être percés,
> Par où l'on peut aller parmi les trépassés?
> Le moindre coup au coeur est une sûre voie
> Pour aller chez les morts; il est ainsi du foie;
> Le rognon n'est pas sain, quand il est entr' ouvert;
> Le poumon n'agit point, quand il est découvert;
> Un artère coupé, Dieu! ce penser me tue,
> J'aimerais bien autant boire de la ciguë.
> Un oeil crevé, mon Dieu! que viens-je faire ici?
> Que je suis un franc sot de m'hasarder ainsi!
> Je n'aime point la mort, parce qu'elle est camuse...

Also, as in the Spanish play, Jodelet stages a duel in which he names all his thrusts. At this point Alphonse arrives, whereupon Jodelet explains that he was merely reciting lines of a play.

Both Moscón and Jodelet try to talk their way out of the duel, but each is confronted with the letter of challenge that he has written his adversary. The letters are quite similar, as may be seen from their beginnings: "Malas lenguas me han dicho que vuesa merced me ha dado un bofetón; yo no lo puedo creer de su cortesía..." (Act III, p. 99). And: "Quelques médisants disent que vous m'avez donné un soufflet: je ne puis croire cela de votre courtoisie" (V, 2). Both Moscón and Jodelet deny having written the letters but to no avail; they both receive another beating from their offenders.

In summary, the seven scenes which constitute the comic subplot of *Le Jodelet duelliste* and which Lancaster thought to be of Scarron's invention were based on, or suggested by, three scenes in Rojas Zorrilla's *No hay amigo para amigo*. In Rojas Scarron found a kindred spirit, one who was a master of burlesque and who, through the antics of cowardly servants, loved to poke fun at the follies of duelling and the code of honor.

LOPE DE VEGA'S *ARTE NUEVO DE HACER COMEDIAS*: POST-CENTENARY REFLECTIONS

by J. H. PARKER
University of Toronto

Recent Lope de Vega bibliography * attests to the continuing interest in the *Arte nuevo de hacer comedias en este tiempo,* a document which is worthy of even more intensive perusal. This *New Art,* we remember, was printed in 1609 in a volume of Lope's *Rimas,* but had been read, or recited, previously, as the complete title indicates, before "the Academy of Madrid." Both the exact date of composition and the literary group involved are somewhat uncertain. Miguel Romera-Navarro, over twenty years ago, stated (in *Hispanic Review,* IX, 1941) that it was his opinion that the Academy of Madrid was really the Academy of the Conde de Saldaña, in which Lope was active, and at which, on one occasion, Lope says in a letter, he borrowed Cervantes' glasses to read some poetry. (This reference has caused some controversy on the part of critics, because Cervantes is not generally believed to have worn spectacles.)

José Sánchez, in his monograph of 1961 on *Academias literarias del Siglo de Oro español,* thinks, however, that the Academy of Madrid was a separate entity, and that the *Arte nuevo* was presented by Lope to an academy bearing that name at the end of 1607 or at the beginning of 1608. The Sánchez arguments

---

* See, for example, José Simón Díaz and Juana de José Prades, *Lope de Vega: Nuevos estudios,* 1961; Parker and Fox (eds.), *Lope de Vega Studies 1937-1962: A Critical Survey and Annotated Bibliography,* 1964; and Raymond L. Grismer, *Bibliography of Lope de Vega,* Vol. I, 1965.

seem plausible, although there is a problem of date in that Lope refers to his *Jerusalén,* published in 1609. However, it is felt, as was the case so frequently at the time, that the epic poem was well known through circulation in manuscript some time before being printed; from 1605 on, says La Barrera, in his *Nueva biografía de Lope de Vega,* in the first volume of the Academy edition, of 1890.

The *Arte nuevo de hacer comedias en este tiempo* is a treatise in poetry of 389 hendecasyllabic lines, divided into a series of strophes in blank verse, each ending in a rhyming couplet. At times the composition shows Lope de Vega's poetic genius, with pleasing rhythm and fluidity of verse; other portions seem prosaic and bogged down with a show of erudition. The all-but-final ten lines are in Latin, as an ending flourish, as if to proclaim to the learned world that Lope was skilled in that language too.

In the first paragraph of the poetic treatise, Lope de Vega explains that he has been asked to present his ideas on dramatic theory and practice. And he hastens to do so, assuring those present that he is providing his "barbaric" ideas, fully aware of the "classical" rules and regulations. One wonders at this point what the constitution of the audience was. It is probable that there were a good many neo-Aristotelians present, and a good many of Lope's supporters too. But since all such details about the many academies and literary groups of the day seem to be unrecorded or lost in oblivion, we shall probably never know.

Throughout the poem, Lope leans heavily on the fourth-century commentaries of Terence by Donatus, on the Italian sixteenth-century preceptist, Robortello, and on other second-hand sources relating to Aristotle and Horace. The purpose of drama is "To imitate the actions of men and to paint the customs of the contemporary age"; and that is of course what Lope generally did in practice. The Lopean theatre, which is designated the *Comedia nueva,* was an idealized portrayal of the seventeenth-century Spaniard, made dramatic and intensified for stage purposes, but whether the play was one of contemporary life, or historical in its setting and background, the Spanish audience was seeing itself as it would like to be. This dating has made Lope de Vega, the dramatic poet of his times and of his native land, less appealing than some of his contemporaries to audiences in other countries and of later centuries.

Referring once again to an imitation of nature and of life, Lope goes on, in the *Arte Nuevo,* to insist that a mixture of tragedy and comedy is the proper thing, since variety brings great enjoyment, and Nature, after all, is beautiful because of her diverse aspects. This combination of *genres,* which is carried out in practice by Lope de Vega and his contemporaries, permits comic relief amid tense situations, and fitted in with the Spanish temperament of the day. But for a dyed-in-the-wool classicist of the later French school, it is one of the shocking characteristics of the Spanish Golden Age drama. The Spanish position, nevertheless, has often been defended, in many countries, for it is the old Italian saying that "Per molto variar Natura è bella" and the French that "La Nature ne fait rien que l'Art ne puisse imiter." This attitude leads naturally to a mingling of high and low, of kings and commoners, and to every conceivable combination which Life provides; in short, to a theatre similar to the English theatre of Lope's unknown contemporary, Shakespeare.

Lope de Vega advocates the unity of action, for he does warn against unrelated elements in plot: "Let the subject have one action only, taking care that the plot be in no way episodic." In practice, I belive, any good play must have that unity, and all of Lope's top plays certainly stand the test. Even though there may be a sub-plot present, or even more than one, there is a tying-together and unification into one whole to meet the restrictions of this canon, as Diego Marín showed in his study of *La intriga secundaria en el teatro de Lope de Vega* (1958). It might be argued that dramatic simplicity demands a one-plot treatment, but the use of a sub-plot does provide enrichment, which I have at times argued was put in for the entertainment and diversion of the popular audience of the day, when a deeper philosophical or psychological study was being attempted for a more cultured listener. However, modern critics of the *Comedia* have come to consider the blending of the various threads as an essential characteristic of Spanish baroque art, but I still question how conscious the baroque procedure was in the minds of the dramatists. I can, on the contrary, hear Lope de Vega reasoning to himself: "My main plot is too serious and too profound to hold the attention of everyone. I shall add another thread, which is connected, but which is lighter and more to the popular taste and inclination."

As far as the other two unities go, Lope de Vega, in the *Arte nuevo*, makes specific reference to the unity of time, confessing that "the period of one sun" is well known to him as being the injunction of Aristotle. Whether or not Lope believed this to be pure-Aristotle is hard to say, but in any event twentieth-century critics like Spingarn, Chaytor, and Romera-Navarro remind us that the only true Aristotelian unity was that of *interest* (or, in a certain sense, of action), and that the other two unities, of time and of place, were interpretations of the sixteenth-century Italian preceptists. Geraldi Cintio is credited with comment on the unity of time in mid-century, and Segni with fixing it at a maxium of twenty-four hours. Maggi has been granted the honour of evolving the unity of place shortly afterwards, and Castelvetro made good use of his predecessors, including Scaliger, to give definitive form to all three unities in 1570. In spite of these "shaky" origins of the unities of times and of place, the Aristotelian preceptists of Lope's day considered the unities to be inviolable rules, and bitter indeed were the quarrels arising therefrom. It is unfortunate that the critics of Lope de Vega's epoch did not have before them, for their enlightenment, Bernard Weinberg's monumental two-volume *History of Literary Criticism in the Italian Renaissance* (1961).

As far as the unity of place is concerned, however, Lope makes no specific reference to it, except that an enigmatic line alluding to a character's moving about, from place to place, seems to deal with that unity. In practice, of course, Lope did not worry about these two unities in his plays, but he did observe some moderation. As he states it in the *Arte nuevo*, the action is to take place in the least time possible, with long intervals occurring between acts, whenever feasible. Naturalness continues to be the dramatist's watchword in this connection; to make his plays as true to life as possible.

In the next paragraph of the *Arte nuevo*, there is a very strange recommendation: "The subject being chosen, write in *prose*." The critic Menéndez Pelayo believes this to be a carry-over of an injunction of an earlier preceptist, and states that Lope is giving a piece of advice which he himself never followed. Indeed, in writing the *comedias,* it is my opinion that prose did not intervene at all. That was not Lope's way of composing. An examination of the extant autographs reveals that while Lope de Vega frequently scratched out and re-wrote, he was always working in verse. He was too skilful and spontaneous a poet, I feel, to enter into the intermediary stage of prose. Subject to correction, I hold that Lope's intended meaning of "escriba en prosa" was certainly "write in verse," for that is what he did.

In the same connection, the Corominas *Diccionario crítico etimológico* contains an enlightening discussion of the word *prosa* in the old language, where there was a strange confusion of terminology. "Prosa" was used by Berceo and by Juan Ruiz for "verse", in a religious sense; and Luis C. Pérez and Federico Sánchez Escribano, in their *Afirmaciones de Lope de Vega sobre preceptiva dramática a base de cien comedias* (1961), state that "para Lope poca diferencia hay entre prosa y poesía." Here the authors are discussing the fact that letters often appear in the *Comedia* in prose, and that in *La dama boba* (Act I) there is a conversation between Nise and Celia regarding "poesía en prosa."

After this controversial point, there follows immediately in the *Arte nuevo* a very reasonable statement on the number of acts which a play should have. A *comedia* is to contain three: which gives the logical sequence of a beginning, a middle and an ending, for exposition, development, and conclusion. The history of the theatre in Spain throughout the sixteenth century, we recall, is one of evolution from the classical five acts recommended by Torres Naharro in the prologue to his collected works of 1517, through four as set down by Juan de la Cueva in his *Ejemplar poético* toward the end of the century, to the three acts which came into fashion in the early 1580's. In these lines of the *Arte nuevo,* Lope declares that he wrote plays in four acts at the age of eleven or twelve years—a statement not accepted by modern critics—which would be about 1573 or 1574; but it is worth while noting that only one play by Lope in four acts has been preserved, and that that one, *Los hechos de Garcilaso de la Vega y moro Tarfe,* has been dated by Morley and Bruerton (*Chronology,* 1940) as 1579?-83? It is a proven fact that Lope de Vega was singularly inaccurate about himself and his activities as he referred to them in later years; nor can too much credence be given to his first biographer, Juan Pérez de Montalván, writing in the *Fama póstuma,* in memory of his friend and mentor, in 1636. It complicates Lopean criticism no end that these firsthand accounts, which one would like to take as accurate and trustworthy, are often far from being so.

"Verisimilitude" is a norm which Lope advocates in the *Arte nuevo,* and one in which he catches the so-called classical spirit. Impossibilities, he says, should be avoided, and decorum, in every regard, should be observed. A king should speak with royal gravity, an old man with sententious modesty; lovers should express their feelings in moving terms; a woman's speech should not belie her name; and the lackey, the famous *gracioso* of the Golden Age theatre, should keep within his station. This likeness of truth, however, permits a wide interpretation, for things may appear, not necessarily as they are, but as they may be found to be.

A variety of verse forms, both native and Italianate, is strongly recommended; and the metre should be prudently chosen to suit the circumstances and the sentiment. The old medieval tradition was continuing, in the use of the octosyllabic line, and enrichment had come to Spain throughout the sixteenth century, with the innovations of Boscán and Garcilaso de la Vega through the use of the Italian hendecasyllabic line. *Décimas,* of the native 8-syllable length, are to be used for complaints; the sonnet, from Italy, is to be used by one who waits, for his soliloquy; ballad metre is to be employed for exposition and the recital of events which have occurred before the play begins, or off-stage; and octaves too serve well, says Lope, for this purpose. Tercets, the Italian *terza rima,* are to be used for serious matters, and *redondillas* are fine for the conversation of love. This is Lope's theory, and to a great extent his practice also (see Diego Marín's *Uso y función de la versificación dramática en Lope de Vega,* 1962), subject, of course, to changing tastes and preferences which evolved throughout the dramatist's career, and whose general principles permitted Morley and Bruerton, twenty-five years ago, to compose one of the most important monographs on Lope de Vega ever written (the *Chronology* of 1940). It is worth noting, as a general tendency, that as the seventeenth century progressed, the popularity of the Italian hendecasyllabic line, and of the native *redondilla* too, decreased, and the old, popular ballad line came more and more into vogue. This evolution, with its ups and downs, is so striking that the study of verse structure, by careful analysts, has led to very fertile and successful results, for authorship and chronology, in the case of almost all of the dramatists of the Spanish Golden Age.

As for the subject matter to be treated in a play, Lope de Vega, in the *Arte nuevo*, seizes upon the mainspring of all *Comedia* action: the honour theme. The seventeenth-century Spaniard's *pundonor* was highly developed, and Lope was stating the truth when he declared that problems of honour make good theatre because they deeply move everyone. It is difficult to find a Lope play, or indeed any play of the time in Spain, where the honour motif is lacking, or where it is not used as the source of action. Conjugal honour, interpreted in the wide sense of the husband protecting the family honour through the wife, or the father through the daughter, or the brother through the sister, is Lope's concern, and the concern too of most of his contemporaries. Sometimes, nevertheless, as we know very well in the case of Juan Ruiz de Alarcón, the honour dealt with is the honour of the gentleman.

The purpose of this theatre, according to Lope in his *Arte nuevo*, or at least the purpose which can be inferred from his constant references to the *vulgo*, his popular audience, is to entertain, to give pleasure. In spite of the contrary opinion firmly expressed by Pérez and Sánchez Escribano in the monograph cited above, it is my considered conclusion that there is no serious intention of instructing beyond the combination of enjoyment plus example-held-before-our-eyes, which may be taken to heart if one chooses. This *ensalzar deleitando* is as far as Lope de Vega ever cared to go. The crowd, he says, pays; the crowd should therefore be amused, and his is a *New Comedy* which will do that very thing. We are reminded of Roosevelt's *New*

Deal of the thirties; and of Vargas' and Salazar's *Estado novo* in Brazil and Portugal respectively. All were attempting to bring about something new, and, in their eyes, improved. Whatever may have been the intention, the success, or failure of the politicians, there is no doubt but that our man of letters succeeded in *his* New Deal to the point of establishing a national theatre which has been unsurpassed.

* * *

The literary polemic in which Lope de Vega was intervening with his *Arte nuevo de hacer comedias en este tiempo* was apparently bitter enough. Critics such as Menéndez Pelayo, Romera-Navarro, and Entrambasaguas, to hurriedly cover the twentieth century, have delved into this complicated problem. The old die-hards, of the neo-Aristotelian camp, were waging a losing battle, but not for that reason were the literary and personal enmities any the less. There seems to have been a great deal of fumbling and confusion at the time on both sides. It was an age of great cultural activity, but also one of concern and uncertainty regarding the principles of literary art, of criticism, and of taste. The authority of the past had been questioned for some time, and innovations were being introduced, but a decisive victory was still to be won.

The *Philosophia Antigua Poética,* by Alonso López Pinciano, which had been published in 1596 and which was the most faithful and learned commentary on Aristotle at the time in Spain, must have been on Lope's mind as he conceived the *Arte nuevo.* Both that treatise, and the *Tablas poéticas,* written in 1604 by Francisco Cascales, censured the "popular" theatre of the day, defended warmly and energetically the rules and regulations of the classics, as they interpreted them, lamented the contempt in which they were held, and recommended a speedy return to them. These poetics did not mention Lope de Vega by name, nor does he mention them, but they certainly must have had his ever-growing success before them. The critics who followed along in the "classical" camp, and poured forth their bitter sarcasm, both of a literary and personal nature, were above all those dramatists who had been put into eclipse by the all-popular Lopean *Comedia*. Their criticism, therefore, is usually not of a logical kind, but, coloured by their deep resentment, gives voice to their personal animosity and frustration. Cervantes, in his prologue to *Don Quixote*, is one of them; as he is also in the forty-eighth chapter of the first part of his famous novel where he denounces the stupidities of the Golden Age theatre of the Lope de Vega style; and again in his volume of 1615, where he is forced to publish his collection of eight plays and eight interludes, *never performed*.

Andrés Rey de Artieda, in his *Discursos*, Cristóbal de Mesa, in his *Epístolas*, filled with sharp barbs of irony and satire, Cristóbal Suárez de Figueroa, in his *Pasagero*, riddled with envy and jealousy—all these are only a few from the enemy camp, but among the most vociferous who, at the time of the *Arte nuevo*, or shortly after, uttered vilifications against the idol of the Spanish stage. And one of the most virulent attacks on Lope personally, and on his literary output, appeared, according to contemporary references, in 1617, with the *Spongia*, by one Pedro de Torres Rámila, the purpose of which was to erase all of Lope's writings from the face of the earth. The curious thing is that not one copy of this "eraser" is extant, for Lope's faithful followers, it seems, immediately sprang to his defence and destroyed every copy, manuscript or printed, in existence. In return, the defenders produced a vigorous reply, the *Expostulatio Spongiae* of 1618. Led by Francisco López de Aguilar, the contributors entered into a nasty personal attack on Torres Rámila and the other Aristotelians, and declared the superiority of Lope's theatre above any other, past or present.

In these charges and counter charges, it is impossible to separate the polemics in theatre from those in poetry in general. Góngora came up from Córdoba to Madrid in 1612 with his learned *Soledades* and *Polifemo*, and Lope de Vega immediately captained the plain-style camp against the obscure gongorists. In the *Arte nuevo*, Lope had already insisted that comic language should be free from rare words, and be pure, clear, easy, and taken from the usage of the people; and from *comedia* to *comedia* and prologue to prologue, he satirized "new" words and expressions,

Latinisms, and Italianisms, in his defence of the purity of the Spanish tongue against those who sought an enrichment to the point of incomprehension. "I do not wish to cast my pearls before swine," said Góngora, but it was this "swine," the common people, whom Lope loved and who gave him their homage and respect, as well as a full purse to provide him with the luxuries of daily life. And so the battle raged, throughout the years following the *Arte nuevo*, through the teens and twenties, and even after Góngora and Lope themselves had passed from the scene.

* * *

The best defence of the Lope system came from another leading dramatist, Tirso de Molina. A chapter in Tirso's *Cigarrales de Toledo*, a kind of Spanish *Decameron*, of the early twenties, stresses the fact that the verisimilitude advocated by Lope de Vega is adhered to in the *Comedia* in general, even though historical truth is frequently altered for the dramatists' purpose. Tirso insists that theatre is "living painting," and that the pen must be granted the same freedom of interpretation as the paint brush. Another point of criticism which Tirso meets very vigorously—one which was the constant source of complaint on the part of the Aristotelian preceptists—is the abovementioned question of the unities of time and place. Tirso's main defence for disregarding them is that Lope de Vega's New Comedy follows the usage of the day, with its modern ways and methods, and is superior to that which was written in the past. Tirso finds the "twenty-four-hours-or-less" rule to be artificial and unnatural, and to even sin against verisimiltude itself. How, in that period of time, he asks, can a young man fall in love with a young woman, pursue her and regale her, beginning his courtship in the morning and bringing about his marriage by evening? Tirso's mouth-piece, don Alejo, finds contemporary art so far superior to that of the past, that in the quarrel of the Ancients and Moderns, there is but one answer: Lope and his school are entirely in the right in disregarding and changing the outmoded ways of centuries gone by.

Other points which were covered by Lope de Vega in the *Arte nuevo* are repeated and stressed by Tirso de Molina in the *Cigarrales de Toledo*: persons of high and low rank are rightly mingled, tragedy and comedy are properly mixed; in short, if the excellences of the Greeks and Romans sufficed to establish the rules and regulations so bitterly defended by the Aristotelian die-hards, the Spaniards of the seventeenth century have a supreme authority for their way of writing plays; they have the excellence of their Spanish poetic leader, the honour of Madrid, Castille, and of the whole nation, the great Lope Félix de Vega Carpio, who has raised the *Comedia* to heights of perfection and subtlety and has formed his new, modern school, with its own rules and regulations, with its numerous pupils who are ever ready and happy to defend their master and his doctrine against anyone who may attack him or it. This indeed did seem to be the case, for the continuing protest of the Aristotelians became weaker and weaker, and although they did go on and on, as has been noted, during many years, they gradually became drowned, as far as the theatre was concerned, in the general shouting in favour of Lope de Vega, and in the defence of the artistic liberties for which he stood. Lope's prestige and his authority to cast aside the classical doctrines were recognized by his contemporaries, almost unanimously, except for the rarest, isolated voice.

Tirso's defence seems to sum up the position of dramatic criticism in Spain at the time when it was written ("aprobación", 1621), about fifteen years after Lope's *Arte nuevo*. Critics of the present century attest to that fact. Pedro Muñoz Peña, writing in 1889, says that it is perhaps the best and most valuable of dramatic treatises written in Spain in the seventeenth century, and calls it a brilliant defence of the dramatic system invented by Lope de Vega. For Menéndez Pelayo, it is the most brilliant and spirited treatise we know on the old theatre, and Menéndez Pidal agrees that it is a magnificent defence. Romera-Navarro declares it to be warm and resolute, well-grounded, brilliant, and filled with reasonable and plausible arguments. One critic, on the contrary, Alfred Morel-Fatio, who has given us a good edition of the *Arte nuevo* (in *Bulletin Hispanique*, III, 1901), has considered the Tirso defence to be over-rated. For him the Apology owes its reputation to Tirso's name, and to the vivacious style employed, rather than to the precision and profundity of its doctrine.

* * *

While the majority of modern critics have praised Tirso's defence of Lope's dramatic system to the skies, they have not been so generous toward our principal treatise, Lope de Vega's own *Arte nuevo de hacer comedias en este tiempo*. The two greatest Spanish critics of recent times, the late Marcelino Menéndez Pelayo, and the respected nonogenarian, Ramón Menéndez Pidal, are poles apart in their evaluation of the *New Art*. Branding it in his *Historia de las ideas estéticas en España*, written at the end of the nineteenth century, as a "lamentable palinodia," Menéndez Pelayo goes on to say that the *Arte nuevo* is the result of a position of doubt. From Lope's classical training and from his very different practice in drama, there arose, according to Menéndez Pelayo, a contradiction and affliction in spirit, which resulted in the "humble and dejected" critical position he assumed in writing the *Arte nuevo*. For Menéndez Pelayo, the treatise is "superficial and of little consequence, ambiguous and contradictory, always fluctuating between rules and practice." (This could be the dichotomy between intention and fulfilment which Alberto Porqueras Mayo found in many Spanish authors in his monograph on *El problema de la verdad poética en el Siglo de Oro*, 1961.) Lope de Vega, continues Menéndez Pelayo, seems to be blushing in shame as he contemplates what he has done theatrically in the light of what he should have done, excusing himself by reference to the harsh law of necessity, as if he had prostituted his art at the caprices of the popular audience, the *vulgo*, and at the same time boasting pedantically that he had Aristotle's *Poetics* and the *Commentaries* at his fingertips. "A sad and pitiful spectacle, concludes Menéndez Pelayo, in the greatest poet which Spain has produced!"

For Schevill (in *The Dramatic Art of Lope de Vega together with La dama boba*, 1918), the *Arte nuevo* is likewise "pedantic ill-combined material drawn from [Lope's] reading." But these destructive ideas are vigorously rejected by Menéndez Pidal, writing in the *Revista de Filología Española* (XXII, 1935) for the tercentenary of Lope's death. Menéndez Pidal looks upon the *Arte nuevo* as the decided and definitive statement of a new aesthetics. Here, insists Menéndez Pidal, is no vacillation; on the contrary, for him it is the firm expression of the artistic principles conceived by Lope in his youth, principles which guided him throughout the long voyage of his life against the wind and tide of Neo-Aristotelian preceptism. Menéndez Pidal's two main arguments for his position are based on the idea that those who take care to keep the rules (of the classics) never share in the riches of natural things. The first argument is that Modern man, man of seventeenth-century Spain, is tapping a new spring of aesthetic pleasure hidden to antiquity, as he mixes the high and the low, tragedy and comedy (Lope's variety of nature, which is, through its diversity, beautiful); and the second, that the pleasure or delight produced therefrom prevails against and overrides all rule and regulation. As the *Arte nuevo* affirms, rightly, taste (in the sense of pleasure or enjoyment) has its own norm which can be contrary to those of cold reason. "Dramatic poetry, concludes Menéndez Pidal, has been decisively drawn out from between the greasy leaves of the precepts, to be set, by Lope de Vega, in the midst of contemporary life."

* * *

For me the true value of Lope de Vega's *Arte nuevo de hacer comedias en este tiempo* resides somewhere between the two extremes expressed by Menéndez Pelayo and Menéndez Pidal. Lope de Vega was too independent of spirit and too successful as a dramatist to be writing a "lamentable palinode," a weak excuse, for what he was triumphantly doing, and had accomplished by that time: indeed "four hundred and eighty-three plays" (with one he had finished that week!), and "all of them," he boasts, except six (which have never been identified), "sinning against the classic art." It may be that Lope *was* indulging in "natural modesty," as his followers seemed to belive, and as Tirso de Molina puts it, when he referred to his theatre as a barbaric *genre*. But there is another possible explanation for this attitude, not attributable to the time, place or surrounding circumstances: and that is *literary tradition*. Inspired by a study of some of the prologues to the *commedie erudite* by Italian dramatists of the sixteenth century, I argue that herein are to be found, much stronger than any immediate influence, the forerunners of Lope's very way of approach to the Academy assembled to listen to him. There is no doubt but that Lope knew the Italian dramatists who preceded him, as did his contemporaries in Spain, and in their introductory remarks are to be found, as models for him, the same type of apparent apology. Ariosto, Della Porta, D'Ambra, Gianotti, Cecchi, and others, while stressing their profound admiration for the classics, refer to the innovations which they deem necessary in the light of the new social order and times. The same caution and prudence is theirs, as is Lope's, as they acknowledge, with questionable sincerity, their indebtedness to the Latin writers, profusely apologize for their presumptuousness, in varying from them, and plead for the kind indulgence and generosity of the critics. Yet, in spite of this, they argue that drama must conform to new times and conditions, (and after all, as we remember, even the "classical" Cervantes said in one of his later plays [*El rufián dichoso*] that "Los tiempos mudan las cosas / y perfeccionan las artes.") Yet at the very moment when these Italian dramatists of the sixteenth century are admitting that it is both preposterous and impudent for any author to try to be original, they are boasting that they are that, and that their innovations have made their plays superior to any written previously in classical times. And just as Lope's creation will be called a *Comedia nueva*, they too are dealing with and producing a "new comedy" (as Marvin T. Herrick has shown in his book on *Italian Comedy in the Renaissance,* 1960), and their idea often is that they are tired of the old art, for the "true art is to please and to delight."

Their apologetic tone, combined with the contrary spirit of originality, which the petty critics were trying to check by weighing every comedy upon the scales of the rigorous and fastidious neo-Aristotelian doctrines, is that of the Lope de Vega of the *Arte nuevo de hacer comedias en este tiempo*. It is my feeling that Lope de Vega was very close indeed in his ideas to these free-thinking Italians, as he was to the dramatic movements in his own country. It is my belief, too, that further research in comparative literature would strengthen the tie with the Italians and explain more fully the development of the Lopean *Comedia*. It does grow out of Lope's own innate dramatic genius: it is a synthesis of all that is best in Spanish drama before him, as is *Don Quixote* in the history of the novel; but it is something more: it is the appropriating of all that came to Lope's hand — digesting it, sifting it, and weighing it on the balance of what the modern, contemporary age required. The Lopean theatre was produced by a man who had a sense of humour, and it was with a twinkle in his eye and tongue in cheek that Lope made his concessive statements to the Aristotelian preceptists who were listening to him in a literary reunion on an unidentified day in an unidentified place in Madrid, the centre of Spain's early seventeenth-century culture.

While Menéndez Pelayo for his criticism of the *Arte nuevo* seizes upon the negative aspects of the treatise, or at least those parts which I look upon as being no more than the sour fruit of misguided literary tradition, Menéndez Pidal goes much too far in seeing in the *Arte nuevo* the wonderful expression of a new aesthetics. Menéndez Pidal is completely right in declaring that Lope recognized that times had changed and that the classic restrictions were outmoded, but to state that Lope's treatise is the dramatic embodiment of this idea is going beyond the truth. Lope admits that his pronouncement regarding drama as the mirror of life is of no originality with him; the important canon of verisimilitude had been frequently stated and restated in his time: it had been systematically expounded by Pinciano at the end of the sixteenth century and had already been referred to by Lope himself in 1604 in his *Peregrino en su patria*. Juan de la Cueva had stated some years before, in his *Ejemplar poético*, the Spaniards' acceptance of the mixing of tragedy and comedy and of the high and low, the disregard of the classical unities of time and place, and the advantage of varied metrical forms for various uses. Honour as an important motif had long been employed in Spain, and the division into three acts had been in vogue for about twenty-five years.

* * *

If then we strip Lope and his *Arte nuevo de hacer comedias en este tiempo* of credit for originality of statement, and blame him for a tongue-in-cheek apology for not doing what he might have done, or for doing what he should not have done, what in it is left to merit attention and consideration? What is its significance, after this dissection? As I see it, the answer lies in the fact that we have the rare example of a top practitioner within modern times laying down the format of the type of play in which he had been, and was continuing to be, extremely successful. The case, too, of a dramatist highly sensitive to the varying theories of drama in the world about him; a dramatist who had come to the conclusion that, after all, there was for him but *one* guiding principle: to please his audience — an audience which had a very good sense of theatre, and recognized what was suitable contemporary art. For Lope's theatre was a theatre written for immediate performance, without any or at most little thought of publication for posterity. The Lopean *Comedia* took the place of the movies, television and the popular stage of today. It delighted an audience which was ever in search of change.

Lope de Vega reveals in the *Arte nuevo* that besides knowing good theatrical structure, as we said before: three acts, the mixture of tragedy and comedy, etc., etc., he knew all the little tricks of the trade; and no doubt his *Arte nuevo* was an immediate chart and compass, as his plays themselves must have been, to the budding dramatists in his talented coterie. If, to hold the attention of his audience, he schemed too obviously, let us not forget the critical students and soldiers standing in the pit ever ready to throw vegetables or other objects if the fare was not to their taste. Lope emphasized what has since become a rule of thumb for thoughtful playwrights: do not leave an empty stage, for as he puts it, "the audience becomes restless and the play is unduly prolonged." Likewise he knew and pointed out that a masculine disguise could often be assumed by a woman character to entertain and intrigue the audience and to complicate and advance the plot. (The study of 1955, *La mujer vestida de hombre en el teatro español. Siglos XVI-XVII,* by Carmen Bravo-Villasante, on this very point, has revealed, through example after example, how often Lope took his own advice, and how profitable it was to others.)

Another trick of the trade advocated in the *Arte nuevo* was what Lope called "engañar con la verdad"; to speak with an ambiguous phrase or statement, which keeps the audience guessing and thus keeps the listeners' interest alive. The insertion of a little bit of satire and of wit served the same purpose. For Lope was not writing a dull drama for a polite audience. The people did not attend his plays because it was the *done* thing. He had to be, and was, a practical man of the theatre. Lope knew that he either had to please or be replaced. And so, for a period of at least fifty-five years, until his death in 1635, he continued to write a superior type of play.

Arnold G. Reichenberger, in his article on "The Uniqueness of the *Comedia*" (*Hispanic Review, XXVII*, 1959), has seen "the *comedia's* greatness" to lie "precisely in its being an unsurpassed instrument of self-expression of a people." "Compact and unitarian as their beliefs," he continues, "is their theater, the artistic re-creation of beliefs in dramatic form. The Spanish nation, united in its social and religious convictions, found its voice in Lope de Vega, this genius of conformity. The dramatic formula he created is just as sturdy, compact, and coherent as is the world his theater brings to the stage. Subject matter, plot structure, *galángracioso* parallelism, poetic imagery, versification of the *comedia* — all is the work of his genius. Its quick and general acceptance by his people is due to Lope's mysterious accord with the collective mentality of the people for whom he wrote."

* * *

To thoroughly comprehend the success and greatness of the Lopean theatre, one must understand the historical-cultural background of the age in which it was flourishing. One must likewise read the hundreds of plays which Lope de Vega has left us. Helpful clues to his purposes and practices may be found from time to time in his prologues, his letters, and in the plays themselves. But a necessary and important beginning is to scrutinize his declarations in the *Arte nuevo de hacer comedias en este tiempo*. In this document, which Brander Matthews in his introduction to the Brewster translation (1914) called "the chief Spanish example of an *Ars poetica,* as Boileau's *Art poétique* is the chief French example and Pope's *Essay on Criticism* is the chief English example," we have Lope de Vega's system, informally given like an after-dinner speech, as a guiding principle.

When all is said and done, Lope was his own justification. For to those who would scoff at his versified suggestions, his plays remain a living proof of their practical virtue. The dramatist's abilities were thoroughly recognized and appreciated during his lifetime, and the Spanish populace, we know very well, followed him and paid court to him. Indeed all good things came to be "things of Lope." A survey of Lope de Vega scholarship made at the time of the quadricentennial celebrations of 1962 was able to declare that such scholarship was "very much alive." The investigators involved found the dramatist "in the full bloom of a flourishing after-life." The Quadricentennial Year is now three years past, but we have not forgotten him!

CERVANTES AND THE *AMADIS* [1]

by EDWIN B. PLACE

Professor Emeritus, Northwestern University

Was Don Quixote merely crazy, or is Cervantes telling us that uncompromising idealists were so rare in the Spain of his time that a decadent and materialistic society would be bound to interpret the Knight's misplaced altruism in no other terms? Be that as it may, literary history is full of paradoxes. Miguel de Cervantes was a man of letters whose highest ambition was indisputably to win recognition as a writer; but nevertheless he permitted the Knight of La Mancha, in one of the latter's most lucid moments, to award the palm to the fighting man, the soldier, as the highest type of self-sacrificing member of society. [2] On the other hand, Cervantes informs us that he wrote the *Quijote* to destroy the prestige of the novels of chivalry, all of whom are concerned with fighting. The earlier commentators found it difficult to resolve this seeming contradiction. Even more paradoxically, the consensus latterly has come to be that the character of Don Quixote himself as it develops subsequent to the First Sally of Part I stems from that of Amadís de Gaula, and that much of the action of the novel is tinctured with motifs drawn from the *Amadis*, by far transcending that of a mere parody. Everybody of course recalls that the *Amadís* proper was saved from the bonfire of Don Quixote's library; whereas Book V, the *Esplandián*, which at least in

---

[1] Much of the material of this paper was originally presented in 1958 as a public lecture at the University of California (Berkeley) under the auspices of the department of Spanish and Portuguese.

[2] Parte I, Cap. xxxviii.

part was Montalvo's own creation, was condemned to the flames. And in Part II of the *Quijote,* when speaking of awarding the government of an *ínsula* to Sancho Panza, the Knight of the Rueful Countenance declares: "...sólo me guío por el ejemplo que me da el grande Amadís de Gaula..." [3]

The *Amadís* seems to have made its first appearance in the Iberian peninsula during the reign of Alfonso XI, who was king from 1312 to 1350, and who was the first Castilian monarch to popularize chivalric practices pertaining to knighthood. This first half of the fourteenth century was also, for the Peninsular literatures, a period in which there appeared reworkings in Spanish of Old French prose versions of the principal Arthurian themes as embodied in the so-called French Vulgate romances. One central figure of these romances is Lancelot; another is Tristan, already mistaken for a knight of the Round Table. The finespun code of courtly love, as it had evolved in Old French literature and in high society from the twelfth century on, is a leading motivation for the exploits of the Arthurian knights. This courtly love is often illicit, and the object of the hero's affections, in coincidence with Ovidian precepts, is most frequently a married woman. The hero himself, like King Arthur, is frequently of illegitimate birth. [4]

Without necessarily accepting Portuguese claims of primacy in the composition of Hispanic romances of chivalry of Arthurian provenance, it does appear probable that the original *Amadís,* now lost, which was in one or two books only, was written in a western Peninsular dialect, very possibly in Leonese, [5] by someone who evinced no compulsive urge whatever to introduce any nationalistic feeling or readily discernible reflection of local color, — into whose diction had filtered not a few syntactical gallicisms. Either this person, or someone back of him in the sequence of events

---

[3] I, 1(50).

[4] For statements in this paper concerning the *Amadís* not otherwise substantiated, see E. B. Place, "Fictional Evolution: the Old French Romances and the Primitive Amadís Reworked by Montalvo," *PMLA* LXXI (1956), 521-9, and the works therein cited; Place, "*Amadís of Gaul, Wales,* or *What?*" *HR* XXIII (1955), 99-107: Place's edition of *Amadís de Gaula* (CSIC, Madrid; T. I, 1959; T. II, 1962; T. III, as of February 1965, soon to come from the press; T. IV, in preparation.)

[5] See Place ed. of *Amadís,* II, Notas sobre el lenguaje.

attendant upon the composition of the work, was thoroughly familiar with the Arthurian prose romances in French as well as their Spanish reworkings, and levied heavily upon them. Whoever he was — and let us bear in mind that during the Middle Ages there were always foreigners at the courts and in the service of the various Hispanic kingdoms, as well as in that of the Church — the fact is that he composed an Arthurian type of romance whose chief deviation from the French concept of courtly love was to cause Amadís, while still a page boy at Languines' court, to conceive a violent passion for the daughter, not the wife, of King Lisuarte of Great Britain. This romance with Oriana is by no means platonic, its immorality being mitigated only by the traditional *palabra de casamiento* ultimately kept by the inflexibly faithful young hero.

But Amadís is much more than a faithful lover and brave knight. I have sought to show elsewhere that he embodies the seven cardinal virtues, that he wages war on the seven deadly sins, and indeed on the Devil himself; and that Books I and II of his life story are in fact a *disciplina regum,* as well as a plea for the mercenary foreign knight as a knight errant.[6] The exemplary quality of these two Books could not have failed to impress the author of the *Novelas ejemplares.*

During the latter part of the fourteenth century a third book was added to the *Amadís.* Recently there have been discovered in Spain and published by the distinguished bibliographer, Antonio Rodríguez Moñino, some fragments of an early fifteenth-century manuscript of this Book III, couched in a Spanish which displays Eastern Leonese traits. These fragments constitute the only known MS version of the *Amadís.*[7]

Shortly after 1492 Garci Rodríguez de Montalvo, an elderly alderman of Medina del Campo, finished reworking the three books of the *Amadís.* This fruit of his efforts was later published along with a fourth book. Soon thereafter there came from the press a fifth book, which he had already advertised throughout Books I to IV. The original Book III must have been very long,

---

[6] See ibid., III, Estudio Literario, passim.
[7] Cf. A. Rodríguez Moñino et al., *El primer manuscrito del Amadís de Gaula...* (Madrid, 1957), p. 31 ff.

since it necessarily covered the action of the work down to the death of Amadís in a duel with his son Esplandián, a *desenlace* first demonstrated by the late Professor María Lida de Malkiel.[8] Since Montalvo had to make wholesale changes as well as excisions in Book III, it appears on linguistic evidence that most of his Book IV and a portion of V (the *Esplandián*) consist of material salvaged from the primitive III. It seems somewhat evident also that the unknown author of this primitive Book III anticipates Montalvo's disapproval of courtly love and avowed dedication to militant Christianity.[9] But Montalvo knew the popular taste for Arthurian romances, so he mainly limited the expression of his disappoval to long moralizing interpolations until he had finished restyling the first three books. But in Book IV he hastened to arrange canonical marriages for each knight and his lady love, despite the longstanding upper class European convention that it was a grave social error to be in love with one's wife. Even Cervantes bears witness to the persistent belief that love matches were bound to turn out badly: in the *Casamiento engañoso* he puts such an opinion into the mouth of the Licenciate Peralta.[10]

Hence Montalvo gave new orientation to his own narration, following the lead of his inmediate predecessor, for in Book IV and its sequel these knights are assigned military adventures in the Near East which involve participation in wars against pagans. Of course, there is also the final rescue of King Lisuarte; and on the side the heroes are permitted to dispatch a few giants and other sinister characters. This love interest, so diluted by Montalvo, gives way completely to parody at the hands of Cervantes whenever it is a question of a potential love scene. Inevitably so, for not only had Montalvo grown old, but Cervantes, his creation Don Quixote, and even the latter's steed, Rocinante, are weighted down with years.

---

[8] In *RPh* VI (1953), 283 ff.; see also C. García de la Riega, *Literatura galaica, el Amadís de Gaula* (Madrid, 1909). p. 102 ff. For my arguments, see above, Note 6.

[9] See S. Gili Gaya, *BBMP* XXIII (1957), 103-11, and Montalvo's Prólogo. On the attitude of the author of Book III, see T. III of my ed., Estudio Literario.

[10] *Novelas ejemplares,* ed. Losada (Buenos Aires, n. d.), in 2 vols., II, 199.

The four-hundredth anniversary of Cervantes' birth occasioned the publication of a vast number of books and articles, thus greatly increasing the already large Cervantine bibliography. Among these anniversary books there is one by Padre Félix Olmedo entitled *El Amadís y el Quijote*.[11] Olmedo's professed admiration for the ideology of Montalvo's own (?) continuations of the *Amadís*, I am in the main unable to share, although I concede the latter's importance in literary and social history, and especially do I agree that the *Amadís* was a prime factor in the composition of the *Quijote*.

The chief stock-in-trade of literary criticism has always been the discovery of hidden meanings — often symbolic, sometimes truly transcendental. Such interpretations, in not a few cases where the author was still living, are known to have occasioned as much surprise for him as for the reading public. Pérez Galdós affords one example, Walt Whitman another.[12] One wonders whether Cervantes would call for a bonfire of Cervantine criticism. Latterly Jorge Mañach, in a book called *Examen del quijotismo*, has made a very discerning statement in explanation of the discovery by others of meanings in books unsuspected by their authors. He says: "Cualquier gran obra artística lleva en sí mucho más de lo que el autor deliberadamente pone... De ahí que una obra de mucha densidad creadora signifique casi siempre más para el lector o para el espectador que para quien la hizo."[13]

In modern times it appears that not many Hispanists read the *Amadís* except in excerpts. However a lot of other people do, for no less than twelve editions of it have been published since 1900 in Spain and Spanish America. In Cervantes' time the flood of continuations and imitations with their crusading, Near East orientation, had already slackened, perhaps partly because they lacked erotic love interest implicit in *el amor cortés artúrico*, and

---

[11] Madrid, 1947.

[12] Cf. the editorial treatment accorded Galdós's play *Electra*, as set forth by H. C. Berkowitz, *Galdós, Spanish Liberal Crusader* (Madison, Wis., 1948), p. 360 ff., in contrast to G.'s own recorded conception of his play. For a record of broadly differing interpretations of Whitman's poetry over the years, see C. B. Willard, *Whitman's American Fame* (Providence, R. I., 1950), passim.

[13] (Buenos Aires, 1950), p. 11.

also because of their increasing lack of realism in style and content. The last *edición antigua* of Books I-IV is of 1586, although translations continued to appear in Italy and England for another quarter-century. It is likely that the real reason why editions of Books I-IV ceased to be printed in Spain until more modern times was the steadily increasing clerical opposition, in the wake of the Spanish Counter Reformation, to its episodes of illicit love.

On the other hand, the work as a whole had already influenced profoundly the upper-class society of Spain and Portugal as well as that of other countries. I have shown elsewhere that its courtly speeches and pronouncements, especially those penned by Montalvo himself, taken as a whole constituted a manual of courtesy, replete with patterns for ethical and moral conduct couched in elegant phraseology. Collected into a book in sixteenth-century France, they alone — not to mention the many editions of Herberay's translation proper—ran through more editions in French translation than Castiglione's *Cortegiano* and della Casa's *Galateo* put together, and were an important factor in the improvement of upper-class deportment. [14]

In view of all this it is not surprising that Cervantes should praise and imitate the *Amadís*, though condemning its sequels. The *Amadís* is in so many respects admirable for its time that it is understandable why most modern critics are of the opinion that the *Quijote*, despite all its humor, basically advocates the chivalric ideals of the *Amadís*. The impact of the latter work on Spanish society unquestionably was from the outset a leading factor in the formation of an upper-class chivalric code — more honored perhaps in the breach than in the observance — whose sources, as time went on, quite naturally tended to be forgotten.

The author of the *Quijote*, a high-minded gentleman unduly buffeted by ill-fortune, could not fail to note the difficulty of maintaining ideals in a period of national maladministration and economic decadence. Launched on an amusing little tale inspired, according to Ramón Menéndez Pidal [15], by an anonymous six-

---

[14] See E. B. Place, "El *Amadís* de Montalvo como manual de cortesanía en Francia," *RFE* XXXVIII (1954), 151-69.

[15] In "Cervantes y la epopeya," *Homenaje a Cervantes*, edited by F. Sánchez Castañer (Valencia, 1950), p. 426 ff; and more especially "The

teenth-century *entremés* in which one Bártolo, a peasant, goes crazy from too much reading of ballads, and believes himself to be the French knight Baldovinos (Baudouin), he dispatches his protagonist on his first sally. Clearly this was a false start for anything more than slapstick humor. But fortunately Cervantes perceived immediately the enormously rich potential of his theme, were he to change his treatment of it. He decided to let his hero keep his own identity, mad only in the sense of believing himself the knight errant Don Quixote of La Mancha, anachronistically imbued with the ideals and following the behavior patterns of an Amadís of Gaul, including the use of an elevated style of oral discourse. He causes him to mingle most frequently with a middle and low-class society contrasting very unfavorably with that of the era of Carlos Quinto and the earlier years of Felipe II.

Thus we find Don Quixote striving to behave like Amadís. At this juncture let us recall that in the latter part of the fifteenth century the Hispanic Peninsula was already conscious of the Italian Renaissance and was reacting to humanistic concepts. At this time the ideal of the *uomo universale*, the composite of sage, courtier, diplomat and soldier was in process of formation. Whoever first reworked Book III of the *Amadís* shows some awareness of it. Montalvo of course feels its impact. Amadís in Montalvo's first known edition, that of Saragossa 1508, is represented not only as a knight who knows thoroughly every detail of combat with sword and lance, but as a linguist capable of speaking various languages, a poet, a singer who can play his own accompaniment, a strategist in the art of mass warfare, and as a diplomat possessed of rare skill in persuasion and command. He knows how to phrase a compliment and he is very witty. But it must be confessed that his greatest virtues are chivalric, just as his greatest weakness is his propensity to weep at the mere thought of his lady. At such times he is literally lovesick, in the most extreme medical and poetic tradition of the Middle Ages.

The composition of the *Amadís de Gaula*, including Montalvo's labors, precedes the vogue in Spain of Renaissance neo-

---

Genesis of Don Quixote", trans. by G. I. Dale, in *Cervantes Across the Centuries*, edited by A. Flores and M. J. Bernardete (New York, 1947), pp. 37-42.

Platonism; whereas Cervantes himself makes reference more than once to its great popularizing medium for the Peninsula, the *Dialoghi d'amore* of León Hebreo, first published in Italy between 1498 and 1502, and first translated into Spanish in 1568.[16] But Cervantes probably read this work in the 1590 translation of the Inca Garcilaso. That Don Quixote's love for Dulcinea should be of the platonic order—so genuinely platonic as to permit the highest idealization—eminently befitted a man of his advanced years. For Don Quixote Dulcinea is from the outset a poetic abstraction having nothing whatever to do with the ill-favored rustic female with breath smelling of garlic. Don Quijote himself explains all this, but attributes Dulcinea's lack of charm to the work of evil enchanters, just as he so explains many other clashes with reality.

This business of enchantments, spells, and the like is not so preposterous as it sounds to modern ears. The ancient and colorful Celtic beliefs in fairies, magicians and such, as elaborated in the Arthurian tales, had been early reinforced by all sorts of other superstitions, as well as by the contemporary Christian belief in evil spirits and in the ability of so-called witches and necromancers to invoke the aid of the devil—a belief which survived until the eighteenth century.

Of course to the ultra-sophisticated such notions were already nonsense, but in the popular fiction of Cervantes' time they could still serve as motivation acceptable to the *vulgo*. The operation of a kind of necromancing marvelous pervades the whole *Amadís*, with an endless struggle in progress between the good fairy and prophetess Urganda — represented in Book IV as a pious Christian! — and the evil Arcaláus. Small wonder, then, that Don Quixote should believe in enchantments.

The episode of the lions (*Don Quijote*, II, xvii) was initiated by the Mad Knight for the obvious purpose of emulating Amadís's daring in loosing two rampaging beasts from inside a castle.[17] In fact Don Quijote is even more valorous than the well-nigh invincible Amadís: little by little in Part II he gives

---

[16] By Juan Costa (Venice, 1568).
[17] Libro I, Cap. xxi.

evidence of a realistic awareness of his own physical insufficiency and of the difficulties posed by his environment; yet despite this, *he never hesitates to do combat.* In short, he becomes a doubly heroic figure, his heroism in adversity paralleling the reckless bravery of the sixteenth-century conquistadores and those who served under Don Juan of Austria at the crucial battle of Lepanto, among whom was Cervantes himself. Like many others, I believe that Cervantes was fully aware of the noble traits of character with which little by little he came to invest his knight errant. And it is likely that in his older years he had been deeply disturbed by reports of the occasional mutinies of Spanish troops, evidence of the increasingly low morale of the ill-maintained armed forces under inept leaders in lost causes. Cervantes, as has been said so many times, was not ridiculing chivalry. But it certainly does appear that he was ridiculing a government and a people which had abdicated the supremacy of the Western World won by its skill at arms. And more than this: in the *Quijote* he was seeking to edify as well as give pleasure. Cervantes was a Christian gentleman, his high principles forged by adversity, his faith almost entirely devoid of bigotry, and his loyalty to the crown unshaken by his dismay at what he had experienced and what he saw about him. He had known Italy when she was still deemed the fountain-head of letters and the arts; there he had fought in the most important naval battle of his younger years. He had suffered five years of captivity in Algiers, punctuated by dangerous attempts to escape. All his life he had read books with rare critical insight, in an age when, according to Américo Castro, books were as real as persons to their readers.[18] And always he had observed people, places, and remembered what he saw. Upon all these experiences he levied when he wrote the *Quijote,* which is peopled with characters who step out of other books as well as from real life, and even from tales interpolated, into the cognizance and companionship of Don Quixote and into the higher reality so peculiarly his. And yet to other characters less

---

[18] Cf. his "Incarnation in Don Quixote," in *Cervantes Across the Centuries,* pp. 160-61.

discerning they are merely ordinary people, such as runaway girls and youths, or galley slaves, or duennas, or even swineherds and prostitutes. And because in not a few instances they come to feel a liking and a respect for the Mad Knight, they are willing to leave their own plane of existence and dwell for short periods in his; thus enabling our knight errant to bridge the gap and restore his battered ego, while Sancho in the meantime could fill his own empty stomach.

The *Amadís* likewise presents a horde of characters of high and low degree in Books I to III, - this with frequent realism and occasional psychological insight. With relative equanimity these people view the magical happenings on the Insula Firme and the awe-inspiring machinations of Urganda and Arcaláus. But one reality suffices, for the age of chivalry was all-inclusive: even Montalvo could not abolish it entirely, despite his own attempts to intrude on the scene with disapproving monologues addressed to the reader. But he did not seek to identify himself with Amadís, as did Cervantes with Don Quixote in I, xlix; he barely succeeded in remolding Esplandián in his own image.

And now to summarize. In my view the first three books of the *Amadís,* especially I and II, present with considerable artistry chivalric ideals in large part rejected by continuators and imitators of the romance, whose works, by the same token and with few exceptions were bound ultimately to be forgotten. With these ideals in combination with the Renaissance notions of the well rounded gentleman, and the lofty concepts of Platonic love, Cervantes caused his hero to be imbued and by them to be motivated. Why did he do this? In my opinion the immortal novelist, after penning the first few chapters of Part I, sensed that here for the first time was at hand for him a God-given opportunity to shape into a masterpiece a lifetime's accumulation of aspirations, hopes, readings, experiences and disillusionments, seasoned with a humor born of sadness, often verging on the tragic, yet ever gay. Amadís de Gaula, Alonso Quijano alias Quijote, and Miguel de Cervantes Saavedra—by the latter's genius these three were fused into one man, Don Quixote, who so loved knight-errantry and felt himself so ennobled by it that he died when it was taken from him.

SOME BAROQUE REFLECTIONS OF THE GREEK ANTHOLOGY IN LOPE DE VEGA

by IRVING P. ROTHBERG
University of Massachusetts

Rich in the symbols, images and wit of classical culture, the epigrams of the Greek Anthology achieved their most notable vogue in Spain among the poets of the seventeenth century. The Anthology's influence was generally not a direct one; indeed, the Greek origin of Anthology themes was rarely acknowledged by the writers who worked them. The Spanish poets of that age were still able to manage Latin but, with the traditional exception of Quevedo, had no Greek. Like their opposite numbers in Italy the vernacular poets of Spain depended normally on Latin intermediaries.[1] Versions of the epigrams made by Ausonius and Alciati appear to have had the strongest appeal.[2]

Given a poet of Lope de Vega's prodigious dimensions, there is little wonder that a sampling of his non-dramatic verse and certain other works yields the best harvest of Anthology themes in the seventeenth century.[3] The intent of the present study

---

[1] See James Hutton, *The Greek Anthology in Italy to the Year 1800* (Cornell University, 1935), p. 49.

[2] Karl-Ludwig Selig's "Notes on Alciato in Spain" (Unpubl. diss., The University of Texas, 1955) is basic to an understanding of the influence of emblem literature in Spain, particularly in humanistic and didactic writing. There has been no systematic study of Ausonius in Spain, but one may refer to Menéndez Pelayo's *Bibliografía hispano-latina clásica* (Santander, 1950), I, 186-247.

[3] Limitations of space preclude discussion of the fifty reminiscences of the Anthology the writer has so far been able to single out in Lope.

is to isolate a few of these ancient motifs in Lope, to examine them within the baroque context Lope creates for them.

One of the better known themes is *A. P. (Anthologia Palatina)* 6.1, a dedicatory epigram ascribed to Plato. The epigram reads: "I, Lais, whose haughty beauty made mock of Greece, I who once had a swarm of young lovers at my doors, dedicate my mirror to Aphrodite, since I wish not to look on myself as I am, and cannot look on myself as I once was." [4] This epigram (with its polished antithesis) attracted many imitators in its long history—Ausonius and Alciati among them—but only an exiguous number of poets in Spain. There are imitations by Hurtado de Mendoza in the sixteenth century and one by Quevedo in the next. [5] Interest in the dedicatory epigrams, of which *A. P.* 6.1 is only one, is wanting in either century. Yet the pagan practice of dedicating an object of strong personal significance is not an unknown motif in Spanish poetry.

Not inappropriately, Lope provides the milieu of an allegorical temple for his version of the epigram, a curious atavism for a theme intended to be originally a literary exercise. Lope's adaptation occurs toward the last of *La Arcadia* in circumstances that are explicitly baroque. His shepherds have come for their final edification to "el templo santo del Desengaño." A white marble statue of "el Desengaño" dominates an array of additional allegorical figures: "la Hermosura," "la Vanagloria," and "el Amor." Hanging on the walls and columns of the temple are "algunas tablas" [6] dedicated by shepherds whom the visitors "conocieron por los nombres ser de amigos." Upon each plaque is painted a scene of symbolic value beneath which the pilgrims may read legends varying from two to four verses. Following is the setting in which Lope's rendition of the Lais theme appears:

---

[4] *The Greek Anthology*, trans. W. R. Paton (London, 1916-1918). This is the source of the four English translations used in this article.

[5] For Mendoza's version see *Biblioteca de autores españoles*, 32, 103; for Quevedo's, see his *Obras completas* (Madrid, 1960), II, 108.

[6] Covarrubias in the *Tesoro de la lengua castellana o española* (Riquer's edition, Barcelona, 1943) offers this in his gloss of *tabla*: "Llamamos tabla una pintura, por estar pintada en la tabla" (p. 949b).

Cerca tenia la suya [tabla] Tisandra, un tiempo pastora bellísima del Arcadia, y ya por larga edad desengañada del tiempo. Víase pintado un espejo sobre el altar del Desengaño, que con esta letra ofrecía:

> Por no ver lo que ya veo,
> Pues no veo lo que vi,
> Aqui os ofrezco y deseo
> Que se mire Silvio en mí.

Parece que habian estado esta pastora y el poeta Ausonio en un mismo pensamiento cuando él escribió aquella [sic] elegante epigrama y ella ofreció este espejo...[7]

It is something in the nature of a conditioned response on Lope's part to evoke the phrase "elegante epigrama" when one by Ausonius is in question. Lope's partiality to learned allusions conveniently reveals his intermediary, though neither conceptually or structurally can his treatment of the theme be said to resemble the Ausonian version which follows the Greek original.[8] In Lope the motif is obliged to harmonize with the pastoral design of the *Arcadia,* and the celebrated Lais exchanges her courtesan's robe for the tunic of the shepherdess Tisandra. Lais' new name and costume are attended by a transformation of character that, in the light of her long history, seems redemptive. The Alciatan emblem deriving from the Greek epigram is captioned "Tumulus Meretricis." It is in effect an epitaph teaching a lesson on *luxuria*. The Spaniard Mal Lara's commentary on this emblem adheres to the lines indicated by both Alciati and Ausonius: "Assi Lays Famosa Ramera de Corintho siendo ya vieja cõsagro su espejo a la Diosa Venus, segun lo trae Ausonio en sus Epigramas."[9] *A. P.* 6.1 displays more conceit

---

[7] *Biblioteca de autores españoles* (Madrid, 1950), 38, 134.

[8] Ausonius reads: "Lais anus Veneri speculum dico: dignum habeat se / aeterna aeternum forma ministerium. / at mihi nullus in hoc usus, quia cernere talem, / qualis sum, nolo, qualis eram, nequeo." *Ausonius* (Cambridge, Mass., 1961), II, 194.

[9] The emblem may be seen in Henry Green's edition, *Alciat's Emblems in their Full Stream* (London, 1871), p. 82. Mal Lara's commentary on the emblem is from *La philosophia vulgar de Ioan de Mal Lara* (Seville, 1568), X/45. See also Karl-Ludwig, "The Commentary of Juan de Mal Lara to Alciato's *Emblemata*," *Hispanic Review*, XXIV (1956), p. 36.

than it evokes imagery. In his version Lope stresses the visual. He has manifestly blunted the point of the original epigram, misplacing its *agudeza* and altering its spirit. The traditional Lais offers up her mirror to Aphrodite in the objective mood of resignation that characterizes the votary epigrams. Tisandra's act of dedication to "el Desengaño" is made prayerfully on a *quid pro quo* basis.

This incidence of the Lais theme is, of course, only a detail in the agglomeration of elements we know as *La Arcadia*. Still, its presence in "el templo del Desengaño" draws our attention to a unique development in the tradition of emblematic literature, the popularity of which there is no need to underscore here. Each of the *tablas* on view in that allegorical structure is essentially an *emblema* which Lope owes to the vogue of Alciati. When his shepherds have read the last of the plaques, Lope cannot forgo defining the kind of literary experience he has given the reader: "Era tanta la variedad de motes, tablas y empresas que fuera imposible referirlos" (p. 135). To his "monstrous accumulation of idealogical and poetical materials," in the apt phraseology of Avalle-Arce, [10] Lope has adjoined, then, a singular collection of *purely verbal* emblems. Within the *Arcadia* the emblems function not only as Lope's *deus ex machina*, but they add another dimension to the allegory of the temple. The effect they create is that of a baroque picture-within-a-picture. As one visualizes the shepherds contemplating the representations on the *tablas*, he may recall the mirror and picture devices in the paintings of Velázquez and, in particular, those of the allegorist Valdés Leal.

In the convergence of influences here, it is mildly ironic that Lope who knew Alciati surpassingly well should utilize the latter's mode but not his version of *A. P.* 6.1. He prefers, as we have seen, to recall Ausonius. In point of fact, however, Lope is pleased to cite Alciati whenever he can remember to do so. The frequency and quality of emblem influence on Lope bespeak an admiration for Alciati which is rather above the mere use of him as a learned source.

---

[10] Juan Bautista Avalle-Arce, "Lope de Vega and Cervantes," *The Texas Quarterly* (Spring, 1963), p. 193.

Certain of the Greek epigrams are descriptive comments on paintings, sculpture and other ancient *objets d'art*. Through Alciati's emblems they attain a type of circular existence. The emblems re-create, after a fashion, the work described by the epigrammatists. In Lope such epigrams are again in a verbal phase. "It follows," writes Mario Praz, "that between an emblem of Alciati and an epigram of the *Anthology* there is a difference only in name." [11] This applies comfortably, at least, to the epigrams on art, but for Lope's purposes a synonymous relationship between the emblems and the Greek epigrams does not really exist. The knowledgeable Lope never appears to be aware of Alciati's source for a given emblem. It is not excessive to suggest that Lope, a writer of seasoned dexterity in the manipulation of source books, knew the erudite commentators who had audited Alciati's substantial debt to the Anthology. This reticence is inconsistent with one of Lope's most persuasive characterizations: the rôle he creates for himself as a pedant unable to repress a learned allusion. It was perhaps inadmissible that a fount of wisdom like Alciati might be beholden to an earlier tradition.

In his story "Guzmán el Bravo," from *Novelas a Marcia Leonarda*, Lope makes reference to two emblems at the same time. These have to do with the prowess of the child Cupid and are based on the epigrams *A. P.* 9.221 and 16.250. The former reads: "I see upon the signet-ring Love, whom none can escape, driving a chariot drawn by mighty lions. One hand menaces their necks with the whip, the other guides the reins; about him is shed abundant bloom of grace. I shudder as I look on the destroyer of men, for he who can tame wild beasts will not show the least mercy to mortals." The latter epigram, a distich in the original Greek, follows: "See how winged Love is breaking the winged thunderbolt, showing that there is a fire stronger than fire." The two themes occur in this passage of Lope's *novela*:

> Descuidado de la fuerza y violencia de amor don Félix, y seguro de la fortuna en su patria, el que tan fuerte había

---

[11] Mario Praz, *Studies in Seventeenth-Century Imagery* (London, 1939), I, 21.

nacido y tanta libertad profesaba, se rindió a un niño, pero niño tan antiguo, que no se llevan él y el tiempo dos horas en tantos años. ¡*Qué bien pintó Alciato su fortaleza, ó ya enfrenando leones, ó ya rompiendo rayos*! [Italics mine]

> De los alíge[r]os rayos
> Rompe el amor el rigor,
> Porque es mas fuerte el amor. [12]

Reduced to its minimal idea this orotund paragraph would read: "Don Félix se enamoró." Yet taking Lope's style at its own baroque value, such a simplification would be beside the point. More concerned with the attributes of Love than with Don Félix, the paragraph is counterpoised to a preceding one delineating the gentleman's invincibility in feats of arms. His powers are necessarily unequal to those of the redoubtable boy who drives lions and smashes thunderbolts. The image of Cupid destroying thunderbolts is one which comes readily to Lope. His use of the motif parallels the number of imitations of it in Italy and France. [13]

Additional reminiscences of the two themes in a looser association may be seen in a lament of love sung by Menalca in the first book of *La Arcadia*. That Lope tends to repeat themes and ideas is evident here where the circumstances—not simply the reflection of the epigrams—recall those of Don Félix's capitulation to Cupid. Basically, both situations in Lope are reverberations of Cupid's triumph over Mars. Menalca's song in the *Arcadia* is a narrative of the encounter, challenge and humiliation of a "capitán valiente" (Menalca) by the "niño en la vista y en la voz gigante." There is an exchange of bravado between

---

[12] *BAE*, 38, 43.

[13] Hutton, op. cit., records four incidences of this theme in Italy (p. 644) and in his *The Greek Anthology in France* (Cornell University, 1946) he registers five versions (p. 800). In Act II of Lope's *Barlaan y Josafat*, vv. 985-989, one may read a clear reflection of it: "No en uano la antigüedad / quebrando rayos te pinta, / Amor, pues que no es distinta / tu deydad de la deydad / de Júpiter soberano, ..." The quotation is from the edition by José F. Montesinos (Madrid, 1935) who associates the reference with Alciati, but is unaware of its Anthology origin.

the two antagonists in which Cupid resorts to a modification of *A. P.* 16.250:

> Que el rayo mas furioso
> Se templa con mis flechas penetrantes,
> ....

Before his subjugation Menalca becomes aware of a phenomenon which is equivalent to the "abundant bloom of grace" described by the poet of *A. P.* 9.221:

> Así le replicaba,
> Cuando de entre unas hiedras
> Una hermosura celestial salía,
> ....

Menalca is swiftly disarmed. A triumphal chariot appears on the field, drawn not by the lions of the epigram and the emblem, but by tigers. Menalca suffers the cruelty—an embellishment in this instance—which the epigram only suggests:

> En esto al verde llano
> Un carro victorioso
> Dos tigres ya domésticos trajeron:
> ....
> Entre sus pies me ataron
> ....
> Llevándome cautivo
> Adonde agora lloro, muero y vivo
>   (pp. 53-54).

The sonnet form is generally thought to be the modern vernacular equivalent of the classical epigram. As a final example of Anthology influence on Lope we may cite a sonnet of his which derives ultimately from *A. P.* 9.12. The theme, which follows, was a popular one among Italian writers, and in Spain there is also a version by Quevedo.[14] "The blind beggar supported the lame one on his feet, and gained in return the help of the other's eyes. Thus the two incomplete beings fitted into each other to form one complete being, each supplying what the other lacked."

---

[14] Quevedo, p. 390.

Lope has this theme from Alciati, not especially as an emblem, but as an "epigramma." One observes that Lope (or perhaps a subsequent editor) fails to acknowledge Alciati, as Fucilla has already indicated.[15]

EPIGRAMMA.

Loripedem sublatum humeris fert, lumine captus:
Et socii haec oculis munera retribuit.

IMITACION

Llevaba un ciego al hombro los despojos
    de un cojo, cuyos ojos le guiaban,
    y andando y viendo, a un tiempo se prestaban,
    este al ciego los pies, y aquel los ojos.

Los dos de su fortuna los enojos
    con amistad reciproca templaban:
    los ojos con los pies del ciego andaban,
    y él trocaba los pies por los antojos.

Assi Firmio a Damon versos neutrales
    en su cerviz incognito dispone,
    y andan entrambos en un cuerpo iguales:

Que este le dá los libros que compone,
    y el otro la vergüenza de ser tales,
    que no sé qual mayor trabajo pone.[16]

The "epigramma" which Lope cites consists of only the initial two verses of Alciati's original four.[17] The first quartet of the sonnet is an adequate rendering of the theme, the second is gratuitous. The whole of the sonnet as an "imitación" requires a lenient interpretation. It is not, in its entirety, a *version* of the emblem or epigram made for the sake of its theme alone. The sonnet form is patently too ample a vessel for the substance of the original, and Lope, moreover, inspirits his "imita-

---

[15] Joseph G. Fucilla, "Concerning the Poetry of Lope de Vega," *Hispania*, XV (1932), 227.
[16] *Colección de las obras sueltas* (Madrid, 1776), I, 275.
[17] The last two verses follow: "Quo caret alteruter, concors sic praestat uterq[ue], / Mutuat hic oculos, mutuat ille pedes." Alciati, p. 173.

ción" with an altogether different sense. The Greek epigram suggests, as it were, the solution to a riddle: it is as if the epigrammatist had been asked to ponder how the lame might walk and the blind might see. The appeal of this theme for the Greek epigrammatists who versified it is the bizarre harmony —the "perfect whole," [18] one poet writes—achieved by two human beings of defective parts. Alciati's version teaches additionally the social value of "Mutuum Auxilium." While Lope prolongs the vogue of the reciprocity motif, his means and purposes are very particularly his own. The positive sense of reciprocity is vitiated, of course, by the antagonism Lope feels toward "Firmio" and "Damon." Too, the sonnet is divided against itself in a competition of ancient and contemporary themes. The sestet rather assuredly matches its own invention against the motif of the quartets. What results, then, is less an "imitación" than a satirical glance at two literary contemporaries of Lope's who have jointly elicited his contempt.

The four themes from the Greek Anthology reviewed here—a fraction of those that may be separated out of Lope's works—are helpful in establishing the character of this influence on him. The epigrams rarely are transmitted directly, but rather are filtered through Latin intermediaries like Ausonius and Alciati, as is the case in the influences studied in this article. Though one tends to speak in terms of "influence upon Lope," it would be just as well to think of him in a more active, independent rôle. He tends to adapt the themes to the variety of his invention, not to cultivate them for their own sake. Further study of Lope and the epigrams promises additional insights into a baroque relationship with a classical tradition. [19]

---

[18] The basis for Aliciati's emblem is the epigram cited, *A. P.* 9.12. There are, however, other versions of this subject in the Anthology. The expression "perfect whole" is drawn from *A. P.* 9.11.

[19] The writer is indebted to the Graduate Research Council of the University of Massachusetts for its generous support of the project of which this article is a segment.

CARA Y CRUZ DE LA NOVELÍSTICA GALDOSIANA*

by William H. Shoemaker
University of Illinois

De Galdós se ha creado, y aún durante su vida se creó una estereotipia de gran patriota (en los *Episodios Nacionales*), observador frío que reflejaba y describía la sociedad contemporánea, en quien elementos imaginativos y de fantasía escaseaban, inventor fecundo de tipos y personajes y de una obra total muy grande cuyo conjunto vale más que ninguna de sus partes. Además de muy incompleta, esta estereotipia falsea en aspectos muy importantes la caracterización de la obra de Galdós. Un ejemplo: Galdós sí inventaba tipos y personajes, pero lo que es mucho más importante, llegó a ser un verdadero creador de un gran número de caracteres, uno o varios en cada novela. Y aunque algunos individuos figuraban en dos o más novelas, como por ejemplo, Francisco Torquemada en diez, el padre de la familia Pez en nueve, y Milagros Botín, la Marquesa de Tellería en ocho, la verdad es que los protagonistas de las novelas, con muy contadas excepciones, aparecieron cada uno en una sola novela: así, Lázaro, Muriel, Doña Perfecta, Marianela, León Roch, Máximo Manso, Alejandro Miquis, José María Bueno de Guzmán, Fortunata, Angel Guerra, Tristana, Halma, Benina de Casia, Albrit, Casandra, Tarsis y Atenaida, para no nombrar más que uno —y el principal— en cada una de las novelas interesadas.[1] Así es que ningún protagonista

---

* En forma algo distinta, este tema fue elaborado en España mientras el autor disfrutaba beneficios de la American Philosophical Society y de la Comisión Fulbright, cuya ayuda acusa aquí con gusto y muy agradecido, y leído en El Ateneo de Madrid el 26 de noviembre de 1963.

[1] Es verdad que algunos de estos nombres se mencionan en otras novelas: Marianela en *El Doctor Centeno*, León Roch en *El Amigo Manso* y *Lo*

de éstos saca valores literarios u otros de un conjunto de obras porque no existe en más que una, a la que en cambio trae esos mismos valores que tenga. Si el conjunto vale y por contener unas creaciones imperecederas, será porque valen esas mismas creaciones, y cada una en su novela.

En este ensayo quiero tratar dos novelas —no precisamente porque los personajes de cada una no aparecieran en otras, aunque sí es verdad que esto no les pasó ni a los principales ni a los secundarios. Quiero comentar *Doña Perfecta* y *Misericordia* porque ilustran unas constantes galdosianas, pero aún más, dentro de las constantes, unas diferencias que marcan el desarrollo espiritual y novelístico experimentado por Galdós durante más de veinte años. No se trata aquí de trazar ese desarrollo, pero sí de llamar la atención a aspectos de las dos novelas en que se parecen y a otros que las diferencian. Estos aspectos son muchísimos —tantísimos, en efecto, que me he de limitar en este ensayo a algunos de tema y contenido, otros de actitud e intención o tendencia del autor, y varios de forma en cuanto a estructura y procedimientos— esto último casi nunca tocado por los críticos.

El tema de las dos novelas es religioso y cristianamente moral, pero con enfoques y acentos muy distintos.

En *Doña Perfecta,* el joven Pepe Rey, ingeniero madrileño, llega a la ciudad provincial y episcopal de Orbajosa para visitar a su tía *Doña Perfecta* y a la hija de ésta, su prima Rosario, con quien tanto su padre como su tía quieren que se case. Llega Doña Perfecta a creer, falsamente, por insinuaciones y hábiles tácticas del sacerdote Don Inocencio, su director espiritual, que su sobrino es ateo (que no lo es por su propia confesión), y que por consiguiente su hija no debe casarse con él. Se las compone para producirle a su sobrino un sinfín de obstáculos y molestias en forma de pleitos legales, prejuicios sociales, el no entregarle su correo, e incluso la destitución de su cargo profesional en unas minas hulleras cerca de la ciudad — todo para que se desanime y se marche de Orbajosa. Sin embargo, Pepe no se va, y por fin su tía le dice directa-

---

Prohibido, Máximo Manso en *La de Bringas* y *Angel Guerra,* Alejandro Miquis en *La Desheredada, Tormento, Fortunata y Jacinta* y *Angel Guerra,* pero los personajes mismos no aparecen, ni siquiera momentáneamente como figura, por ejemplo, Gloria, de niña, en *La de Bringas.*

mente que se vaya. Pero ya es tarde. Los jóvenes se han enamorado y se han prometido mutuamente para esposos. El amor lo puede y lo justifica todo, como siempre en Galdós. Pepe se niega a marcharse, se retira de la casa de Doña Perfecta, y espera, con la ayuda de las tropas del gobierno, poder libertar a Rosario y llevársela. Doña Perfecta, a pesar de haber inspirado a los caciques facciosos de la región a que rompieran la palabra dada al gobernador de no levantar la partida rebelde, tiene miedo, y cuando le avisan una noche que Pepe está en el jardín, ella, enfurecida, le grita a su leal y devoto cartero-guerrillero Caballuco: —Mátale. Así lo hace efectivamente. Y Galdós termina la novela escribiendo:

"Es cuanto por ahora podemos decir de las personas que parecen buenas y no lo son."

Se ve en la novela *Doña Perfecta* que la protagonista titular, que tiene fama entre los suyos de piedad, de beata, y de una acendrada fe católica, se deja llevar al pecado y al crimen por las malas indicaciones y direcciones de Don Inocencio y por la intolerancia de su propio fanatismo.

La novela *Doña Perfecta* pertenece a la juventud literaria de Galdós, a la llamada "primera época" de sus novelas sociales, y es en efecto la primera de ellas, publicada en cinco números de *La Revista de España* en 1876 y en forma de libro en el mes de abril de este último año. El novelista tenía a la sazón treinta y dos años de edad. Todavía no era Don Benito, sino sólo Galdós o con mucha frecuencia Pérez a secas.

La otra novela que voy a comentar aquí, *Misericordia*, se escribió veintiuno o veintidós años más tarde, se publicó en 1897, cerrando en realidad si no literalmente la serie de las llamadas "novelas españolas contemporáneas". Pertenece a la plena, la máxima madurez de Galdós como creador novelístico, cuando tenía cincuenta y cuatro años, y aunque es verdad que siguió escribiendo veinte años y cuarenta y tantas obras más, las novelas sociales ya escasean a partir del 97. Y de las pocas, ninguna merece ser colocada en el mismo nivel de calidad artística y literaria, con ninguna de las veintidós escritas en los años que separaban *Doña Perfecta* y *Misericordia*. Es decir, en efecto, que si aquélla dio principio al ciclo novelístico de Galdós en cuanto sea éste de índole social y realista, *Misericordia* casi lo acabó.

En *Misericordia,* la protagonista Benina de Casia es una vieja criada de sesenta años de edad en la casa de Doña Francisca Juárez, viuda de Zapata, señora de una antes acomodada familia andaluza, quien está en la época de esta novela, por sus descuidos, irresponsabilidades, y despilfarros, completamente sin fondos. Poco a poco pero irremisiblemente lo ha perdido todo, y la leal y cariñosa criada Benina la sostiene a ella y aun a sus dos hijos Antoñito y Obdulia, que viven fuera de la casa — económicamente muy mal casados. Los sostiene pidiendo limosnas, y para no ofender la dignidad y el amor propio de su ama, encubre la fuente de los pocos reales que puede traer a casa con el engaño de una explicación falsa, que es de que un cura, llamado Don Romualdo, le ha dado un pequeño empleo y le paga el poco trabajo que le hace. Benina socorre también a otros muy necesitados, notablemente a dos solterones. Uno de éstos es Don Francisco Ponte Delgado, un señorito contemporáneo de Doña Paca, venido tan a menos como ella, y admitido por ella a su casa cuando le falta alojamiento. El otro socorrido de Benina es el moro Almudena, ciego y fervoroso admirador de Benina, al que Doña Paca echa de la casa cuando Benina le trae enfermo y rendido de fuerzas. Un día la policía echa una redada y detienen a Benina, acompañada de Almudena, por mendigar en lugar prohibido y los encarcela en el Asilo Municipal de San Bernardino, de donde los trasladan después a un recogimiento de pobres que había en El Pardo. Durante esta ausencia, Doña Paca recibe una visita en la persona de un cura llamado Don Romualdo, que le trae una pequeña fortuna, herencia de un pariente recién fallecido en Andalucía. Cuando Benina vuelve, encuentra instalada en la casa a la nuera de Doña Paca, Juliana, quien le pasa un duro y la despide negándole la entrada. Doña Paca no contradice a su nuera, y Benina — incrédula, entristecida, y hasta amargada brevemente de tanta ingratitud, se va con Almudena, quien ahora tiene una sarna y un salpullido de que Juliana está segura es lepra. Pasa un mes, y viene Juliana en busca de Benina, para que venga a curar a sus niños que teme estén enfermos o vayan a estarlo, y desea la ayuda de la que ahora cree que es una santa. Benina le asegura que sus hijos sanarán, diciéndole las palabras con que termina la novela: "Vete a tu casa y no vuelvas a pecar."

Es evidente que *Misericordia* es también una novela religiosa. No figura la iglesia más que como lugar o escena —"lugar de la escena" según decía Clarín— en cuyos portales pordiosean las mendigas, compañeras y rivales de Benina; y en la novela no aparecen más curas que Don Romualdo, y ninguno como director espiritual de nadie. Sin embargo, la novela contiene, como dijo Menéndez y Pelayo, "ráfagas de cristianismo positivo." Pero también es evidente que el sentido de religiosidad es muy distinto al que se presentaba en *Doña Perfecta*. La primera novela fue una obra de ataque contra el clericalismo, la intolerancia, y el fanatismo, fue una novela demoledora, fue esencialmente una obra negativa. *Misericordia* en cambio es una novela afirmativa, de una persona humilde cuya vida personifica una caridad amorosa y cristiana, una vida de abnegaciones altruistas de un continuo sacrificio del propio yo. Las palabras concluyentes ya citadas de las dos novelas llevan bien patentes las dos actitudes de su autor.

En 1876 Galdós habla por sí mismo, como lo hacían Larra y Mesonero y los otros articulistas de costumbres de la generación anterior. Como ellos, Galdós explica verbalmente cuál ha sido su intención moral al escribir la novela que acaba de concluir. Dos decenios más tarde el novelista deja hablar a su protagonista misma, ya con palabras que quienes conocen el texto del Evangelio de San Lucas sabrán que son las mismas de Nuestro Señor, dirigidas a otra clase de pecadora, es verdad, pero pasadas ahora apropiadas a la boca de Benina. También, aunque es obvia su intención, Galdós la deja implícita para que el lector la infiera y la formule según la novela misma se la haya dado a entender. La diferencia entre las conclusiones de estas dos novelas de tema religioso que se acaba de apuntar representa una diferencia de actitud del autor que recorre enteramente los dos textos, pero que representa incluso una diferencia muy importante de método, de procedimientos, y de técnica novelísticos.

Pero antes de observar de cerca estos aspectos literarios, quiero hacer constar la honda humanidad de las dos protagonistas. Porque ni es Doña Perfecta enteramente mala ni Benina la bondad sin mancha. No son personificaciones abstractas ni siquiera increíblemente exageradas. Doña Perfecta no fue una hipócrita, aunque a menudo esto se ha dicho. Es verdad que escondía la mano al tratar de conseguir la marcha voluntaria de Pepe Rey de Orbajosa, pero cuando esos métodos indirectos no traían éxito, no dudó en declararse abiertamente para decirle a su sobrino que se fuera. Doña Perfecta fue una mujer de principios profundamente arraigados, en los que creía tan sincera como firmemente. Amaba a su hija aunque no tanto como a sus principios. Era más bien víctima de defectos suyos y de otros que influían malamente en su vida y en sus acciones. Asimismo, no fue Benina, aunque encarnaba lo que era para Galdós lo esencial, una cristiana perfecta. Tenía debilidades o defectos muy humanos. Víctima de larga costumbre, no podía dejar de sisarle dinero a su ama, aun cuando el origen de ese dinero venía a ser su propia persona. Por sisona había sido despedida por Doña Paca dos veces anteriormente al tiempo de la acción propia de la novela. Además de engañar a su ama, Benina fingió conformidad con la recomendación de Don Carlos Moreno Trujillo de que hiciera un presupuesto y llevara la contabilidad de sus ingresos y gastos. Don Carlos era un benefactor ocasional de Doña Paca por cierto parentesco familiar, pero como era muy avaro y mezquino, Benina le engañaba para poder sacarle unas cuantas pesetas más. Además, tan desesperada se veía la situación económica de la casa que Benina experimentaba dudas religiosas y se dejaba creer —supersticiosa y provisionalmente por lo menos— en un Dios subterráneo que le predicaba el ciego Almudena; según éste el Rey Samdai les traería oro y fortuna. Y, finalmente, cuando Doña Paca la echó de la casa, Benina no pudo reprimir un estallido de cólera y amargura que formuló en el grito, tres veces repetido, de "Ingrata".

Pasemos ahora a ciertas consideraciones de elementos formales de la novelística galdosiana, especialmente notables en estas dos obras. Si estas consideraciones tienen que ver a veces con el estilo, sépase de una vez que no me meto con el lenguaje de Galdós, muy censurado por algunos críticos sobre todo a partir del 98, siempre en términos generales, y nunca estudiado a fondo ni analizado detalladamente. Los hay que sostienen que el elemento canario, por ejemplo, se nota por toda la obra galdosiana, pero nadie se ha ocupado en explicarlo con referencia a una sola novela ni siquiera a un solo párrafo. No comento el estilo de *Doña Perfecta* y *Misericordia* porque me estimo francamente, no siendo español, sin competencia para hacerlo con la debida sensibilidad y aprecio. Lo único que diré a este respecto es una respuesta a los que decían y quizá sigan diciendo muy pintorescamente, es verdad, que el lenguaje de Galdós "huele a cocido", o su variante "huele a puchero". La respuesta es: Puede ser, pero será porque Galdós escribe de cocidos, de pucheros y de otras cosas caseras, callejeras, diarias y hasta rutinarias, casi siempre sencillas, vulgares, y humildes. Un estilo que representa bien, que corresponde bien al asunto a que se dedica, y no oliendo a otra cosa ajena por bonita y estética que ésta pueda ser en sí, ese será un estilo que obedece a las rigorosas reglas clásicas (moratinianas, digamos, en España) del decoro.

El escenario y el ambiente de *Doña Perfecta* y de *Misericordia* es la ciudad. No mencionaría esta perogrullada galdosiana, porque como se sabrá perfectamente, con excepción parcial de *Marianela* y de *Nazarín-Halma* no hay novela suya desde *Doña Perfecta* hasta *Misericordia* cuya acción pase en el campo y que en ellas no hay más paisaje que el urbano — ni la mencionaría, digo, si no fuera por apuntar sus características distintivas. Orbajosa es una ciudad provincial y episcopal, pero es imaginaria y sintética; en otras palabras, es una ciudad idealista que corresponde a un concepto que hubo de tener su creador — *urbs augusta* o orbe del ajo, su producto agrícola principal. Pero tanta verdad les parecía tener a los lectores de 1876 que buscaban, asidua y claro que frustradamente, en el mapa de España la población que correspondiera a las características y a la distancia de Madrid que Galdós pone en el primer capítulo cerca de un apeadero de ferrocarril entre ciertos kilómetros. Varias ciudades —una, según me acuerdo, era Soria, y otra, Burgo de Osma— fueron sugeridas. Y Galdós no sólo tuvo que declarar que había inventado Orbajosa sino que se creyó obligado a decir de Ficóbriga, ciudad en donde situó la acción de su próxima novela *Gloria,* que no figuraba más que en el *mapa moral* de España.

Pero Galdós era el novelista de Madrid. A partir de *La Familia de León Roch* sus novelas son madrileñas. Con la excepción de en dos tomos de *Angel Guerra* y en la parte principal de la pareja *Nazarín-Halma* Galdós no sale —novelísticamente— de Madrid. En *Misericordia* el fondo que Galdós presenta —de calles, de plazas, de iglesias desde la Plaza Mayor hacia la de Santa Ana y la del Ángel, las iglesias de San Sebastián y San Andrés, hasta la

Calle y el Paseo de Atocha y aun las Cambroneras a orillas del Manzanares;— este fondo era tan conocido al lector contemporáneo (de la capital, sobre todo) y constituía un ambiente tan exacto que prestaba su olor de realidad —por mera asociación y propincuidad— a lo puramente imaginado e imaginario. El lector de 1897 pudo seguir los pasos de Benina por esos barrios bajos muy fácilmente con su imaginación o en algún paseo si quería. Cuesta más trabajo ahora, como yo puedo certificar, por los cambios que en el transcurso de sesenta y ocho años han sufrido muchos edificios y algunas calles. Sin embargo, la técnica de especificar y de concretizar todavía nos convence de la exactitud descriptiva, externa, sensible del cuadro que Galdós presenta.

Ironía y símbolos son características persistentes de la novelística de Galdós, y ambas forman parte esencial de las dos novelas que comentamos ahora. En *Doña Perfecta* la idea temática más abstracta es la dicotomía entre ser y parecer. Antes de llegar al comentario final con lo de las personas que parecen buenas y no lo son, Galdós nos ha dejado ver muy a las claras la índole de esta trágica situación en los individuos y en la sociedad orbajosense. Pero muy temprano —ya en el segundo capítulo— nos prepara para la grande y última ironía con "un viaje por el corazón de España" (que es el título del capítulo). En este viaje que Pepe Rey hace a caballo para llegar desde el apeadero hasta la ciudad de Orbajosa, su compañero es un leal devoto de Doña Perfecta, a quien han apodado Tío Licurgo. Los jinetes pasan por unas tierras feas, desnudas y desoladas; sin embargo, tienen nombres bonitos como Valleameno, Villarrica, Valdeflores, Cerrillo de los Lirios, donde no hay amenidad, riqueza, flores ni lirios, Galdós observa por boca de Pepe y de su propia parte que la gente de ahí debe ver las cosas no con los ojos de la cara sino soñando.

Estos nombres de lugar y varios otros como los Alamillos de Bustamante y la Estancia de los Caballeros, donde habitan unos bandidos, son símbolos irónicos, como pronto ven los lectores que es el caso también de un gran número de nombres de persona. Doña Perfecta es algo menos que perfecta y Don Inocencio es todo lo contrario. Tío Licurgo es más tío que émulo del gran legislador griego y llega a ser pleitista implacable contra Pepe. Caballuco debe ese apodo suyo a su gran pericia como caballista. Monta a caballo con tanta belleza y velocidad que parece un centauro, pero más tarde se ve que la semejanza es irónicamente falsa cuando Galdós nos dice en otro contexto que se parece a los héroes épicos castellanos como el mulo al caballo. Así se ve que muchos nombres de lugar y de persona en *Doña Perfecta* son a la vez símbolos e ironías, que quedan explicados en el texto, y en seguida o pronto le resultan obvios al lector.

En *Misericordia*, en cambio, aunque el nombre de Benina de Casia llega pronto a corresponder al carácter de la vieja protagonista y a las imposibilidades de la causa que, como Santa Rita, aboga, no tiene nada de irónico. Asimismo los apodos carecen de ironía, y en ellos no se ve ninguna intención ni tendencia más que la de reflejar la costumbre popular de pegar remoquetes que hagan resaltar características destacadas de las personas. A la mendiga que manda en las puertas de San Sebastián la llamaban "la Caporala" y a una mujer borracha y diminuta, de nombre la Diega, la apodaban "cuarto de kilo." Estos no sirven más finalidades literarias que las de un realismo pintoresco y algo cómico.

Mucho más profundas son las ironías de *Misericordia*, cuyo título mismo significa la cualidad que le falta a la mayor parte de los personajes de la novela, cualidad que Galdós busca y que encarna en su protagonista Benina. Pero también Misericordia es el nombre de un Asilo de Pobres a donde varios personajes recomiendan que vaya Benina, la que en su propia vida personifica la misericordia, o sea, la que es la misericordia misma. La humorística ironía verbal se acerca al problema más profundo de cómo una puede serlo y no estar en ella, y comienza a acercarnos a otro tema importante de la novela, que es el de la verdad y la mentira, en que hemos de detenernos un poco más adelante y que no es más que otro aspecto del de ser y parecer de *Doña Perfecta* veintidós años antes.

De las varias ironías en *Misericordia* que no dependen de elementos lingüísticos sino que son de situación y de caracteres, quizá la más notable es la de la liberación de Benina del Asilo de El Pardo. Antoñito, el hijo de Doña Paca, había visto a Benina en el recogimiento de pobres, se lo dice como por casualidad a un compañero Polidura y a Ponte, y los tres se deciden a sacarla, dicen que mañana mismo. Pero no lo hacen tan pronto, pues sólo "el siguiente domingo" se realizó la misión, la cual se convirtió en una juerga de muchos individuos, Antonio y amigos en sendas bicicletas, Polidura y otros a pie, y Ponte a caballo. Lo primero que hacen al llegar a El Pardo es "almorzar gozosos." El rescate de los prisioneros es lo último que hacen después de días de tardanza y las horas dedicadas a comer, aunque se sabía antes por Antonio que Benina vivía descalza, hambrienta y "con los trapitos en jirones." La misión caritativa de los tan misericordiosos merece del autor la calificación de "aquella excursión alegre." Además, es cómica, y sumamente ridícula, en contraste con lo amargamente triste de la situación de Benina. Y las buenas intenciones de Ponte y los otros están contrapesadas con la tardanza, la negligencia y la despreocupación con que las llevan a cabo.

Otro aspecto muy persistente de la novelística de Galdós es su carácter dramático. Como se sabe muy bien, Galdós escribió, además de sus 31 novelas y 46 *Episodios Nacionales,* nada menos que 26 obras teatrales. Algunas piezas dramáticas, a lo menos dos de ellas, fueron escritas antes de que pusiera mano a la primera novela. No se representaron nunca, fueron rechazadas por los empresarios, y tardó Galdós veinticinco años en darle al público la primera representación de un drama suyo —*Realidad,* en 1892. Recuerdo esto ahora como indicación de esas tendencias suyas desde fecha muy temprana y para que no deba extrañarnos encontrar aspectos dramáticos en las novelas durante su cuarto de siglo de silencio teatral. Unas veintitantas obras de este período —novelas y Episodios— fueron adaptadas más tarde al teatro por varios autores, entre ellos Benavente y los hermanos Quintero e incluso siete por el mismo Galdós.

Una de estas siete fue *Doña Perfecta,* y era de las de más éxito sin duda porque la novela misma ya tenía un carácter y hasta una forma y estructura muy dramáticas.[2] Si lo esencial de lo dramático es lucha, conflicto —sea entre ideas o pasiones, sea entre intereses y prejuicios, sea entre personas, elementos sociales o nacionales— entonces *Doña Perfecta* posee lo esencial a partir del capítulo quinto hasta el asesinato de Pepe Rey. Ese capítulo temprano tiene el título: "¿Habrá desavenencia?" y lue-

---

[2] No quiero decir que la obra teatral siga técnicamente la estructura de la novela, porque en muchas partes y en el ordenamiento de las escenas no es así.

go, en una serie de doce y otros tres capítulos siguientes, sus títulos correspondientes marcan el desarrollo de la intensidad del conflicto desde desavenencia dudosa, después asegurada y crecida, pasando por discordia amenazada y luego evidente para llegar hasta batalla abierta, guerra, y combate terrible. Además, la forma y estructura de una lucha, un conflicto, es decir, un drama literario en el teatro, es necesariamente la de la agrupación de los personajes en la escena, o sea una serie de escenas o cuadros y la de un texto que tiene mucho diálogo y una cantidad limitada de elementos descriptivos, narrativos y explicativos. En las tablas un drama se desarrolla hablando y con un mínimo de acotaciones. Algo muy parecido ocurre en la novela *Doña Perfecta*. En como la mitad de la obra el escenario es o el comedor o el jardín de la casa de Doña Perfecta, donde los personajes principales y a veces otros secundarios se reúnen, y donde se desarrolla el drama entre Pepe y su tía.

En *Misericordia*, en cambio, se encuentra otra modalidad literaria, procedimientos superficialmente parecidos pero cuya finalidad esencial es muy distinta. No es *Misericordia* una novela esencialmente dramática. Es verdad que Benina vive en una lucha constante por la vida, por el pan diario, pero en esa lucha no sale ni vencida ni vencedora, ni es ésa la intención ni la dirección de la novela. Además, la acción pasa, no en pocos, sino en muchos escenarios distintos. Sin embargo, la inmensamente mayor parte del texto de la novela es el lenguaje del teatro, es decir, el diálogo de los personajes y otras formas relacionadas técnicamente al diálogo. Estas otras formas, muy frecuentes en *Misericordia*, son el monólogo y varias combinaciones de diálogo y monólogo de tercera persona o sean indirectos, y aún éstos dispuestos con trozos descriptivos, en que escribe el autor omnisciente intercambiando como quiera dos o más puntos de vista: el suyo y el de un personaje determinado. Galdós manejaba estas combinaciones con una habilidad extraordinaria en *Misericordia* y lamento no poder ahora desarrollar más este tema que merecerá algún día un estudio detenido y separado, porque Galdós no estrenó este procedimiento en *Misericordia* sino mucho antes; pero tampoco lo emplea en *Doña Perfecta*. Lo que nos importa aquí es que el diálogo y dichas formas análogas sirven principalmente para desarrollar no un drama sino un personaje, el carácter y la personalidad de Benina. Todas las escenitas, las pequeñas luchas cotidianas presentadas principalmente en estas formas son pasos, como ha dicho algún crítico, pasos en el camino de perfección de Benina, a quien Ponte llama un ángel y Juliana, por fin, una santa; son, como otro crítico ha procurado demostrar, una serie de pruebas de dificultad creciente que progresivamente experimenta la vieja Benina. Sea como sea, todos los elementos de la novela sirven para que sea Benina como es. En *Doña Perfecta* el diálogo revela y expresa la creciente, feroz y trágica lucha de un drama externo entre personas y gentes; en *Misericordia* el diálogo y las otras formas de ahí derivadas y refinadas presentan, tal vez el desarrollo, y seguramente el desenvolvimiento interno, del carácter de Benina.

Lo mismo ocurre con los personajes secundarios. En *Doña Perfecta*, casi todos se presentan en función de correligionarios de Don Inocencio y de Doña Perfecta, o como partidarios de Pepe Rey. En *Misericordia*, todos los otros personajes —los secundarios y aun los principales de Doña Paca y de Almudena— tienen la finalidad principal de hacer destacar los atributos y rasgos de carácter y personalidad de Benina. Don Carlos Moreno Trujillo, rico concuñado de Doña Paca desaparece por completo de la novela después del capítulo doce —la cuarta parte de la novela— al haber dejado bien e irónicamente claro el contraste entre su mezquina y calculada caridad de pesetas bien contadas y la de Benina, natural, espontánea y sin medida. De cada uno de hasta diez o doce de los personajes de *Misericordia* Galdós escribió un retrato descriptivo y explicativo. Estos retratos tienen el efecto también de hacer parar breve pero inevitablemente el movimiento del argumento de la novela. El empleo del retrato no es nada nuevo en *Misericodia*, pero en la novela de acción dramática que es *Doña Perfecta*, es un recurso muy poco usado, y con una sola excepción, el retrato es brevísimo.

Esa excepción es el retrato de María Remedios, sobrina de Don Inocencio, antes criada de Doña Perfecta, mujer social y financieramente ambiciosa, madre ambiciosísima por que su hijo Jacinto se case con la hija de Doña Perfecta. La presencia de Pepe Rey amenaza acabar con la posibilidad de realizar esa ambición. Cuando la situación llega a mostrarse violenta, su tío se lava las manos a lo Pilatos, pero la sobrina no. Galdós había presentado muy fragmentariamente a esta mujer en capítulos anteriores, dotándola con el irrisorio apodo de *Suspiritos,* de índole beatona y sospechadamente hipócrita. Pero ahora que la necesita para llevar la novela a su trágica y criminal conclusión, se encuentra en la necesidad de explicarla para que resulte creíble esa conclusión y también para que se vea que la terrible lucha no se fundara sólo, ni siquiera fundamentalmente, en diferencias ideológicas sino en deseos, pasiones e intereses muy humanos. Un papel parecido hace Juliana en *Misericordia.* El lector la conoce mejor que a María Remedios por un breve retrato que el autor le dedica anteriormente, pero Galdós se sirve de ella para llevar la novela a su conclusión, o sea para llevar a Benina a lo alto de su escala o al final de su camino. Por muchas que fueran las influencias y reminiscencias clásicas en la obra de Galdós, y desde luego que eran muchas, muy poco estudiadas hasta ahora, ninguna de estas dos mujeres —ni María Remedios ni Juliana— es una *dea ex machina,* como algunos han supuesto, por el mero y manifiesto hecho de haber sido presentada mucho antes y de quedar engranada íntegramente cada una en el desarrollo de su novela, aunque no se la veía con toda la fuerza de su interés y de su voluntad dominadora.

Desde hace tiempo muchos son los temas que se han pretendido ver en *Doña Perfecta*: que el gran conflicto ha sido entre la ciudad y el campo, o mejor dicho, entre la capital y la ciudad provincial; o que ha sido entre lo liberal, lo progresivo, lo nuevo de un lado y lo viejo, lo tradicional, lo reaccionario del otro; y hasta de la fe religiosa y sus mitos contra los conocimientos de la ciencia y por los métodos científicos. Creo yo que todas estas pretensiones pueden tener su verdad pero siempre como extensiones más o menos lógicas y válidas del tema central de ser y parecer que en su aspecto moral se ve en la lucha contra la intolerancia promovida por el fanatismo fomentado a su vez por un peligroso, pecaminoso y criminal clericalismo.

En *Misericordia* no ha habido tantas interpretaciones diversas del significado de la novela. Su tema principal es para todos la caridad cristiana hecha carne en una persona humilde y abnegada. Pero al lado de la presentación de este tema van relacionados otros del tipo del de ser y parecer en *Doña Perfecta,* que podríamos expresar como el de imaginación y realidad, o verdad y mentira. El ciego Almudena encuentra bella y joven a la fea y sesentona Benina; le ve el alma con los ojos del espíritu. ¿Cuál es la verdad? ¿Es fea o bella Benina? [3] Doña Paca sueña varias veces con una fortuna que le traen o que se encuentra escondida en la casa; cuando llega la noticia de la herencia, ella dice: 'Esto no puede ser; esto es un sueño.' Al lado de la práctica y positiva Nina, Galdós pone los románticos fantaseadores Ponte y Obdulia, quienes hablan de viajes, de lugares hermosos por lejanos, y de emperadores y emperatrices desconocidos, mientras Benina les prepara la comida que ha comprado con sus limosnas mendigadas. Almudena habla del Rey Samdai "de baixo terra" que le traerá oro y joyas; Benina no cree pero quiere creer, porque, como Sancho finge por codicia creer en la ínsula que le promete Don Quijote, parecidamente Benina se deja seducir por su grande necesidad.

Pero lo que más confunde y perturba a Benina es el problema de verdad y mentira encarnado en el personaje imaginado o inventado por ella misma con el nombre de Don Romualdo y en el de carne y hueso del mismo nombre y de parecidas facciones y atributos físicos que le trae a Doña Paca la fortunita. ¿Es una sola persona o son dos? Si es uno y otro, entonces, cómo hubiera dicho Unamuno, ¿cuál es el otro? Todo esto tiene su aspecto cómico, que, dicho sea de paso, falta mucho en *Doña Perfecta.* Galdós no da más respuesta a estas preguntas que las que andando andando Benina se da a sí misma. Después de la primera visita de Don Romualdo a su casa, cuando no estaban ni Doña Paca ni Benina, ésta sintió "que lo real y lo imaginario se revolvían y entrelazaban en su cerebro"; después de la segunda visita infructuosa, Benina "tenía... un espantoso lío en la cabeza." Más tarde "llegó al mayor grado de confusión y vértigo de su mente", tanto que pensaba en ir a buscar a Don Ro-

---

[3] Piénsese en la muy distinta resolución positivista que había dado Galdós a este problema hacía diez y nueve años en *Marianela,* de que tampoco renegó nunca, que yo sepa, sino todo lo contrario, para que nos demos cuenta de que muchas ideas con sus variantes y con sus contradicciones aparentes han cabido en el pensamiento de don Benito.

mualdo "para pedirle perdón por haberle inventado." Cuando vuelve de El Pardo y la enteran de la herencia, Galdós nos relata en monólogo de tercera persona en que adopta el punto de vista psicológico de Benina: "¡Vaya con don Romualdo! Le había inventado ella, y de los senos obscuros de la invención salía persona de verdad, haciendo milagros..." Pero su veredicto último es una humorística reconciliación: "Ya estoy segura, después de mucho cavilar, que no es el Don Romualdo que yo inventé, sino otro que se parece a él como se parecen dos gotas de agua."

Para concluir vale llamar la atención en cómo concuerdan o dejan de concordar las dos novelas con los teóricos "ismos" literarios del día. *Doña Perfecta* se escribió en los primeros años del realismo en la novela moderna española. Contribuyó mayormente al desarrollo español de ese realismo. Fruto de una actitud aparentemente objetiva y observadora de la vida contemporánea, *Doña Perfecta* presenta una gran cantidad de detalles de tipos, costumbres y modos de ser cuya gran totalidad anonada y convence, de su propio peso, al lector. Excepto que se le deja transparentar a veces la actitud idealista del yo del autor, esta novela corresponde a estos y otros criterios del realismo. Pero hacia el final Galdós deja ver bien a las claras sus dudas y su propia desconfianza en uno de los métodos más empleados por los realistas — es decir, los comentarios de un observador y testigo diario de la vida. Me refiero a las cartas de Don Cayetano Polentinos, historiador de Orbajosa y hermano político de Doña Perfecta que vive en su misma casa. En estas cartas se ve que Don Cayetano no sabe lo que pasó ni se da verdadera cuenta de nada. Podría bien ser esto una sátira que Galdós hace del tipo de cronista local que saca verdades de los documentos históricos y no ve lo que tiene delante de las narices. Pero también es seguramente un rechazo del método realista de observaciones objetivas que años más tarde Galdós presenta en la novela *La Incógnita,* cuyo fracaso metódico en la busca de la verdad, él mismo reconoce y corrige en seguida con la novela *Realidad.*

En los veintidós años transcurridos entre *Doña Perfecta* y *Misericordia,* Galdós y ciertos contemporáneos suyos habían sufrido la influencia del naturalismo francés de Taine y Zola. En *Misericordia* vemos en las descripciones de la pobretería, la abyecta miseria y suciedad en que pasa su siempre hambrienta vida, claras continuaciones de esa dedicación naturalista a lo feo, lo fétido, lo enfermo y lo nauseabundo. Como Don Quijote en Sierra Morena, Almudena hace penitencia por su amada, pero ya "en un vertedero de escorias, cascote y basuras" por las Cambroneras, "en medio de una aridez absoluta..." Y a ese contrahecho Quijote le apedrean unos gitanos, como los galeotes al ingenioso hidalgo. En esto va acompañado de su Sancho de Benina si no es ésta más bien lazarillo de ciego, como en casa de Doña Paca no es solamente criada sino sustento de su ama como lo había sido Lazarillo de Tormes con la uña de vaca para su amo el escudero. Pero si en el naturalismo, tales fealdades son la consecuencia ineludible del determinismo ambiental o hereditario, aquí en *Misericordia* falta lo principal, porque dentro de tal ambiente que no pudiera producirla de sí, sale una flor de alma de las más hermosas creadas en la literatura, un rechazo directo y sublime de las pretensiones del naturalismo.

En años recientes se ha hecho frecuente y hasta popular, tanto en la ciencia como en la literatura, el estudio de la psicosomatía, o sea la influencia de factores psíquicos en el estado o la salud del cuerpo. En esta extensión obvia del naturalismo primicial, Galdós, sin ser necesariamente original, se ha adelantado bastante en varios casos novelísticos, entre los que *Doña Perfecta* y *Misericordia* nos dan ejemplos de su cara y cruz. Después del crimen del asesinato, Doña Perfecta sufre un cambio de color de su tez que amarillece notablemente. Don Cayetano, que da la noticia, no sabe la causa del malestar de su cuñada, pero el lector, mejor enterado, cree firmemente que se debe a la conciencia perturbada de la señora y el sentido del mal que la había poseído. Igualmente Juliana, al poco tiempo de haber rechazado de casa a Benina, de haberla negado (con resonancias evangélicas), empieza a sufrir insomnios, pérdida del apetito, temores vagos, melancolías y la medrosa convicción de que sus hijos enfermaban a menos que Benina le afirmara lo contrario, porque, como decía, "lo digo claro: yo he pecado, yo soy mala."

Y aquí, dejando todavía en el tintero mucho más de lo sacado, termino este comentario de la cara y la cruz de la novelística de Galdós sin haber podido concluir —naturalmente— cuál es cara y cuál cruz.

THE CHARACTER OF DON JUAN OF *EL BURLADOR DE SEVILLA*

by GERALD E. WADE
Vanderbilt University

If measured by its progeny in world literature, *El burlador de Sevilla y convidado de piedra* is the most important play of all time.[1] Surprisingly, no book of criticism has been written about the play; one may contrast *Hamlet*, for example, about which many volumes and thousands of pages have been composed. It is true that numerous editions have been made of the *Burlador* (and none of them really adequate), and certain things have been said about some of its aspects, especially its possible sources. But the paucity of material is striking for such an important play, and the lack of commentary will surely be remedied as scholars begin to appreciate better the drama's supreme significance.

One element of the *Burlador* that demands careful consideration is the character of Don Juan. Again, surprisingly, there has been little comment on this most important element of the play. The present brief paper is an effort to remedy this lack. In the space permitted we shall have opportunity only to approach Don

---

[1] We choose to base what we shall say here on the *Burlador de Sevilla* rather than on the first version of the play, *Tan largo me lo fiáis*, that initially gave the definitive Don Juan figure to the world. Actually, the Don Juan of *Tan largo* is fundamentally the same character as in the *Burlador*, and since the latter version is much the better known to scholars, it seems preferable to use it for our present purpose. (For the relationship between the two versions of the play, see Wade and Mayberry in the *Bulletin of the Comediantes*, XIV, No. 1 [Spring, 1962] and also María Rosa Lida de Malkiel in the *Hispanic Review*, XXX, 275-295.)

Juan in the most elementary way, to delineate his character as this is offered directly by the lines of the play itself. We shall recall those words and passages that describe his actions, hear his utterances about himself, examine the passages that tell us about him as others remark on his actions. What we shall hope to compile is a set of statements on which scholars may agree and on which subsequent comment of a less elementary nature may be based. Lest the reader regard our effort as trivial — since we shall often make statements about what seems to be obvious — we may perhaps be permitted the reminder that this is a necessary task that has demanded doing for a long time.

We shall attempt to make our delineation of Don Juan's character as *descriptive* as possible. We shall therefore try to keep at a minimum an *explanation* of the character, for explanation—indeed a necessary, and a standard, procedure in criticism but one that may not always be based on verifiable *facts* within the play — is likely to be more open to controversy than is description. Most of all we shall try avoid *evaluation,* for this procedure — again a very effective one as a major approach to literature — is not as elementary and fundamental as is needed for this first systematic assessment of Don Juan's character.[2] We shall assume that our interpretation of those words, lines and stanzas that help to describe his character is not too far from their original meaning to have reasonable adequacy for the twentieth-century reader, even though it is realized that the meaning we now attach to the play's language can never be exactly that which the author and his contemporaries understood by it.[3]

---

[2] We find it desirable to base our procedure partly on that explicated by Morris Weitz in his *Hamlet and the Philosophy of Literary Criticism* (Chicago, 1964). Professor Weitz, whether or not he succeeds in convincing scholars of the validity of his approach to literature, is at least to be commended for his effort to order the philosophy of criticism so that scholars may criticize on a more meaningful basis. In passing, our own previous comment on Don Juan's character is quite different from that which we are making in the present article. See our "Camus' Absurd Don Juan," *Romance Notes*, I, 85-91, for an interpretation of the Don Juan figure of the *Burlador* in the light of Camus' delineation of his "absurd" type of man.

[3] If the reader is skeptical of the thesis that our contemporary understanding of the language of the seventeenth century and of the mind that

Our first task, then, is to examine those lines in which Don Juan's character is given direct elucidation by word or deed. These passages reveal first of all that Don Juan did certain things, committed certain deeds that are facts of the play and hence offer a minimum of danger for misinterpretation. It is entirely obvious, for example, that Don Juan did seduce Isabela and Tisbea, that he tried unsuccessfully to seduce Ana and then killed her father when the latter intervened at her call against the attempted seduction. He betrayed Aminta, first having driven off her *novio* Batricio by threatening him and by lying to him about a previous intimate relationship with Aminta. He met the ghostly statue of Don Gonzalo twice for interviews and was killed by the statue's handclasp as a punishment by heaven.

These very important facts of the action, and without which there would indeed be no play, are clear enough, but their bald recital gives little hint at Don Juan's character except the obvious conclusion (and here we must for a moment have recourse to *explanation* rather than description) that as a seducer and murderer he is driven presumably by whatever motives and impulses seducers and murderers are moved to do what they do. These motives might of course have an attempt at an elucidation at this point without examining the play's lines in detail for data, but, to repeat, it is our aim to seek out all possible help from the lines before drawing conclusions about the protagonist's character, conclusions that we hope scholars may accept as accurate according to the *facts* of the play. That is, we should like to offer conclusions that are open to the least possible debate. This will of course hold true not only for the action that involves the seductions but also for the action surrounding Don Juan's interviews with Don Gonzalo and the young libertine's punishment.

It is convenient to begin with the fundamental facts of Don Juan's identity. He is Don Juan Tenorio (I, 577-578; II, 668), son of the *camarero mayor* of King Alfonso de Castilla (I, 570-

---

produced it is to a degree incomprehensible to us, he may find it profitable to consult Professor Weitz's book in those portions where it is shown that critics of *Hamlet* have found it impossible to agree on just how the Elizabethan mind approached its thought material. See also my "Interpretation of the *Comedia*," *Bulletin of the Comediantes*, XI, No. 1, Spring, 1959.

571; II, 697-698). The father's name is Diego, as numerous lines of the play make clear (although the name is implied as being Juan rather than Diego at II, 669, where the error of the *Burlador's* reviser from the earlier *Tan largo* version of the play is amusingly manifest). Don Diego, by virtue of his high office, is "el dueño de la justicia, / y es la privanza del rey," as Don Juan reminds Catalinón at III, 164-165. (See also III, 238-242, 330.) The Tenorio family, which includes Don Juan's uncle Don Pedro (whom we meet at the beginning of the play in Naples), is of noble ancestry; "antiguos ganadores de Sevilla," as Don Juan tells Aminta (III, 237-238).

Tisbea recognizes in Don Juan his status as an *hidalgo* (I, 667), a status made clear repeatedly, and so plain a fact of the play as to make unnecessary further references to substantiate it. Only a gentleman, in the meaning of the term at that time, could be given the title of *conde* granted him by the King (III, 328, 760-761). He is very much of the inner circle at the court, for King Alfonso, before he learns of Don Juan's multiple crimes, refers to him (III, 777-778) as an "gentilhombre de mi cámara,... y hechura mía." The King's willingness to favor Don Juan (again until he learns of his many crimes), is based on his great liking for Don Diego; see II, 12, 20-21; III, 705-707.

Don Juan, then, is of the select inner circle, in favor with Alfonso until his exceptionally scandalous and criminal conduct causes even the King as well as the boy's own father to decide that he must be punished—and with death. (The King's decision is at III, 1021-1022, and Don Diego's concurrence in the immediately following lines.) Until destruction falls upon him during his second interview with the statue (at III, 969-970), Don Juan refuses to belive that he will be punished by the law or, until on some far off day, by heaven. His conviction on this score is voiced repeatedly throughout the play. He considers secular punishment as very improbable because of his father's power in the court, and because of the father's unwillingness to punish a son (III, 164-165). He is even so bold as to return to Sevilla against Alfonso's orders (III, 175-176); the latter had exiled him to Lebrija (II, 386-419), the town of which he is to be made *conde*.

Thus Don Juan is what we should today call an incorrigible youth, a perhaps not-so-juvenile delinquent. (We are never told his age, but this is perhaps less than twenty; we recall the *mocedades* of Pedro Girón, later the famous duque de Osuna, when he was still in his 'teens.) That he belongs to a social circle whose men are likely to bear a bad name is indicated by the remark of Aminta at III, 131-132: "La desvergüenza en España / se ha hecho caballería." A further indication of this is made clear by the long conversation between Don Juan and Mota in II, 154-213; here, one of the favored pursuits of our two young gentlemen is seen to be whoring, and Mota's exploits in the same passage betray him as the wenching trickster of Don Juan's own stripe. (Cf. also the intrusion of the name of Don Pedro de Esquivel at line 207 of the passage; Don Pedro is obviously another young blood of their own kind.) It is also clear that the exploits of the type preferred by Don Juan are looked upon with disapproval by other members of the court circles both in Italy and in Spain. Don Pedro in Italy is shocked by his nephew's seduction of Isabela (I, 81-93), just as he had been upset by the boy's previous exploit with the unnamed lady of reference above. The King of Naples is greatly concerned at the action of Isabela and her lover at the beginning of the play; in Spain, Don Juan's father tries unsuccessfully to get him to mend his ways (II, 378-425), [4] while King Alfonso, at first indulgent

---

[4] There is an interesting passage at II, 40-44, where Don Juan's father Don Diego is speaking:

> ...aunque mozo, gallardo y valeroso,
> y le llaman los mozos de su tiempo
> el Héctor de Sevilla, porque ha hecho
> tantas y tan extrañas mocedades,
> la razón puede mucho.

The last line indicates the father's hope that reason may yet induce his wayward son to mend his ways; his had been a type of conduct that involves the "extrañas mocedades" that cause other young men to name him after the much-admired Trojan hero Hector, usually pictured, as is Don Juan in the play, as "mozo, gallardo y valeroso." We are not told what the *extrañas mocedades* were, but it is quite certain that they were concerned mostly with *burlas* of the type perpetrated by Don Juan in the play. One of these would be the adventure with an unnamed lady referred to in I, 77-80.

toward the youth whom he so far considers only wayward (even though he calls Don Juan's exploit in Naples an "atrevimiento temerario" at II, 8) is, as we have seen, determined on his severe punishment at the end of the play. Even Catalinón, largely although not completely inured to his master's delinquency, expresses his dismay as also his conviction that Don Juan is making sure for himself of the severe punishment that is to be the inevitable reward for such conduct. (Catalinón's expressions of his belief, inspired at times by his fear for himself as an accomplice in his master's crimes, hay be read at I, 901-903; II, 308-314; III, 166-174, 178-181.)

That Don Juan has a clear knowledge that he is violating both secular and divine law is a fact of the play. That he is perverse as moralists define the term is also a fact. We have already seen that he depends on his father's influence at court to avoid castigation by the King, while his scorn at the idea of heavenly punishment is revealed in the famous refrain, "¡*Qué* (or *tan*) *largo me lo fiáis!*"[5] This exclamation occurs nine times in the play (at I, 904, 944, 960; II, 405; III, 120, 473, 585, 601, 940), and its expression leaves no room for doubting Don Juan's satirical and cynical rejection of the idea that his misdeeds may receive punishment at any early date. He does believe in the idea orthodox for his time that one will be punished eventually for evil-doing; we recall his desperate plea for confession and absolution at III, 966-967. But to him it is quite incredible until his very last moment that it is he who can be punished, and moreover by a special dispensation of heaven. (The fact of his punishment by God's decision is made clear by the statue's pronouncement in lines 952-958 of the third Act.)

Thus it is a fact of the play that Don Juan is perverse, and this in accordance with his own ideas of what perversity is; that is, a deliberate flouting of civilized custom, of statute law and of the moralistic bases on which his society rests. He is intensely evil, as he himself of course knows. Not that he ever uses this term to himself, however. It is not a desire for evil for its

---

[5] This exclamation has more detailed comment in our "*El burlador de Sevilla*: Some Annotations," *Hispania*, XLVII, 751.

own sake that drives him; he is not first of all deliberately satanic in his perversity, even though Catalinón refers to him as Lucifer at II, 729. Rather, it is the pleasurable fruits of his evil that seduce him (is he not first of all the hedonist?), and he prefers to seek out the *burla* for the titillation it provides his (to us) grotesque and cruel sense of humor rather than the sexual pleasure of the love trysts.[6] Hence our recollection of his own words at the beginning of this study:

> Sevilla a voces me llama
> *el Burlador,* y el mayor
> gusto que en mí puede haber
> es burlar una mujer
> y dejalla sin honor.

If these words are not sufficient to betray him as first of all the *burlador,* the trickster, rather than the relatively uncomplicated and merely sensual lover driven only by his lust, let us recall other lines to help clarify the point. At I, 891-894, in answer to Catalinón's query whether he plans to seduce Tisbea, Don Juan replies,

> Si burlar
> es hábito antiguo mío,
> ¿qué me preguntas, sabiendo
> mi condición?

Again, he savors in advance his conquest of Ana: "Ya de la burla me río" (II, 301). And, enjoying in acticipation his deceiving of Aminta, he exclaims: "La burla más escogida / de todas ha de ser ésta" (III, 160-161). A little later, when he enters Aminta's bedroom and she looks at him at first surely with eyes of

---

[6] As Eric Bentley has it (*The Life of the Drama,* New York, 1964, p. 50), although his reference is to Molière's Don Juan rather than to the *Burlador*'s, "his seductions are not displays of sensuality but of technique." Oscar Mandel, in *The Theater of Don Juan* (University of Nebraska Press, Lincoln, 1963), proposes (p. 16) that Don Juan is first of all the sensualist. For the figure in its evolution subsequent to the *Burlador* this may indeed be true, but for our *burlador* it is not quite accurate.

disbelief and then with increasing fright, he prolongs the pleasure of his trickery by exclaiming,

Mira
despacio, Aminta, quién soy.

(It is at the end of this scene where he refers to himself in an aside as "el Burlador de Sevilla.") The word *burla* comes out again as the predominat element of the Aminta exploit, for at III, 812 Octavio recognizes Don Juan's conduct with her as a *burla*. When Catalinón calls him "El Burlador de España," his master replies, "Tú me has dado gentil nombre." (II, 445). Again, when Catalinón, preceding his master's attempt at the seduction of Ana, asks him, "¿Dónde vamos?" (II, 500), Don Juan responds, "adonde la burla mía / ejecute," and a line further along he exclaims, "El trueque adoro." The *trueque* refers to his exchange of cloaks with Mota so as to betray him as well as Ana, a joke that is to be double; that is, not only sexual but *cuernal*:

CATALINÓN. Echaste la capa al toro.
D. JUAN   No, el toro me echó la capa.

(The same kind of double *burla* is of course directly involved in three of his four exploits, for with Isabela he deceives Octavio, with the abortive attempt to seduce Ana he plans to betray Mota, and with Aminta he batrays Batricio. The joke at Batricio's expense concerns also Don Juan's mocking his rustic table manners: III, 17-42. Only with Tisbea is there no direct involvement of a deceived male.) Even as death stalks him unbeknownst to him— for he is soon to have the first of his two fateful interviews with the statue—he savors his deceit of Aminta: "Graciosa burla será" (III, 441).

Having, then, seen what Don Juan thinks of himself and his actions as the *burlador* and as the lover (but this latter only secondarily to the other), we might examine the words of some of the other characters about him. Catalinón refers to him as "castigo de las mujeres" (I, 895), as "el gran Burlador de España" (II, 236), as "langosta de las mujeres" (II, 436), and describes in this passage the omnivorous quality of his sexuality (exercised habitually as an expression of his love of the *burla* even though the passage lacks the word):

> Fuerza al turco, fuerza al scita,
> al persa y al garamante,
> al gallego, al troglodita,
> al alemán y al japón,
> al sastre con la agujita
> de oro en la mano, imitando
> contino a la *Blanca niña*.
>   (III, 186-193) [7]

His pursuit of sex wherewith to perpetrate his *burlas* is accented by his conduct with Mota at II, 154-205, where the two exchange notes on the courtesans of Sevilla. Thus although Mota's words with Don Juan help to characterize the latter only as a gentleman, a friend and a boon companion in sexual exploits, their *actions* do indeed speak louder than Mota's words. Again, in his social intercourse with Octavio and Mota in II, 106-377, 466-506, Don Juan is the suave and courteous *caballero* whose demeanor leaves nothing to be desired, but Catalinón characterizes him in his *burlas* as "cruel" (II, 164), and the term is quite acceptable for the four seductions in which Don Juan becomes involved. For his attitude toward the courtesans he and Mota talk about, "cruel" is admirably descriptive, since, among other matters, it concerns the heartless *perros muertos* of II, 206-213, 483-497. Don Juan's attitude toward his father as Don Diego urges him to mend his ways (II, 378-425) is obviously one of impatience at the older man's insistence on a more moral type of conduct, and it also involves again a contemptuous disregard of what to the reader is seen to be heaven's warning to him to change his ways before it is too late. When he decides to re-enter Sevilla against the King's orders, his attitude is insolent in the extreme; his

---

[7] We are quite doubtful that Catalinón's words are to be taken literally as an indication of homosexuality on his master's part. There is nothing else of this nature in the play. There is indeed an unsavory passage of similar kind at II, 334-337, but we take this passage, as we prefer to take that at III, 186-193, as Catalinón's greatly exaggerated way of commenting on his master's excessive sexual energy.

decision (one soon to be carried out) startles even Catalinón, used to his extremes (III, 175-177).

Commentators on the Don Juan world figure have made much of his personal valor, which shrinks from facing nothing, not even the evident danger of hell's punishment. This courage is often mentioned as the trait that more than any other makes him admirable to those who like him. (The other most admired trait is his insistence on personal freedom against all restraint, whether of this world of the next. Commentators, however, are careful not directly to base their praise of this drive for personal freedon on his sadism and his animalistic urge to mate with all possible females.) Let us see whether the *Burlador's* Don Juan has this personal courage.

It is apparent that the maximum of courage is shown when Don Juan faces the statue, for he of course recognizes it as supernatural. (The servants are extremely fearful at the apparition, thus accentuating their master's valor.) Having faced the ordeal of the first interview unflinchingly (cf., for example, III, 548-550, 634-639, 645-647), and having promised the statue to visit him the next day in his chapel, Don Juan then confesses (664-675) that he has been greatly afraid: "se me hiela el corazón." Thus he exhibits what we often are told is the height of courage: having felt and confessed his fear, he overcomes it and reassures himself of his own valor (676-687), resolved to keep the second appointment with the statue. It is a part of his courage to be the exhibitionist: "por que se admire y espante / Sevilla de mi valor." He has been the exhibitionist all along, as we have seen a number of times when he confesses to his pleasure at having been known as the *burlador* of Sevilla and indeed of all Spain.

Don Juan does keep his second appointment with the statue, having suppressed his fear and having brushed off Catalinón's remonstrances; he feels, for one thing, that his gentlemanly honor as well as his courage is involved; cf. 642-643 with 871-872. He greets the statue with equanimity although fearful within (937); at 891-892, and 895-896 he denies that he was afraid at the time of Don Gonzalo's murder. In a moment or two the statue agrees that he shows courage, "Valiente estás," surely knowing that very soon now heaven will strike down this criminal who has flouted God's will. Again denying his fear, Don Juan gives the statue his hand, even though he knows of its infernal heat from the first interview (668-670). As he takes the hand he is unable to restrain his cry of terrible pain from its burning, and it is hell's own fire that now consumes him.

So Don Juan has great, well-nigh superhuman courage. Other of its evidences are minor in comparison with that shown during the interviews with the statue, and after this proof, one is willing to accept his words and actions at other places in the play as evidence of genuine courage rather than braggadocio. He did save Catalinón from the sea in Act I, risking death to the point of having become unconscious from near drowning. At the beginning of the play, he is willing to face the palace guard in sword play although badly outnumbered (I, 37-40, 42). Altogether, there is no reason at all to doubt his physical courage as a fact of the play.

CONCLUSIONS

And so we have reached the end of those major evidences in the play that tell us directly who and what Don Juan is. Once more we stress the word "directly," for, as was made clear at the beginning of the study, we have desired only to state what the *facts* of the drama are as regards Don Juan's character. (Of the major inferences that may be drawn through *explanation* of the facts we shall offer no account here; it is in these inferences that scholars are quite certain to present controversial matter on which agreement may be difficult, as on certain past occasions.)

In conclusion, then, we have seen that the *Burlador's* Don Juan, the young noble of exalted lineage, is a gentleman, as this term was understood then. But beneath the suavity of his manners is the savage trickster who, often irresistible to women (cf. Tisbea's expression of attraction to him at I, 579-580), victimizes them through the *burla*, That is, he seduces them either through imposture (Isabela, Ana—although the seduction of the latter failed) or by a promise of marriage (Tisbea, Aminta). He is aware of the enormity of his offenses against secular and divine law, but is not evil only for the sake of evil. Rather, he is the hedonist who performs his deeds for the pleasure they afford, and this pleasure dwells not purely in the sensual thrill of his encounters, but, more substantially, in the jokes played on his victims and their menfolk. His deeds involve a large element of cruelty. In order to achieve his goals, he is willing to deceive even those who have most reason to assume his loyalty to them, his friends Octavio and Mota, his uncle Pedro, his benefactor and sovereign Alfonso. He is even willing to kill in order to escape the consequences of his misdeeds, and does kill Don Gonzalo. He takes advantage of his father's position of power at the court to perform acts he knows are evil, and for a time is successful in avoiding a day of reckoning. His unwillingness to face up to the fact of the inevitability of heavenly punishment unless he repents is made clear by his oft-repeated and scornful "¡Qué largo me lo fiáis!," a hallmark of most of the Don Juans of world literature, for, as Stendhal observed of the Don Juan figure, "In the great market of life he is a dishonest merchant, who is always buying and never paying." That is, Don Juan, a believer in the orthodox Catholicism of his time, knows he will be punished, but he wishes as long as possible to postpone giving thought to his own dreadful day of reckoning. His refusal to give consideration to his fate does not spring from his lack of physical courage, for this he possesses in major degree. He is an exhibitionist, performing his acts partly to gain the applause of others who approve of his behavior even though they may not dare to imitate it (or to gain the shocked disapproval of others whom he despises as less than truly virile). He is insolent toward the King, disrespectful of his father's wishes, headstrong in his exaggerated waywardness. May we not agree that it is a fact of the play that, as the moralist saw him in his own time and as moralists see him now, he has only one major virtue, his physical courage? All of his other major traits are evil, tending toward the destruction of the culture that begot and nourished him.

CALDERÓN'S COMEDY AND HIS SERIOUS SENSE OF LIFE

by BRUCE W. WARDROPPER
Duke University

Most students of Calderón base their interpretation of his dramaturgy on a handful of plays: the *dramas de honor, La vida es sueño, El alcalde le Zalamea,* and a very few others. A. A. Parker, it is true, has studied the *autos sacramentales,* and Kenneth R. Scholberg the *obras cortas.* [1] But ever since Calderón studies emerged from the well-meaning floundering of Menéndez Pelayo to become a serious discipline, a major aspect of his drama has been largely ignored by the critics. *Casa con dos puertas mala es de guardar* may be taken to represent this other, quite neglected, side of Calderón's dramatic art. It belongs to the genre we call *comedia de capa y espada.* The genre— roughly speaking, a fusion of the comedy of manners with the comedy of intrigue—was given this name by Calderón's contemporaries, not because these are savage or bloodthirsty plays—as one might be tempted to infer from the nearest English equivalent, "cloak and dagger" — but because they required a minimum of props. The conventional masculine costume, a cloak and a sword, was available to the most modest producer, whereas in the antithetical dramatic category, denominated *comedia de ruido,* a great deal of pomp and circumstance called for a more spectacular production.

---

[1] A. A. Parker, *The Allegorical Drama of Calderón* (Oxford, 1943); K. R. Scholberg, "Las obras cortas de Calderón," *Clavileño,* No. 5 (1954), 13-19.

No one is too sure what to make of the cloak-and-sword plays. There is no good or recent criticism of them. References to them in standard literary histories do not begin to grapple with the esthetic problems involved. Calderón's intense seriousness as a writer makes it hard to believe that he could have written so many mere entertainments. "Mere," indeed, they were not; but entertainment did fall within his understanding of the dramatist's mission. I do not, however, regard the cloak-and-sword plays as entirely trivial.

In these plays Calderón, a most consistent thinker, expresses the same attitudes to the world as in his serious plays: in both kinds he conveys its confusing reality, the disastrous effects of human frailty and sinfulness, problems of cognition and identification, the deceptive appearances of both truth and falsehood. This is his coherent, if pessimistic, view of his world, the world of man. His age, his country—the ephemeral and the localized—concern him far less than the human condition. Since this condition, whether mocked or admired, is a matter of essence, it is not surprising to find the same themes repeated in his serious and in his comic theatre. But the treatment of these themes is necessarily different at either end of the spectrum of his dramaturgy. In the comedy they are exploited for comic purposes: we laugh at man's predicament. In the drama they are exploited to bring out the tragedy of man: we see this stranger from the world of eternity struggling to find his way in an alien world of time, in which contours are blurred, the meaning of life is elusive, and wickedness often overcomes good. In the comedy the pathos of man's condition in a world of deception is diluted to such an extent that the difficulties along the path of salvation are seen as nothing more significant than the artificial and amusing contraptions set up on an obstacle course. We concentrate on the sport, on the fun-and-games, and ignore the tragic implications. But in spite of this de-emphasis of all intellectually challenging considerations, it is still the same world of deception in which the characters gyrate, pirouette, and maneuver.

In all of Calderón's plays human beings are presented as creatures deficient in logic, as playthings of hazard, as victims of misunderstanding and deceit. Yet because their goal in life is a reasonable one—through mutual aid, through acts of faith and gifts of grace, through belief in an eternal life, to achieve the soul's salvation—Calderón imposes on the labyrinthine confusion of human life a pattern of reasonable order. In terms of his art this means that he reduces the darting hither and thither of wayward men to a set of logical schemes; over the natural disorder of life he lays a stencil of rigorous art so that the gallivanting becomes the set moves of pieces on a chess board. In the serious plays the effect of this strict control over the characters' actions is to heighten the meaning of life: providence, destiny, religious dogma gradually wear down man's rebelliousness until, at the end of each play, he accepts the dramatist's vision of order as his directive in life. In the comic plays, on the other hand, the effect of the symmetry and the intricate patterns of art is merely zany: the characters struggle grotesquely in straitjackets of Calderón's design.

Before I can attempt to illustrate this thesis by reference to *Casa con dos puertas* let me remind the reader briefly of the nature of its plot. The play tells the story of how Lisardo, a guest in the house of his friend, Don Félix, falls in love with Don Félix's sister, Marcela, without knowing who she is or even that she lives in the house in which he is staying. At the same time Don Félix loves his sister's friend, Laura. Incredible cases of mistaken identity, deliberate obfuscation, ruses and schemes, exchanging of houses, wrong interpretations of evidence, ill-founded jealousy, misapplied acts of friendship—all conspire to turn this initially simple, if artificial, situation into the most frightful confusion. Add to this the fact that Laura's house has two doors, while Félix's house has a two-doored room, not to mention a walled-off apartment for Marcela's use, and one realizes that the poet has designedly stacked the cards against the creatures of his imagination. By the time Calderón has finished with his characters they have had to submit to two shot-gun marriages as the only possible way to prevent wholesale murder. Since our heroes are forced to marry the girls they want to marry—and who want to marry them—the events turn out happily in the end, but it is nothing short of a miracle that they do. Amusing as the comedy is, it is for ever teetering on the brink of tragedy.

Only the grace of God, and the intention of the dramatist, prevent a blood bath.

This play, then, presents an excessively artificial picture of the labyrinthine confusion which Calderón habitually sees in the world of men. The actions, the ill-laid schemes, and the overhasty assumptions of the men and women in the play create the confusion to some extent. But fate, in the unexpected return of Laura's father, Fabio, is also responsible. And the house with its two doors — the environment itself — contributes no little to the general turmoil. As Don Félix puts it at the end of the play:

> el haber tenido
> dos puertas ésta y tu casa
> causa fue de los engaños
> que a mí y Lisardo pasan.[2]

The nature of man and the nature of the world he lives in are, taken together, a source of error. The characters in the play know this; they are filled with doubts about reality. Appearances do not reflect the real. And yet, being fallible men, they give credence to their observations. They are hard put to it to deny the evidence of their senses. "¿Puede ser mentira esto?," Don Félix asks Laura. "Sí, bien puede ser mentira," she replies. "¿Mentira lo que estoy viendo?," he exclaims unbelievingly (1620-22). This propensity of man to interpret his environment wrongly is a serious issue in Calderón's dramas. In *Casa con dos puertas* the intensity of the theme is diminished: it leads not to the great eternal verities but to silly blunders. It is not for this reason any the less a part of Calderón's understanding of his world.

The same is true of the question of identity. Calderón's tragic heroes persist in asking themselves who they are. "Know thyself" is for them the precept underlying all correct human be-

---

[2] 3211-14. Verse references are to George Tyler Northup, ed., *Three Plays by Calderón* (Boston, 1926); except for the prudish omission of verses 118-120 this edition is acceptable. The translation by Kenneth Muir, published in *TDR*, VIII, No. 1 (Fall 1963), 157-217, is extremely unsatisfactory because it is too independent of Calderón's text: the imagery is ruined, important passages are omitted, the overall design of the play is lost.

havior. Once a man knows who he is he can behave as who he is is supposed to behave. Following the phrase *sé quien soy* we find the equally important assertion *soy quien soy*. A character may observe: "I behave in this way because I am who I am." Man must discover his essence as a man, and an individual must discover his personal limitations and fortes, in order to conduct himself in such a way that he shall be saved. How to gain self-knowledge is the existential anguish of baroque man. In the cloak-sword plays this grand theme is reduced to a simple, and superficial, question of mistaken identity. Who is Lisardo's mysterious lady? Is she the beloved of his friend, Don Félix? His actions—just like those of the tragic heroes in other plays by Calderón—depend on answers to questions of this sort. When he learns that the mysterious lady is none other than his friend's sister, the marriage he desires becomes possible, his friendship with Félix can be sustained, he can act *differently*. And then, the confusion of which we have spoken is compounded by the failure of the characters to identify one another. Who is that woman concealed by a veil? Is it Nise, Don Félix's allegedly former beloved, who suddenly appears before Laura's eyes in his house? If a total breakdown between the characters does not occur, it is because two of them, Félix and Lisardo, know— to the limit of human cognition—the identity of each other. At the end of the play Lisardo will twice say to Félix: "Sabéis quién soy" (3185; 3187-88), and in this way resolve his friend's doubts about the honorableness of his conduct. One might say that in the cloak-and-sword plays we have the *reductio ad absurdum* of the metaphysical problem of identity: "I am who I am." But the failure to recognize and to identify leads these characters as close to the abyss as it leads the characters in Calderón's more serious plays. In Calderón's art anagnorisis is never a gimmick.

Another great theme common to *Casa con dos puertas* and Calderón's more transcendental works is that of honor, with its concomitant emotion, jealousy. One of the greatest sources of misunderstanding in our play is jealousy. Don Félix is jealous of Laura, Laura of Don Félix and Nise, Lisardo of Don Félix and Marcela, and so on. In the warped logic of the irrational emotions the characters have grounds for jealousy. For jealousy springs not from the reason or from such moral qualities as trust, but from suspicion and the evidence of the senses. The presence of a veiled woman in Don Félix's house (whom she sees with her eyes), and the knowledge of Don Félix's love affair with Nise (which she refuses to believe over and done with) are enough to turn the gentle Laura into a raging beast. Jealousy and a sense of outraged honor appeal to the subhuman in man. Calderón must therefore condemn them on the level of both comedy and tragedy.[3] In an honor play like *El médico de su honra* knowledge of an affair his wife had before their marriage, circumstantial evidence suggesting she may still be unfaithful to him, and a nature too prone to jump to unwarranted conclusions make Don Gutierre commit one of the more gruesome crimes in the Spanish theatre: in his jealousy he leads a surgeon, blindfolded, to his house, where he forces him to bleed his in fact innocent wife— bleed her to death. Gutierre's justification of this act is quite metaphorical: since he regards himself as the healer of his own honor, he must cure it when it is diseased. In this case, the only cure is death—and, above all, a secretive and metaphorically appropriate death. The senseless brutality of murder for the sake of honor, so prevalent in Calderón's theatre, is the one thing most apt to disconcert and alienate modern readers. If jealousy and a, to us, exaggerated respect for reputation do not lead the characters in our play—Lisardo, Don Félix, and Fabio—to such extremes, there must be some rationale to explain it. There is indeed, and a very simple one. In the comedies the characters are unmarried; in the tragedies they are married.

Let us allow one of Cervantes' characters, in an unsufficiently noticed passage from *Don Quixote,* to explain to us the think-

---

[3] It is obvious that a Catholic intellectual cannot reconcile (in his personal life and in his ethical thought) the savage honor code with the religion of charity. In the last decade or so much critical labor on the part of British Calderonists — E. M. Wilson, A. A. Parker, P. N. Dunn — has been devoted to a vindication of the Catholic poet's stance. The consequence of making the assumption that Calderón could not have condoned in his writing murder for the sake of honor has been a series of totally new and ingenious interpretations of his honor plays. Such critical casuistry is not always convincing.

ing of his age on the subject of matrimony. It is a marvellously clear statement that illuminates as does none other the nagging problem of honor in the Spanish theatre.

> Cuando Dios crió a nuestro primero padre en el Paraíso Terrenal, dice la Divina Escritura que infundió Dios sueño en Adán, y que, estando durmiendo, le sacó una costilla del lado siniestro, de la cual formó a nuestra madre Eva; y así como Adán despertó y la miró, dijo: "Esta es carne de mi carne y hueso de mis huesos." Y Dios dijo: "Por ésta dejará el hombre a su padre y madre, y serán dos en una carne misma." Y entonces fue instituido el divino sacramento del matrimonio, con tales lazos que sólo la muerte puede desatarlos. Y tiene tanta fuerza y virtud este milagroso sacramento que hace que dos diferentes personas sean una misma carne; y aún hace más en los buenos casados, que, aunque tienen dos almas, no tienen más de una voluntad. Y de aquí viene que, como la carne de la esposa sea una misma con la del esposo, las manchas que en ella caen, o los defectos que se procura, redundan en la carne del marido, aunque él no haya dado, como queda dicho, ocasión para aquel daño. Porque así como el dolor del pie, o de cualquier miembro del cuerpo humano, le siente todo el cuerpo, por ser todo de una carne misma, y la cabeza siente el daño del tobillo, sin que ella se le haya causado, así el marido es participante de la deshonra de la mujer por ser una misma cosa con ella. Y como las honras y deshonras del mundo sean todas y nazcan de carne y sangre, y las de la mujer mala sean de este género, es forzoso que al marido le quepa parte de ellas y sea tenido por deshonrado sin que él lo sepa.[4]

The honor problem arises, then, as a result of a belief in the *literalness* of the foundation of a sacrament: Spanish Catholics believed in the one-flesh doctrine just as firmly as they believed that transubstantiation—the *literal* change of wafer and wine into Christ's Body and Blood—took place in the sacrament of the Eucharist. The harm would not perhaps have been excessive, would not have led to such disastrous results, if some of them had not gone on to combine this belief with a too literal interpretation of Christ's injunction to cut off an offending hand or

---

[4] *Don Quixote*, Part I, Chapter 33.

foot, and pluck out an offending eye. A wife being her husband's limb, of his own flesh and blood, he had an obligation to amputate her if she gave offence. The legitimacy of slaughtering a suspect, even if innocent, wife is a logical enough conclusion to draw from these two premises. If in the act another's soul is destroyed—Cervantes does not claim that a man and his wife share the same soul—that is an unfortunate side-effect of a powerful medication. Let us not imagine that Calderón condoned such sloppy thinking. But he found in the honor theme an excellent tragic mode, and in the sloppy thinking an excellent tragic flaw, of which many humans are the victims.

In a comedy like *Casa con dos puertas* these tragic dimensions are missing. The bachelors and spinsters in our kind of play are not one flesh. At most they are bound by a promise of marriage which society and the Church recognize as provisional. It is no crime, no sin, to break off an engagement. And in the skirmishings of courtship, in the prelude to marriage, what will, after the ceremony, be a matter of life and death is just a risky game. Yet the potential, the future, consequences of all this light-heartedness, since by the conventions of the genre it leads to matrimony, are death. *El médico de su honra*, in which the catastrophe is caused initially by pre-marital errors, is, so to speak, the sequel of a never-written cloak-and-sword play. So in Calderón's comedies, though there is no death on stage, the presence of death is always in the minds of the characters and the spectators. This is a far cry from the social comedy of Molière, where ostracism is the final penalty. As we watch Calderón's fun-making, our heart is in our mouth. Those we watch fear; and we who watch them fear for them.

Let there be no misunderstanding. The swords in the cloak-and-sword plays are kept sharpened. The situations are fraught with danger. When Marcela and Laura exchange houses, they know perfectly well that they are prejudicing the honor, respectively, of a brother and a father. And when Fabio finds his daughter in a compromising situation, he immediately looks for someone to run his sword through. In the words of the play the characters are like a moth which

> sobre la llama flamante
> las alas de vidrio mueve,
> las hojas de carmín bate.

Just so the human being in a *comedia de capa y espada*

> ronda el peligro sin ver
> quien al peligro le trae (295-304).

Yet these same charaters feel that, to accomplish their ends, their intimate desires, risks simply must be run. Marcela at one point observes "que, ya preciso un pesar, / algo se ha de aventurar" (2141-42). She acts out of desperation, with consequences that cannot fail to be uncomfortable. But since the play is an artistic joke, which by convention must turn out happily, the dangers are accepted with alacrity and even with joy. Marcela at one point goes so far as to speak of "el más hermoso peligro" (1133). But, notwithstanding these reservations, the peril of which the people in our comedy speak is not the embarrassment of being caught *in flagrante* while flirting, or the discomfiture which follows peccadilloes in a French farce; their fear is of death, and it is a very real fear. If their fear does not materialize, it is because they have in their hands the remedy for they dishonor, which is marriage. In the honor plays themselves, the savage barbaric tragedies, this remedy has already been used up before the play opens. It is in the nature of marriage that the remedy for dishonor is a one-shot vaccination.

We have, to this point, been thinking about the nature of Calderón's dangerous comedy. Little has been said about the art of this same comedy. It is obvious that in his serious plays Calderón is above all a thinker, a man of logic, a lover of order. He is therefore a conscious artist. This means that he recognizes, to a far greater degree than his predecessor Lope de Vega or our Shakespeare, the frontier between those two areas of beauty which, in the baroque age, were neatly labelled Art and Nature. Art usually works with materials drawn from Nature. Thus, a painter may transfer to canvas a natural scene which he thinks is beautiful. But if he is a good artist, he will reorganize that natural scene. He may, for example, move trees, or even a mountain, in order to improve the design of his painting. Strictly speaking, it is the design, and not the raw materials of Nature, that constitutes Art. The purest artist, then, is the best mathematician, the best logician, the one who understands balance and symmetry, the one who imposes an intellectual order on the anarchy of Nature. The artist repeats the act of God the Creator, but because he does so in miniature, his sense of order must be even more apparent than that of the Creator of the natural world. Just such a baroque artist is Calderón, as much in the frivolous cloak-and-sword plays as in the massive dramas of ideas. If there is some blending of Art and Nature, as when in our play Laura is seen to resemble and blend with the statuary by the pool at Aranjuez,[5] this is a deliberate part of the playful blurring of reality in the comedy, not the result of any confusion between the two concepts on the dramatist's part.

Symmetry of thought and the symmetrical arrangements of words imply the perfect logical form of the syllogism. A contemporary of Calderón's, indeed, praises him for having given to the drama the form of a syllogism. The Schoolmen of the Middle Ages (and their successors, the theologians of the Spanish Baroque) knew that syllogistic reasoning was a mental mechanism which reaches conclusions *vi formae*, without interference from the content the form might hold. The content might be replaced by symbolic letters: thus, $a=b$; $b=c$; therefore, $a=c$. It is possible, then, to think of Calderón's dramaturgy as a complicated algebraic system. In fact, a French critic, Micheline Sauvage, has, as a *tour de force,* reduced *Casa con dos puertas* to a long theorem in algebra.[6] When one notes how in the play even the lovers' quarrels follow the lines of a syllogism, Mlle. Sauvage's notion does not seem far-fetched. We may take as an example Don

---

[5] 305-351. Don Félix, seeing Laura motionless, imagines Nature saying to Art: "No blasones..." (328-330).
[6] *Calderón* (Paris, 1959), pp. 120-129.

Félix, trying to make Laura listen to his explanation of his love affair with Nise:

> O tienes celos o no:
> si dices que no los tienes,
> ¿para qué finges enojos,
> Laura, de lo que no sientes?
> Si los tienes, ¿por qué, Laura,
> desengañarte no quieres?,
> pues ninguno al desengaño
> celoso la espalda vuelve.
> Luego para disculparme,
> o para satisfacerte,
> si los tienes, has de oírme,
> o hablarme, si no los tienes (873-884).

Time and again, in Calderón's comedy, the lovers' tiffs become quasi-theological disputations, organized with the technical terms of scholastic debate: ergo, I infer, exordium, premise, I prove.[7] But when all this is said, the play is more than algebra or logic. The symmetry, the pattern, the design are there, keeping the characters moving in harmonious circles, but, after all, if they are not quite humans, they are at the very least puppets symbolizing humans. They have their weaknesses and their free will, and if they argue professionally, they sometimes argue badly. Marcela, for instance, introduces a false premise into one of her syllogisms. Persuading Laura that she must be allowed to borrow her house so that she can continue to pretend to be Lisardo's mysterious lady, she runs into Laura's objection: "But what if my father returns home?" Marcela's answer is, in effect, that one is never caught out in a first offence:

> ¿Luego ha de venir por fuerza
> hoy [tu padre], luego han de cogernos
> en el primer hurto? (1208-10)

---

[7] Calderón is apt to identify scholastic logic with art: "regla es del arte / que la pregunta y respuesta / siempre un mismo exordio guarden" (218-220).

She is caught out, of course,[8] because her premise is inadmissible, and bedlam breaks out. The design loses its purity of form, but it is quickly replaced by another which is just as pure in form until errant man causes it to break down again.

This high degree of organization extends even to the area where one would least expect to find it: the poetic imagery. Calderón employs some beautiful, poetically conceived images, as telling as any of Shakespeare's. Some of them remind us of those of our own metaphysical poets. The picture with which the play opens, of the sunflower following the sun, and the magnet the North Star, may remind us of John Donne's daring image of the lovers as the legs of a pair of compasses. But Calderón, being an organizer of poetic ingredients, also contrives images with, as it were, an image-making machine.[9] In his scheme of things there are four elements: earth, water, air, and fire. Each element has its creature. For example, the creature of earth might be the beast, of air the bird, of fire the salamander, of water the fish. Each creature has its attributes: the beast has fur, the fish has scales. By transferring the attribute of the creature of one element to the creature of another element Calderón manages to produce, automatically and with little effort, a perfect baroque image embracing his entire cosmology. A fast horse may turn up as a winged or finned beast (because birds dart through the air and fishes through the water at high speed). Sometimes this system creates some remarkable hybrids, like the hippogryff at the beginning of *La vida es sueño*. In the description of the royal hunt, at the beginning of Act III of our play, we have a splendid example of a Calderonian horse:

> Tomó un caballo luego,
> el cuerpo monte, si los ojos fuego,
> mas lagos cada espuma de la boca
> entre el bufido que embestir provoca.
> Un mapa componía;
> pues, a partes manchado, en él se vía

---

[8] *Laura*: "¿Ves, Marcela? En el primero / hurto al fin nos han cogido" (1335-36).

[9] This mechanism was first described by E. M. Wilson, "The Four Elements in the Imagery of Calderón," *MLR*, XXXI (1936), 34-47.

> fuego, agua, tierra, y viento
> a un tiempo en el aliento
> con hermosura suma
> en el cuerpo, en los ojos, y en la espuma (2210-19).

Even in this gay comedy one can see the intricate weaving of the elements that make up Calderón's poetic universe. The horse, a symbol of unbridled passion, has its place in the comedy as well as in the tragedy of our author.

This highly conscious, or self-conscious, organization of the poetic and the dramatic material is characteristic of all of Calderón's work. The sheer logic of it is extremely effective, but it is often lost on American readers, more attuned to the shifting nuances of Shakespeare or Lope de Vega. Our post-Romantic training has accustomed us to look for subtlety, for variation in patterns, for idiosyncracies (like false starts and false leads) in the construction of drama. We do not like to see the scaffolding of the construction worker holding up what we would prefer to regard as an organic work of art. The dramatist's plan, we feel, should not be apparent. We like to see a good deal of the arbitrariness of our world reflected not only in the themes but in the form of drama. We do not — not even in the works of a Pirandello or a Ionesco — care for a dehumanized theatre. Man — the constituent of the *dramatis personae* — must impose his presence on the form. When, in Calderón, we find a rigid form imposing its will on man, we are uneasy. We think the dramatist has gone too far. This hypothetical position of the common reader is not one I personally share. But I must admit that in the cloak-and-sword plays the dehumanization process has gone a long way. Calderón may well be the first author of anti-plays. His ironic detachment from his material is such that the figure of the artist protrudes in his comedies. He does not try to seduce us into participation in his imaginary world. He never lets us forget that we are on our side of the footlights, spectators looking at an artificial performance. In *Casa con dos puertas* Lisardo describes his meeting with Marcela as if it were — as it is! — a fictitious adventure: "la más extraña novela / de amor que escribió Cervantes" (599-600).[10] The

---

[10] Cf, verse 2805, Félix, speaking to Lisardo: "Mucho me he holgado de oíros / por ser la novela extraña."

clown Calabazas, asked to identify himself to Fabio, does so in severely literary terms, citing the title of a short story intercalated in *Don Quixote*: "Si es que el miedo no me engaña, / un curioso impertinente" (3006-07). Fabio's fall from a horse parodies self-consciously the many symbolic falls from horses in Calderón's own high drama; what elsewhere is hybris falling Icarus-like because of the "unbridled passion" of the horse here is just a comic tumble. The opening situation is a repeat of the beginning of another well-known play by Calderón, *La dama duende*. This fact reduces both plays to, as it were, exercises in dramatic writing; to compound further the self-consciousness of this technique of self-quotation, the poet has one of his characters draw attention to it: "La Dama Duende habrá sido / que volver a vivir quiere" (185-186). Celia adapts — debases, parodies — a fine poem by Góngora on the fleetingness of human time in order to comment wryly on the vertiginous speed with which events occur in the play: "Aprended, damas, de aquí / lo que va desde hoy a ayer" (2391-92). The characters are well aware that they are not human beings living in the world of real men, but actors in a play. (But, as with *El gran teatro del mundo*, this, for Calderón, is a valid allegory of human life.) Calabazas and Don Félix's servant go off to eat breakfast as their masters are both going to trot out long speeches:

> En tanto que ellos se pegan
> dos grandísimos romances,
> ¿tendréis, Herrera, algo que
> se atreva a desayunarme? (231-234)

An interrupted conversation in Act III is resumed when Don Félix, using a technical term from the dramatic art, says to Lisardo: "he suspendido / *la relación* que empecé" (2705-06; italics supplied). And Laura explains her actions directly to the audience on a couple of occasions.[11] What other playwright allows us to see so clearly the strings that move his marionettes?

Casa con dos puertas, it is scarcely an exaggeration to say, is art looking at art, a deviously contrived artifice designed to give

---

[11] E. g. "*Aparte*. (Esto / digo por asegurar / el paso al que está acá dentro)" (1460-62).

entertainment, a *Much Ado About Nothing*. In the final scene Calabazas makes the comment: "¡Qué linda danza / se va urdiendo!" (3194-95) That is surely an accurate way of summarizing the play. It is not just a game of chess, not just mathematics, but a baroque dance. The beauty of a game of chess or of a problem in algebra consists in the severity of the form. Choreography, on the other hand, is formalism embellished, and embellished with the appearances, the artistic imitation, of human actions. Man has, after all, his place in *Casa con dos puertas*. He is stylized man, almost a puppet, functioning in a stylized poetic world. But the resemblance is close enough for recognition. The play is Art with its baroque capital A, but it is not Abstract Art.

TABULA GRATULATORIA

George C. S. Adams
John N. Alley
Fred J. Allred
Hymen Alpern
F. Dewey Amner
S. W. Baldwin, Jr.
D. L. Bolinger
José A. Balseiro
J. Worth Banner
Rose Bartsch
James Rush Beeler
Violet Bergguist
Elizabeth S. Bibb
Kenneth E. Bunting
James and Nancy Burke
D. Lincoln Canfield
María de la Soledad Carrasco
Melisa A. Cilley
J. D. Charron
Edmund de Chasca
Gilbert Chase
Calvin A. Claudel
Martha J. Cleveland
John A. Crow
Mary Jane Culverhouse
Elizabeth R. Daniel
George B. Daniel
Frank Dauster
J. Cary Davis
Gifford Davis
Frederick H. Dedmond
Lucille K. Delano
Diana Y. Delgado
Arnold A. Del Greco
Russell D. DeMent
William J. DeSua
C. Francis Drake
Dana B. Drake
F. M. Duffey

Robert Duke
Lowell Dunham
Sherman Eoff
Mr. & Mrs. Charles Edward Eaton
Marilyn Lamond Eddington
Sergio D. Elizondo
John E. Englekirk
Mary Claire Randolph Engstrom
Alfred Garvin Engstrom
F. S. Escribano
Virginia C. Farinholt
Louise Sand Faye
John M. Fein
Weston Flint
Eugenio Florit
Richard L. Frautschi
Herschel J. Frey
Werner P. Friederich
Joseph G. Fucilla
Bernard Gicovate
Bruce R. Gorden
Evelyn P. Graham
John J. Guilbeau
Henry S. Hackney
John Ward Hamilton
Jacques Hardré
George M. Harper
Walter R. Heilman, Jr.
Gustavo R. Hernández
Everett W. Hesse
Dorothy L. Hoffman
Urban T. Holmes, Jr.
Glen W. Hudson
Charles Javens
Harvey L. Johnson
Joseph R. Jones
Lloyd Kasten
J. P. Keller
Philip H. Kennedy

F. M. Kercheville
Robert Kirsner
Milan S. LaDu
Robert R. LaDu
Gregory G. LaGrone
George S. Lane
John H. LaPrade
Sturgis E. Leavitt
Clara Jean Leith
Irving A. Leonard
John Kenneth Leslie
Kurt Levy
Robert W. Linker
A. G. LoRé
Mary Loud
Patricia C. Lowenberg
Leon F. Lyday
Raymond R. MacCurdy
Norris MacKinnon
Dougald MacMillan
Juan Marichal
Quino Martínez
Hester P. Matthews
Wm. C. McCrary
W. T. McCready
William A. McKnight
Robert G. Mead, Jr.
Seymour Menton
John V. Meyers
Gustavus H. Miller
Elsie Minter
William J. Monahan
Edwin S. Morby
S. G. Morley
Gerald M. Moser
E. R. Mulvihill
Lucy Ann Neblett
Charles L. Nelson
Edward J. Neugaard
Carl J. Odenkirchen
William Olsen
Federico de Onís
J. Riis Owre
J. H. Parker
Emmett M. Partin
Anthony M. Pasquariello
John W. Peters
Myron A. Peyton
Rupert T. Pickens
Wyatt A. Pickens
Dorothy Pitts
George W. Poland

Karl S. Pond
C. E. Pupo-Walker
Manuel D. Ramírez
Daniel R. Reedy
Arnold G. Reichenberger
Russell Reynolds
W. W. Ritter
Elias L. Rivers
Gino L. Rizzo
Paul Rogers
Renato Rosaldo
Irving P. Rothberg
Molly Ryland
Norman P. Sacks
George A. C. Scherer
Isabel M. Schevill
Kessel Schwartz
Jerome W. Schweitzer
Mr. & Mrs. Hugh N. Seay, Jr.
Frank Sedwick
Lawrence A. Sharpe
Wm. H. Shuford
James M. Smith
Mary Jean Smith
William F. Smith
Frank E. Snow
Jackson G. Sparks
Robert K. Spaulding
Geoffrey Stagg
Daniel D. Stanley
Julia Britt Steanson
Bob R. Stinson
H. Reynolds Stone
Sterling A. Stoudemire
Lilia Dapaz de Strout
Albert Suskin
James O. Swain
Cecil G. Taylor
Edward Terry
John A. Thompson
A. Torres-Ríoseco
Pedro N. Trakas
E. Daymond Turner, Jr.
R. W. Tyler
C. A. Tyre
B. L. Ullman
Frederick W. Vogler
Donald D. Walsh
Bruce Wardropper
Shirley B. Whitaker
William M. Whitby
Julian Eugene White, Jr.

Joseph W. Whitted
W. L. Wiley
Edward E. Wilson
James Williams
Louis J. Zahn

Bryn Mawr College Library
Library at University of Illinois
University of Oregon Library
Queens College

www.ingramcontent.com/pod-product-compliance
Lightning Source LLC
Chambersburg PA
CBHW030236240426
43663CB00037B/1167